Implementing Effective Instruction for English Language Learners

Implementing Effective Instruction for English Language Learners

12 KEY PRACTICES FOR ADMINISTRATORS, TEACHERS, AND LEADERSHIP TEAMS

Suzanne Wagner

Tamara King

Caslon Publishing | Philadelphia

Caslon, Inc.
Post Office Box 3248
Philadelphia, PA 19130

caslonpublishing.com

9 8 7 6 5 4 3 2

Library of Congress
Cataloging-in-Publication Data
Wagner, Suzanne, 1943–
Implementing effective instruction for English language learners : 12 key practices
for administrators, teachers, leadership teams / Suzanne Wagner, Tamara King.
p. cm
Includes bibliographical references.
ISBN 978-1-934000-10-6 (alk. paper)
1. English language Foreign speakers.—Study and teaching 2. English teachers—
Training of. I. King, Tamara, 1977– II. Title.
PE1128.A2W15 2012
428.0071—dc23   2012014748

FOREWORD

One of my earliest school memories is of my mother getting me ready for kindergarten. I can remember the smell of my mother's hands as she buttoned my blouse and the crisp feel of my cotton uniform against my body. I also remember my mother's voice reminding me about *respeto* for my teacher. "*Los maestros son como segundos padres*" (teachers are like second parents), she would say. It was a phrase I remember my mother repeating throughout the years and a phrase that I have often heard while working with other Mexican students. As an educator, I see no greater responsibility or commitment than the one we accept when parents entrust us with the *educación* and *respeto* of their children.

As educators of culturally and linguistically diverse students, we must remember we are engaged in, and responsible for, the education of other people's children (Delpit, 1995). The education of these children requires not only engaging them in learning but also meeting the increasing accountability requirements, monitoring their academic and linguistic progress, collaborating with other educators, and involving the community and families of the students we serve—all this and more with shrinking resources. Educational leadership is key in supporting educators to achieve these goals and is one of the most powerful factors in the promotion and realization of school success for students of color and students of low socioeconomic status (Delpit, 1988; Macedo, 2000; Ogbu, 1990; Watkin, 2000).

The body of work that Wagner and King offer in this book is invaluable to educators and educational leaders who have committed to this great responsibility of providing students with tools, skills, and resources to achieve in our schools. As I visit and consult with educators across the country, I find outstanding teachers scattered throughout our educational system. Nevertheless, without a coherent and systematic approach to the education of culturally and linguistically diverse students, these teachers do not have the same impact on students' educational success and their positive influence on students is easily lost or overpowered by programs and curriculum based on "deficit thinking" (Valencia, 2010). Wagner and King offer a comprehensive approach to systems ready to bring children back, front and center, to our job as educators. Their key practices focus on creating opportunities for educational equity within and throughout educational systems, from classroom instruction to professional development and program configurations. Through a systematic approach, Wagner and King provide guidance to educators on how to build spaces for participation of all students, specifically culturally and linguistically diverse students.

I see this book as one of the tools educational leaders can use to plan, organize, and transform the teaching and learning at their schools and districts. Through its use, we can honor the trust parents have gifted us in naming us *los segundos padres* of their children.

Mariana Castro
Director of Professional Development
WIDA Consortium
University of Wisconsin-Madison

References

Delpit, L. (1988). The silenced dialogue: Power and pedagogy in educating other people's children. *Harvard Educational Review, 58* (3), 280–299.

Delpit, L. (1995). *Other people's children: Cultural conflict in the classroom.* NY: New Press.

Macedo, S. (2000). *Diversity and distrust: Civic education in a multicultural democracy.* Cambridge, MA: Harvard University Press.

Ogbu, J. U. (1990). Minority status and literacy in comparative perspective. *Daedalus, 119,* 141–168.

Valencia, R. R. (2010). *Dismantling comtemporary deficit thinking: Educational thought and practice.* NY: Routledge.

Watkin, C. (2000). The leadership programme for serving head teachers: Probably the world's largest leadership development initiative. *Leadership & Organization Development Journal, 21* (1), 13–19.

This book is a practical implementation guide for administrators, teachers, and leadership teams charged with improving the instruction and achievement of English language learners (ELLs) in their districts, schools, and classrooms. The driving forces behind this work are our experiences as teachers and administrators, our ongoing review of research in the field, and the knowledge we have gained working with educators in scores of diverse school districts in rural communities and small towns as well as in large suburban and urban school districts.

Implementing Effective Instruction for English Language Learners provides step-by-step guidance for district-wide committees, school leadership teams, and teacher teams committed to ensuring that the ELLs in their classes, schools, and districts are successful and reach high content and language development standards. All of our recommendations are grounded in research-based principles that inform pedagogically sound, well-implemented instructional programs for ELLs. These include programs that provide content-area instruction exclusively in English (e.g., sheltered English immersion, ESL) or in two languages (e.g., dual language, transitional bilingual programs).

Implementing Effective Instruction for English Language Learners identifies twelve key practices that are found in all quality instructional programs for ELLs. These practices are organized into a flexible framework that is based on two fundamental assumptions. First, improving instruction and achievement for ELLs is a systemic challenge that requires strategic planning and action on the district, school, and classroom levels over time. Second, ELLs are everyone's responsibility, including school and district administrators, coaches and professional development providers, mainstream teachers and support staff, and ESL and bilingual specialists. Using the 12 Key Practices Framework, educators can improve the instruction and achievement of ELLs in any K–12 context.

The Power of the Twelve Key Practices Framework

We know that when teachers and administrators collaborate to implement the twelve key practices into carefully planned comprehensive language education programs,[1] ELL students have optimal opportunities to be successful at school. We also know that the challenges of implementation are best addressed through collaborative teams at the district, school, and classroom levels over time.

---

[1] We use the term *comprehensive language education program* to refer to the carefully-planned content, literacy, and ESL instruction that ELLs receive, including their instruction in mainstream classes.

The 12 Key Practices Framework requires educational leaders to look at instruction for ELLs in relation to the larger school and district vision, mission, and goals for all students with attention to how ELL education fits into the overall district and school organizational culture. The framework is divided into four parts that provide the overarching structure of the book: (1) shared practices at the district, school, and classroom levels, (2) common classroom practices for all ELL teachers, (3) core instructional practices of every program for ELLs, and (4) effective program configurations. The 12 Key Practices Framework and corresponding checklist provide a common language and a common practice for ELL-focused professional learning communities as they plan, implement, monitor, evaluate, and improve as necessary the ELL services and professional development they provide.

1. Shared practices at the district, school, and classroom levels

The first four key practices are big picture practices, and they provide a strong foundation and organizational structure for effective ELL instruction in any K–12 system.

- Key Practice 1 is about **equity** and shows how to create enriching school and classroom environments that affirm linguistic and cultural diversity at every level of implementation.

- Key Practice 2 is about **collaboration** and outlines how teams working at different levels of decision-making can adapt and apply the key practices in locally appropriate ways.

- Key Practice 3 emphasizes the need to implement **balanced student assessment systems** that use multiple measures of formative assessment data to complement state-mandated standardized test scores of ELLs' academic achievement and English language proficiency. This key practice shows educators how to gather and use information about students' strengths and needs to identify and appropriately place ELLs, and to use evidence of their growth and achievement in content, language, and literacy to inform instruction and guide program and professional development.

- Key Practice 4 is about **embracing an additive bilingualism perspective** and emphasizes the difference that a language-as-resource orientation makes in educating ELLs. This key practice shows teachers how to draw on the linguistic and cultural resources that ELLs bring with them to school to make grade-level academic content comprehensible, scaffold literacy, and support academic English language development.

When administrators, teachers, and leadership teams make their district, school, and classroom-level decisions about instruction for ELLs with equity, collaboration, authentic assessment, and a resource orientation toward linguistic and cultural diversity in mind, they create a district and school environment that makes effective instruction for ELLs possible.

2. Common classroom practices for ALL English language learner educators

The next four key practices are common teaching practices that enhance instruction and maximize learning in all classes (not just in ESL or bilingual education classes).

- Key Practice 5 is about **big ideas** and shows teachers how to target the enduring understandings that are aligned with core state content standards in ways that are comprehensible for ELLs at all stages of language and literacy development.
- Key Practice 6 is about **meaningful vocabulary-building instruction** and demonstrates how to pre-teach and reinforce key content vocabulary across the curriculum.
- Key Practice 7 is about **activating prior knowledge** as a means of building a comprehensible context for ELL learning.
- Key Practice 8 is about **structuring student interaction** during content, literacy, and ESL instruction in ways that engage ELLs in academically challenging, language-rich classroom activities all day every day.

When all teachers who have ELLs in their classes target the big ideas, teach key vocabulary, activate and build on students' prior knowledge, and structure engaging learning opportunities, ELLs can and do learn academic content, develop literacy, and acquire the academic English they need for school success.

3. Core instructional practices of every program for ELLs

These three key practices are at the heart of every effective instructional program for ELLs. Regardless of program model, the core instructional goals for ELLs are academic achievement and English language and literacy development. Equitable education for ELLs therefore must include (a) ESL instruction that targets the oral and written academic English needed for school success, (b) meaning-based literacy instruction, and (c) comprehensible content-area instruction in all subject areas. While ESL instruction is an integral component of all comprehensive language education programs, ELLs cannot reach high content and language development standards in isolated ESL or bilingual classes or programs. Content, language, and literacy teachers and specialists must share responsibility to ensure that every ELL can reach the same high content and language standards as all other students in developmentally appropriate ways.

- Key Practice 9 focuses on the **English as a second language component,** which includes daily content-based second language instruction that targets the oral and written English that ELLs need for school success. All state English language development (ELD) standards divide language into four domains (listening, speaking, reading, and writing), and many state systems have created separate ELD standards that focus on (1) social and instructional language, (2) the language of language arts, (3) the language of math, (4) the language of science, and (5) the language of social studies.

- Key Practice 10 is about **meaning-based literacy instruction** in English and explains how to teach literacy skills within the context of comprehensible texts. This key practice also highlights the relationship between English literacy and home language literacy and emphasizes the importance of including literacy instruction in an ELLs' home language whenever feasible.

- Key Practice 11 is about **comprehensible academic content instruction** and shows teachers how to make grade-level content-area concepts and skills accessible to ELLs at different stages of oral and written English language development.

There are many different ways that districts and schools can organize their instructional programs for ELLs. However, administrators, teachers, and leadership teams must remember that equitable instruction for ELLs includes content-based ESL instruction, meaning-based literacy instruction, and comprehensible content-area instruction in every subject area. This instruction must be aligned with state content and language standards and configured in ways that are locally appropriate given consideration of the number of ELLs in the school, the languages they speak, the number of ESL teachers, and the languages used for instructional purposes.

One of the distinguishing features of the 12 Key Practices Framework is that we do not ask administrators, teachers, and leadership teams to carefully consider specific program models until they have carefully considered how to implement Key Practices 1–11 in relation to their district and school context. However, we know that when teams understand Key Practices 1–11, they are prepared to consider the most effective ways to configure a comprehensive language education program that improves instruction and achievement for the ELLs in their districts, schools, and classes.

4. Organizing the key practices into effective program configurations

Key Practice 12 is about **program configuration,** and it shows administrators, teachers, and leadership teams how to plan and implement effective comprehensive language education programs in any K–12 system. This key practice explores the strengths and challenges of different options available to districts and schools given consideration of

- the size of the ELL population relative to the overall student population
- the number of languages spoken by ELLs
- the differences in program configurations at the elementary and secondary levels, and
- the languages used for instructional purposes (English-only, bilingual education).

We know that there is no one-size-fits-all program model that is appropriate for ELLs in every educational context. In all districts and schools there are diverse ELL student populations that will change over time. Changes in school personnel, board members, and material resources will also occur. In addition, there will be changes in state content and language development standards, new mandates, and revised accountability requirements. However, when administrators, teachers, and leadership teams use research-based principles, flexible frameworks, and templates and checklists to guide their work, they can improve instruction and achievement of ELLs in their districts and schools.

Using the 12 Key Practices Framework on the Local Level

The opening chapter of this book introduces the 12 Key Practices Framework and Checklist in their entirety. After reading this introductory chapter, administrators, teachers, and leadership teams can use the 12 Key Practices Checklist that is included at the end of the chapter to review their current practices for ELLs at the district, school, and classroom levels. This checklist invites educators to identify the degree to which they implement each key practice, and they can use this information as a form of baseline data. Implementing effective instruction for ELLs is a dynamic, recursive process, and teams are encouraged to revisit the entire checklist again at different points in their planning, implementing, monitoring, and evaluating cycles in order to gauge improvement and plan professional development.

Each subsequent chapter focuses on one key practice in isolation, but each practice should always be considered in relation to the rest of the key practices. Moreover, each part of the book focuses on a particular level of planning and implementation, and each level should be considered in relation to the other levels. Teams are encouraged to begin by reading the entire book and then to return to specific key practices as necessary.

We have worked to make each chapter as clear and easy to use as possible. Each chapter begins with the title of the focal key practice, which is followed by a directive statement that tells teams what to do in order to reach this key practice. Each key practice directive is then followed by a bulleted list of implementation guideposts. Next we include a statement of the big ideas of that key practice, which are the enduring understandings that readers should take away from that practice.

Each chapter is organized around the implementation guideposts, and each section suggests specific planning processes, strategic how-to information, tasks, and examples that demonstrate how the key practice may be implemented. Each chapter concludes with Questions for Reflection and Action that are related to the big ideas of the chapter. This section provides questions and activities that ask administrators, teachers, planning teams, and study groups to relate the big ideas of the focal key practice to their context. These questions for reflection and action are intended to stimulate critical thinking and concrete action planning. At the end of each chapter we include a short list of Recommended Readings, additional templates called out in the chapter that can guide planning and implementation, and one section of the Key Practice Checklist that encourages users to assess current practice and note areas in need of improvement. We also include a glossary of terms at the end of the book.

Throughout this book we share "Reflections from the Field" vignettes that exemplify the topics discussed in the text. Many of these vignettes relate "a ha!" moments that we have experienced as teachers and as professional developers. We also include experiences, events, and stories that teachers have shared with us about their learning experience as they work with linguistically and culturally diverse students. Finally, as an important supplement to the book, we have posted Frequently Asked Questions, a Glossary of Teaching Strategies, and downloadable Templates at caslon publishing.com/pd-resources/twelve-key-practices.

Acknowledgements

Over the years, we have had the opportunity to be part of several remarkable learning communities. With our colleagues at the Illinois Resource Center, we have been able to discuss research, share ideas and reflect on the task that educators face as they develop effective instruction for ELLs. For these conversations, we thank our colleagues, Karen Beeman, Jeanette Gordon, Margo Gottlieb, Else Hamayan, John Hilliard, John Kibler, Barbara Marler, Cristina Sanchez-Lopez, Cheryl Urow, Adela Weinstein, and Josie Yanguas. We also thank Norm Stahl and Karen Carrier from Northern Illinois University for their tireless efforts providing professional development for rural school districts. Sue thanks her colleagues at the University of Illinois at Chicago for their heart-felt commitment to diverse learners in city schools. Special thanks to Flora Rodriguez-Brown, who taught Sue so much about involving parents in their children's learning. Tammy thanks the staff at the WIDA Consortium, especially Mariana Castro, Maureen Keithley, and Robert Kohl, for helping broaden her perspective. By collaborating with these professionals and working with administrators and teachers in various states, we have gained confidence that our twelve key practices are relevant and useful in large and small school districts across the country.

We also would like to thank several contributors to this book: Michelle Cubero, Jeanette Gordon, Margo Gottlieb, Doris Reynolds, Megan Salgado, Cristina Sanchez-Lopez, Shalley Wakeman, and Magali Williams. We are very grateful for their willingness to share their knowledge and write up their stories. Special thanks to our mentor and editor, Rebecca Freeman Field, who guided us through the writing and revision process.

For their love, patience and unwavering support, we want to thank our husbands, Rog and Rob, for understanding our goals and supporting our task in every way. Sue would like to thank Grace, Jack, Emily, Sam, and Harper for being the best grandkids on the planet. Tammy thanks the Marrah clan and the King family, especially for the thoughts and prayers from Joey and Hope.

Lastly, we thank the makers of trail mix and the staff at Macy's on State Street for the sustenance to keep working and the place to have our "*Macy's moments*," the term we use to describe our working retreats in the not-so-secret basement food court.

CONTENTS

The Twelve Key Practices Framework

Shared Practices at The District, School, and Classroom Levels

1. Structuring Equitable School and Classroom Environments
2. Educating English Language Learners through Collaboration
3. Implementing a Balanced Student Assessment System
4. Embracing an Additive Bilingualism Perspective

Common Classroom Practices for All English Language Learner Educators

5. Using Big Ideas to Plan Instruction
6. Implementing Meaningful Vocabulary Building Instruction
7. Activating Students' Prior Knowledge
8. Structuring Student Interaction

Core Instructional Practices of Every Program for English Language Learners

9. Implementing English as a Second Language Instruction
10. Implementing Meaning-Based Literacy Instruction
11. Implementing Comprehensible Academic Content Instruction

Organizing the Key Practices into Effective Program Configurations

12. Structuring the Language Education Program

THE BIG IDEAS

- The twelve key practices can help educators build successful instructional environments that enable English language learners (ELLs) to meet core state standards and English language proficiency standards.

- Effective implementation of the twelve key practices is most thoroughly realized when collaborative teams at the district-wide, school-wide, and classroom levels all work toward the common goal of school success for ELLs.

- The twelve key practices provide a common focus, a common language, and shared goals for the collaborative teams.

An important implication of the increased focus on standards and accountability is that all educators must be prepared to effectively teach diverse learners in their classrooms and caseloads. Traditionally, the English as a second language (ESL) and bilingual teachers have assumed exclusive responsibility for educating English language learners. Today mainstream educators at all levels must share the responsibility for educating all students, including ELLs.

Researchers, practitioners, and resource centers working in the language education field have developed research-based principles for educating ELLs in K-12 schools. These principles serve as a foundation to guide educators as they plan, implement, monitor, and evaluate instruction and achievement of ELLs in their schools. For example, the George Washington University Center for Equity and Excellence in Education (GWCEE) sponsored the development of the *Promoting Excellence Series: Guiding Principles* to ensure academic success for ELLs. The World-Class Instructional Design and Assessment (WIDA) Consortium, a consortium of 27 states that has developed the WIDA English language development (ELD) standards and the ACCESS for ELLs English language proficiency test, outlined ten guiding principles of language development that serve as the cornerstone of their ELD standards. Miramontes et al. (2011) identify and discuss ten comprehensive organizing principles that structure all educational programs in linguistically diverse settings. DeJong (2011) proposes four core principles that guide local decision-making. DeJong's principles reflect a holistic sociocultural perspective on the education of ELLs. These principles are based on over forty years of research, a commitment to equity and academic achievement, as well as an enrichment orientation toward linguistic and cultural diversity.

In the following pages, we introduce twelve research-based key practices that we have identified as critical components of language education programs, the term we use to describe all types of program configurations that provide instruction and services for ELLs. These key practices are consistent with the preceding guiding principles and are designed to clearly demonstrate what principle-based language education instruction looks like in practice. The twelve key practices, along with the information, templates, strategies, and examples in this book, provide a user-friendly guide toward the implementation of everyday educational practices that are grounded in well-established guiding principles. These essential practices can be implemented by administrators and teachers in small and large school districts with varying ELL populations. The twelve key practices provide strategic processes, how-to information, and useful examples to help educators gain the knowledge they need to ensure that the ELLs in their schools have ample opportunities to develop strong literacy skills, learn standards-based academic content, and meet English language development standards.

Implementation of the twelve key practices is most effective when collaborative teams at the district-wide level, school-wide level, and classroom level embrace the notion that it is everyone's responsibility to provide equitable, successful learning environments for ELLs. These teams can work and learn together as a professional learning community (PLC), a term that describes a group of teams that work and learn interdependently to achieve a common goal, share the vision that all students can learn, and take on the challenge by meeting regularly to have reflective conversations and solve problems (DuFour & Eaker, 1998; DuFour et al., 2006). The ELL-focused PLC can share the common goal to provide instruction and programming that enables ELLs to be active, engaged learners who meet core state standards and English language development standards. This PLC network, consisting of a district-level language education committee, school leadership teams, grade-level teams (or other subgroups) can use the twelve key practices to provide a common focus and a common language for the work of the various committees.

The twelve key practices are presented within four categories: (1) The "big picture" practices that are shared by educators at the district, school, and classroom levels, (2) the common classroom practices for all ELL educators (the teachers who share the responsibility to teach the same ELLs), (3) the core instructional practices (ESL, literacy, and academic content), designed for teachers in every type of program for ELLs, and (4) the final programming practice that organizes all of the practices into effective program configurations. In this introductory chapter, the twelve key practices are written as practical, useful directive statements. In the following chapters, each of the key practice statements is followed by several bulleted directives we call instructional guideposts. These guideposts indicate the tasks, processes, practices, and/or strategies that are realistic, achievable, and measurable ways to successfully implement the research-based practices.

In many ways, the twelve key practices can be characterized as a "systems approach." In a systems approach, the tasks are generally divided into smaller components that allow for concentrated efforts on particular components by groups with various specializations. As the various PLCs work, it is necessary for them to coordinate their efforts. All of the work is designed to develop a particular product or, in this case, reach the common goal of academic success for ELLs.

Shared Practices at the District, School, and Classroom Levels (Practices 1–4)

In this book, we use the term *English language learners* (*ELLs*) to describe the linguistically and culturally diverse students who have been identified as having levels of English language proficiency that preclude them from accessing, processing, and acquiring unmodified grade-level content instruction in English (Gottlieb et al. 2007a). In almost all school districts, specific English as a Second Language (ESL) instruction is provided to help these students develop English language skills. In some states, educators use the term English for Speakers Other than English (ESOL) and English language development (ELD). This component of the instructional program is often called the *ESL (or ESOL or ELD) program*. In many school districts, in addition to teaching ESL, certified bilingual teachers provide academic instruction in the primary language. Regardless of the extent of use of the primary language, these instructional approaches are usually referred to as *bilingual education programs*.

Over the years, many districts with a small number of ELLs have tried to address their ELLs' needs by simply hiring an ESL or bilingual teacher. It was (and is) not uncommon for these teachers to be assigned to provide ESL instruction and/or primary language support to numerous ELLs— often in multiple buildings. Unfortunately, as the number of ELLs grew, the initial program configuration may have remained the same. Such a program's very design is all about organizing instruction around the ESL or bilingual teacher's schedule rather than meeting the specific needs of the diverse ELLs. In many of these school districts, the responsibilities for educating the ELLs seem to be squarely placed on the shoulders of the ESL and bilingual teachers, even though the ELLs spend part (or sometimes most) of their day in general education classrooms. In many cases, there was (or is) little time for collaboration between the ESL and/or bilingual teacher and the mainstream classroom teachers who also teach the ELLs.

In this book, we use the term *language education teachers* to refer collectively to the certified ESL and bilingual teachers who have the primary responsibility for teaching the ELLs. Twenty-first century schools have increasing numbers of linguistically and culturally diverse students at all grade levels. The reality is that the responsibility for educating ELLs does not just fall to the language education teachers, but rather is shared by all educators who have contact with ELLs. When administrators and teachers have ELLs in their schools, classrooms, or on their caseloads, they become *stakeholders*, a term that we use to describe the adults who have specific roles in the ELLs' progress and, therefore, share the responsibility for the students' success. Principals, school leadership teams, and grade-level teacher teams generally have the primary responsibility for planning the implementation of the first four key practices that are designed to be used by all educators.

Key Practice 1. Structuring Equitable School and Classroom Environments

Implement literacy, content, and ESL instruction in language-rich, low-anxiety environments that affirm diversity and value bilingualism.

Everyone thought ESL was the answer to what has generally been framed as a "language problem" for ELLs. However, there is more to equity for ELLs than comprehensible content and English language development. Learning a second language and learning school subjects through a

Getting to Know about the Backgrounds of ELL students   *Tammy King*

I was working in a suburban school where nearly 80% of the district's student population spoke a language other than English at home. The district's families spoke over fifty different primary languages. I wasn't familiar with all of my students' native cultures. I read what I could find about each country and culture because I desperately wanted my students to feel safe and welcome in my classroom. The reading helped, but it wasn't enough. By getting to know my students and their families, I learned much more about their home countries and what life is like immigrating to the United States as a child.

Sherif, a fourth grader, often popped into my room before school, during recess or after school to see if I needed help. At the beginning of the school year, he barely spoke to the other students or to me, despite moving to the United States almost a year prior. We didn't have the ELD standards at that time, but if we had, I would have estimated that Sherif was at a level 2 proficiency. Over the course of the school year, Sherif and I had many conversations, and I learned that his father was an electrical engineer in Egypt and his mother was a chemistry professor. In December, Sherif excitedly told me what his father had taught him over the weekend—the difference between series and parallel electrical circuits! Even though he didn't know the specific vocabulary of electricity in English, he drew a picture for me and made numerous references to strings of Christmas tree lights. Ultimately he successfully taught me about the advantages and disadvantages of each type of circuit. It was obvious that he had a wealth of background knowledge and interest in the topic despite his limited proficiency in English. By creating a safe and welcoming classroom environment and showing an interest in getting to know my students, Sherif opened up about his family's experiences and I learned the benefits of parallel and series circuits.

second language also involves entering a new cultural group. Improving ELL instruction and achievement requires addressing the sociocultural and affective issues that influence ELL engagement in classroom activities and integration into the school community. "All the best strategies will likely be insufficient if they are employed in a setting where students do not feel valued or have confidence that they can succeed. Simply put, second language learners are more likely to succeed when their teachers create safe, caring environments that promote risk-taking" (Commins & Miramontes, 2005, p. 141). Beyond their homeroom classrooms, ELLs need school environments that demonstrate that their home cultures and languages are important and valued. The school leadership team can take on the challenge to make all school settings safe, caring, and language-rich.

Commins and Miramontes also point out that second language learners experience tremendous stress during the difficult and sometimes embarrassing task of learning another language. "Their language learning is enhanced when affective factors are addressed and when they find themselves in settings that allow them to develop a sense of security" (2005, p. 141). Elementary and secondary teachers can learn how to provide curriculum and instruction that includes learning activities that recognize the diversity of their student populations. Grade-level teacher teams can work together to find materials, share ideas, and plan lessons that utilize the students' languages and cultures in classroom lessons and experiences. Implementing these activities means that teachers need to get to know more about their ELLs' educational and cultural backgrounds. Nothing makes ELLs feel more ready to learn than having teachers who are interested in their languages, countries, cultures, and previous experiences.

Teachers can also make sure that their classrooms are rich in language learning prompts and supports. They can display charts with visuals that explain key concepts and provide useful word walls that assist language development. They can gather multiple trade books about topics the students are currently studying and place them in classrooms in ways that are available for student use. Trade books, which are commercially available content books, are filled with interesting facts, multiple pictures, charts, captions, and graphics. In addition to trade books written in English, curriculum teams can locate trade books in the primary languages of the ELLs.

Key Practice 2. Educating English Language Learners through Collaboration

Address the challenges of educating ELL student populations through collaborative teams who share common goals, common language, and common practices.

Through our work with administrators and teachers in numerous school districts, we have often facilitated collaborative efforts of district-wide language education committees that worked and learned together to design, develop, and/or restructure the language education program. As the committee members completed their tasks and made their decisions, they planned short- and long-term professional development, disseminated information, and communicated the research and rationale for the restructured programs. However, we have learned that the collaborative work of one committee does not always effect change in all classrooms. For example, in a few cases, we have facilitated the work of small committees consisting of the district language education coordinator and a few ESL and/or bilingual teachers within the program. All too often, the effective programs and practices for ELLs developed by the language education teams were not sustained when the administrator or teachers left the district or moved on to other assignments. We have learned that developing successful programs and instruction for ELLs requires a PLC of a wide range of educators dedicated to on-going collaborative efforts at the district, school, and classroom levels.

Organizing instruction and curriculum for ELLs means that administrators, language education teachers, mainstream teachers, and ancillary school staff members must work together. We suggest that the superintendent establish a district-wide language education committee that serves as the hub of this PLC network. Using the twelve key practices framework as a common focus and a common language, the district-level and school-

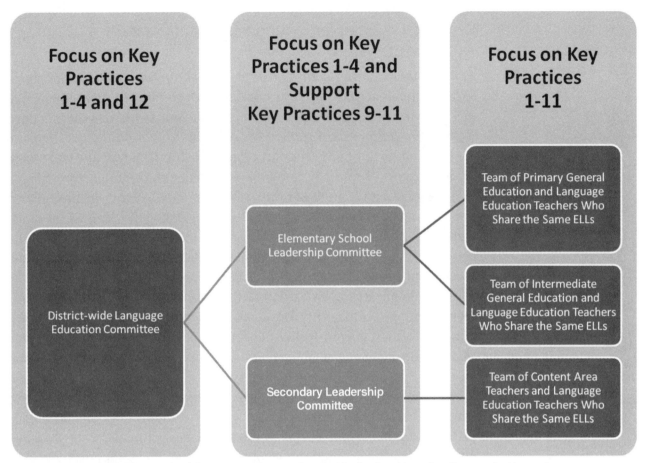

FIGURE 1.1   English Language Learner-focused Professional Learning Community Network

level teams can determine responsibilities and converse with one another. District administrators and principals can find ways to provide professional development and set aside time for school collaborative teams to work and learn together toward their common goal. School-wide teams can focus on ensuring that all school settings are equitable environments for all learners. They can also develop guidelines for implementing common assessment practices and discuss and share effective use of the primary language as a pathway to learning. Mainstream and language education teacher teams can discuss the ELLs' English language development and coordinate ESL, literacy, and content instruction. They can develop common classroom practices and share effective teaching strategies. In addition, they can discuss and share ways to provide meaningful integrated activities with the students in their respective classrooms. These teams can communicate with each other about their progress, share their ideas, and reflect about what works and what doesn't. Figure 1.1 shows how the various PLC teams can use the twelve key practices system to plan and implement ways to improve instruction for ELLs.

Key Practice 3. Implementing a Balanced Student Assessment System

Complement standardized measures with common and classroom assessments that yield evidence of ELL performance in literacy, academic achievement, and language proficiency, and use that assessment data to inform instructional and programmatic decisions.

Keeping track of ELL students' academic performance and analyzing student data over time are tasks that take place at both the district level and the school level. Both of these tasks help measure the effectiveness of the program and highlight instructional areas that need attention. Working with the district's language education coordinator, the language education committee may have the responsibility to facilitate specific district-wide assessment procedures (e.g., report cards, progress reports, and district-wide academic standards-based assessments and English language proficiency testing). At the school level, however, rather than having to rely on mandated standardized testing that may not provide timely and useful information, an assessment team can develop guidelines about how ELLs can be appropriately assessed through common measures at all grade levels. The team can help general education and language education teachers balance a range of meaningful assessment data. For example, using information in this book, the team can develop authentic student-centered measures to find out what newly arrived ELLs already know and can do. These entry procedures will help all general education and language education teachers initiate appropriate instruction and develop meaningful classroom assessments. The team will also want to ensure that ELL students are held accountable for their learning in all classrooms in ways that are appropriate for their English language proficiency levels. At the classroom level, mainstream and language education teacher teams can work together to monitor the progress of the ELLs that they teach in their respective classrooms. They can plan common authentic assessments (e.g., rubrics, checklists), transform classroom activities into classroom-based assessments, and collect evidence of students' learning in portfolios. When the mainstream and language education teachers share and discuss assessment data with one another, they can more effectively design learning activities that support instruction for the ELLs in all classrooms.

Key Practice 4. Embracing an Additive Bilingualism Perspective

Make instructional and linguistic decisions about ELLs based on an understanding of these learners as emerging bilingual students who use two languages for social and academic purposes.

Although all students are unique, the majority of monolingual English-speaking students within the boundaries of a school district are likely to have similar school and community experiences. ELLs from immigrant families, however, come to school with a variety of cultural backgrounds, have varying school knowledge, and may have many different home, school, and community experiences. Just like their English-speaking peers, they use their experiences, social/cultural values, and linguistic knowledge to understand what they are experiencing and learning in school. However, ELLs use both of their languages at school (their primary language and English, their second language) to understand and process the language and instruction of the classroom in order to participate in learning activities. They use their linguistic skills in both languages even when English is the only language of instruction.

In this handbook, we promote *additive bilingualism*, a term coined by Lambert (1975) to describe the language learning process in which ELLs add a new language as they maintain and improve their existing language. The opposite notion, called *subtractive bilingualism*, suggests that immigrants need to exchange their primary language for English, their new language. We believe that being proficient in English plus other languages makes us stronger individually and as a society. For more than two decades, research has shown that it takes five years or more for ELLs to learn the type of academic language skills needed for successful participation in English-speaking content classrooms (Cummins 1980, 2006; Hakuta et al., 2000; Thomas & Collier, 2002; TESOL, 2006; NCTE, 2008). Therefore, throughout this book, we recommend that administrators and teachers provide a well-articulated sequence of comprehensible academic ESL instruction for several years so that ELLs can achieve high levels of academic English language proficiency. At the same time, educators can value and use the primary language to support or teach school concepts. In this way, they are helping ELLs maintain and improve their first language.[1]

Throughout the chapters, we differentiate the use of the ELLs' primary language through two approaches: *primary language instruction* and *primary language support*. School districts with large numbers of ELL students from a single language group (e.g., Spanish, Arabic, Polish) are likely to have the resources to implement primary language *instruction* in bilingual classrooms where certified bilingual teachers strategically teach in both the primary language and in English. In this way, ELLs have immediate and complete access to grade-level academic instruction leading to core state standards. Perhaps the strongest rationale for primary language instruction, however, begins with literacy development in the primary grades. When children learn to read in the language they know best, they can fully utilize their prior knowledge, oral language competence, and linguistic skills. Studies have demonstrated that promoting first language

---

[1] The terms *primary language, first language, native language,* and *home language* are mostly synonymous.

literacy development supports language and literacy development in English, two key goals of all programs for ELLs (Escamilla, 2000; Cummins, 1989; Genesee et al., 2006).

School districts with diverse ELL populations, small numbers of ELLs spread out in many grade levels, and/or limited primary language resources often choose to provide primary language *support*. When bilingual adults preview and clarify classroom lessons in the students' primary language, they are providing the scaffolding necessary to students' understanding of important concepts. As the bilingual assistants work with the ELLs using the primary language, the ELLs can learn specific academic skills (e.g., analyzing, retelling, predicting, questioning, clarifying) that are hard to teach using visuals and graphics. When teachers and other adults speak the students' language and show positive regard for the home culture, children are more likely to be engaged learners and acquire a sense of belonging in the school. By using the children's primary language, these adults can model academic language and share complex ideas with children. With the help of the bilingual adult role models, the ELLs can improve their primary language skills and learn interpersonal skills that will stay with them throughout their schooling and in their adult lives (Lucas & Katz, 1993).

Common Classroom Practices for All English Language Learner Educators (Practices 5–8)

Elementary ELLs generally spend part of their day in at least two different classrooms: a grade-level general education classroom and an ESL or bilingual classroom. Middle and high school ELLs generally receive instruction in multiple classrooms. Furthermore, ELLs at all grade levels receive instruction from various teacher specialists (physical education teachers, fine arts teachers, etc.). In essence, we believe that all of the teachers who have ELLs in their classrooms or caseloads are, by default, language education teachers since all teachers help their students develop language skills. However, to clarify, we use the term *general education teachers* to describe classroom teachers who teach children at all grade levels in elementary schools. We use the term *content teachers* to describe specialized elementary content teachers and middle and high school teachers. We use the term *mainstream teachers* to refer collectively to both elementary general education and secondary content teachers.

Grade-level teacher teams often meet to plan and coordinate curriculum, develop objectives, and divide assessment responsibilities. It is important that the language education teachers be part of this collaborative process, even when the ESL and/or bilingual teachers have ELL students at more than one grade level. In this way, the teachers who share the responsibility of teaching the same group of ELLs can work together to coordinate their respective lessons and develop common classroom instructional practices so that their ELLs become more actively engaged in all classrooms.

In our work, we have identified four common classroom practices (key practices 5–8) that maximize ELL students' learning: (key practice 5) using big ideas to plan instruction; (key practice 6) implementing meaningful vocabulary-building instruction; (key practice 7) activating students' prior knowledge; and (key practice 8) structuring student interaction. These practices, while important for all learners, are especially critical for ELLs, who benefit from consistent, comprehensible instruction across content areas and classrooms.

Within these essential teaching practices, mainstream and language education teachers can develop comprehensible lessons by planning to use various instructional supports. Gottlieb et al. (2007a) describe instructional supports more specifically as *sensory, graphic,* and *interactive. Sensory* supports include visuals, real-life objects, chants, drawings, videos, manipulatives, etc. These hands-on supports provide concrete, comprehensible examples of classroom topics. *Graphic* supports include multiple ways in which information can be organized through graphic representation. Teachers can use charts, timelines, concept webs, cause and effect diagrams, Venn diagrams and other graphic organizers to clarify information found in students' texts and passages. *Interactive* supports include small-group interaction, role play, working with partners, native language support, internet websites, instructional software, etc. Interactive supports encourage language learners to talk about newly learned information. The WIDA Consortium's Resource Guide (2010) provides useful information and examples that clearly demonstrate how these instructional supports help teachers plan comprehensible academic instruction.

Key Practice 5. Using Big Ideas to Plan Instruction

Plan curriculum and instruction that specifically targets the "big ideas" (statements of essential learning) that lead to core state standards.

Big ideas are broad, general statements that describe purposes, functions, patterns, processes, perspectives, and relationships among main ideas and concepts that are grounded in core state standards. Examples of big ideas are: "Conflicts over natural resources are often a cause for war" and "Sound is a kind of energy in the form of waves" (Gordon, 2007). When content and ESL teachers write their lesson plans, listing the big ideas helps them identify essential vocabulary, plan comprehensible instruction, select readings, and develop appropriate assessment strategies. General education and content teachers identify the big ideas so that they can focus on standards-based concepts and essential knowledge that their students must learn. ESL teachers use the big ideas to plan and teach the requisite vocabulary and language skills that the ELL students will need to know in order to understand and express the concepts that they are learning in the mainstream classrooms. Using multiple strategies with sensory, graphic, and interactive instructional supports helps teach and clarify big ideas so that ELL students understand the key points of the lesson even though they may not understand some of the complex details in the textbook and other classroom presentations. Although the notion of big ideas is generally related to content area instruction in math, science, and social studies, literacy teachers can provide learning activities around the big ideas of the language arts topics (e.g., literary themes, author's intent, reading skills/strategies, language genres).

Key Practice 6. Implementing Meaningful Vocabulary-Building Instruction

Pre-teach vocabulary words necessary to understand lessons and readings, teach new words in context during the lessons and readings, and provide practice for students to use the words in various contexts after the lessons and readings.

Teachers intuitively understand the importance of teaching vocabulary to ELLs. For example, kindergarten teachers prominently display the labels of classroom objects (e.g., clock, desk, book, chair). They teach the ELLs the terms used for classroom tasks (e.g., underline, circle, write, open, find, point to). These fundamental steps help ELLs build the confidence they need to be successful learners. A continual emphasis on vocabulary development is a significant component of academic and ESL instruction. Working with a small number of new academic words at a time, teachers can model, illustrate, and use visuals to explicitly teach grade-level vocabulary. Fortunately, the ELLs' social language helps build the bridge to academic language. When teachers identify and teach the vocabulary needed to understand the big ideas, they immediately focus on age-appropriate knowledge and help reduce the gap between the ELLs' developing English language proficiency and the ever-expanding vocabulary of the ELLs' English-speaking peers. Mainstream and language education teachers can work together to identify essential vocabulary and plan how to reinforce, practice, and revisit vocabulary words before, during, and after lessons.

Key Practice 7. Activating Students' Prior Knowledge

Structure activities that connect ELLs' previous knowledge and cultural experiences to current lessons and build a comprehensible context for learning.

Teachers generally initiate a discussion that activates and connects students' experiences to the current lesson. This classroom talk about known topics and concepts builds a contextual bridge to concepts and themes that students will be studying. The difference for ELLs is that teachers need to plan and implement more than just one prior knowledge activity. Many ELLs come to English-speaking classrooms with home, school, and cultural experiences that may be quite different than the experiences of their English-speaking mainstream classmates. Other ELLs who have relocated from other districts may have social English fluency but may have missed major concepts while sitting in English-only classroom settings where they were not actively engaged. Both groups of ELLs need several experiential, hands-on oral activities that access and build upon their prior knowledge in order to have a foundation for the reading passage or lesson. Many of the ELLs need vocabulary assists and instructional supports during the prior knowledge activities (e.g., pictures, demonstrations, videos, role play). When teachers plan and implement several prior knowledge activities, including oral activities that require student interaction, the resulting classroom lessons and reading passages become more comprehensible for all learners, not just the ELLs.

Key Practice 8. Structuring Student Interaction

Provide opportunities for academic development and language practice by implementing activities that require students to talk with each other about what they are learning.

A key factor in the second language acquisition process is the opportunity for the learner to negotiate meaning with a language model who has more linguistic resources than the learner and who is adept at speaking comprehensibly to language learners (Ellis, 1984). In other words, ELLs need quality interaction with teachers and students who have higher levels of English proficiency: the teachers model and teach academic English and the English-proficient children are age-appropriate language models. In addition, the students model the cultural norms and expected behaviors of English-speaking classrooms. Vygotsky (1978) suggests that children learn more successfully by participating with other learners in goal-directed activities that provide social interaction and peer support. Planned, structured student interaction allows ELLs to watch, acquire, and practice the behavior and learning styles that are expected in English-speaking classrooms.

Elementary general education and secondary content teachers can plan cooperative learning activities to engage the ELLs in conversations with their peers. They can provide visuals, charts, specific writing prompts, or questions to talk about as they complete their assignment. When working in small groups, students converse socially, talk about their tasks, give each other examples, and share ways of thinking and problem solving. These conversations make instruction comprehensible and provide low-risk opportunities for ELLs to try out classroom discourse. Meaningful small-group interactions allow ELLs to become active participants in classroom activities rather than sitting on the sidelines as onlookers. When the children move from their small groups to whole-group discussion, all learners are more likely to raise their hands and participate.

Core Instructional Practices of Every Program for English Language Learners (Practices 9–11)

Effective programming for meeting the needs of ELLs must address how these learners will attain academic language proficiency in English, develop or improve literacy skills, and learn grade-level academic concepts. Depending on the design of the language education program, ELLs receive their literacy, academic, and ESL instruction in general education classrooms, secondary content classrooms, ESL classrooms, and/or bilingual classrooms. Their teachers hold various types of certification. Key practice 2 (Educating English Language Learners through Collaboration) affirms our belief that that it is crucial that all of the teachers who share the same groups of ELLs coordinate the instruction of the core key practices: (key practice 9) implementing ESL instruction, (key practice 10) implementing meaning-based literacy instruction, and (key practice 11) implementing comprehensible academic content instruction.

Key Practice 9. Implementing English as a Second Language Instruction

Plan and implement daily content-based ESL instruction in the four language domains (listening, speaking, reading, and writing), focusing on the academic language needed to understand and express essential grade-level concepts.

For decades, researchers have studied various approaches to teaching a second language. Second language methods of the 1970's and 1980's emphasized oral language development first, followed by written work (e.g., the direct method, the audio-lingual method, communicative competence, and the silent way (Ovando et al., 2006). Krashen and Terrell (1983) first introduced the notion that children learn a second language in stages, best through a natural, communicative approach, similar to how young children learn their first language. Meanwhile Cummins (1980, 1984, 1989) worked to define the difference between social and academic language proficiency and to clarify how knowledge learned in one's first language transfers to the second language.

When the No Child Left Behind Act of 2001 mandated that every state adopt English Language Proficiency (ELP) standards and accompanying assessment measures, states began to implement plans to comply with the new federal mandates. In several instances, states decided to come together and share their areas of expertise as they developed their standards and assessments. The WIDA Consortium is the largest and currently includes 27 member states. WIDA and another major organization, Teachers of English to Speakers of Other Languages (TESOL), have developed standards for English language acquisition. The WIDA and TESOL authors, working with task forces of second language experts, have worked to articulate much of what is now understood about second language acquisition theory in a way that helps educators plan instruction and assessment of ELLs. The five language proficiency levels that were created by the WIDA and TESOL authors are reminiscent of Krashen's stages, but they take into account the unique types of language needed to succeed in specific content areas. The WIDA and TESOL English language proficiency levels have slightly different names (e.g. level 1(starting, entering) and level 2 (emerging, beginning). Therefore, in this book, when we refer to students' ELP levels, rather than using terms, we state the ELP level by a number only (e.g., levels 1 through 5, with level 6 meaning English-proficient).

Researchers in the language education field today continue to focus their attention on the development of academic language proficiency and literacy skills (reading and writing). Recent research and legislation have broadened the concept of English language proficiency and/or development to include both social and academic contexts tied to schooling, standards, curriculum, and instruction. (Gottlieb et al., 2006) Responses to these initiatives have led to a deeper understanding of the complexities of academic language and the levels students pass through as they learn how to read, write, listen, and speak in English. At this writing, the WIDA Consortium is in the process of renaming their ELP standards to the more universal and useful term English Language Development (ELD) standards. We use the WIDA ELD standards as the focus of academic instruction and assessment procedures.

Children typically progress rapidly through the first few ELP levels in the early grades. It takes longer, however, for students to move up to the upper language proficiency levels as academic language demands become more complex at higher grade levels. As Cook (2007) succinctly states, "lower is faster and higher is slower." In fact, many students typically go through a period in which it appears as if their language skills have reached a plateau. These plateaus are then interspersed with bursts of development in their language skills (Van Lier, 2004). Therefore, it cannot be assumed that a student will progress one level each year. Language proficiency levels are independent of the students' grade levels or the number of years in a language education program.

ELLs with ELP levels 1 and 2 usually understand more than they can say. However, children need to talk well in order to learn well (Shore, 1997); sitting quietly in the back of the room won't work. ESL teachers can work with the mainstream teachers to plan ways to utilize classroom talk to convert receptive language into expressive language. ESL teachers with beginning levels of ELL students get their students talking by implementing oral language activities, teaching vocabulary, and making sure that the language learners have daily opportunities to listen, speak, read, and write in English. As the ELLs become more socially fluent, the ESL and mainstream teachers can use the language that the students know to teach the vocabulary and the concepts that they are learning in the mainstream classroom. This important collaborative process allows the ESL teacher to plan *content-based* ESL lessons to teach the academic English language that the learners need to succeed in general education classrooms.

A content-based ESL instructional component is at the heart of an effective, comprehensive language education program. In this handbook, when we use the term *ESL instruction,* we are describing ESL as comprehensible English instruction in which learning academic language is the goal. Sometimes we place the term "content-based" in front of the term "ESL" to emphasize that ESL instruction is *not* taught through a traditional approach in which conversational English is taught through grammar structures and discrete language skills. In the traditional ESL approach, lessons are designed to produce correct forms of the English language; there is often little focus on learning language for meaningful academic purposes. On the contrary, in comprehensible ESL instruction, the big ideas and requisite terminology of a particular content topic are the focus. Language instruction is designed to reach ELD standards. ESL teachers use multiple instructional supports to teach academic English in meaningful contexts. These supports include visuals, graphics, real-life objects, videos, charts, timelines, small-group interaction, and working with partners.

Key Practice 10. Implementing Meaning-Based Literacy Instruction

Whenever possible, begin literacy instruction in the primary language; when literacy is taught in English, plan and implement meaning-based literacy instruction that builds on students' oral language and uses comprehensible text at appropriate English language proficiency levels.

Just like their English-speaking peers, when ELLs enter kindergarten and first grade, they have remarkable oral language competence in their primary language. It makes complete sense to offer formal literacy instruction in the language in which they can construct meaning from sight words, phonics work, basic sentences, and text. Unfortunately, in many school districts, primary language literacy instruction in bilingual classrooms is not an option, so the young ELLs must learn to read in English, along with their English-speaking peers.

Whereas their fluent English-speaking peers come to the task of reading with substantial English vocabulary and the ability to use a full repertoire of linguistic skills, the ELLs have various levels of social English fluency and are just beginning the process of acquiring academic English. When teachers must teach ELLs to read in English, they can strategically utilize the ELL children's oral English to provide a pathway to literacy. By reducing the language demands and teaching *meaning-based literacy,* they can ensure that the ELLs are actively engaged in reading and writing. Literacy instruction is meaning based when the text, writing activities, skills, and tasks are meaningful and functional for the emergent reader (Fife, 2006). Teaching ELLs how to read in English is similar to the emergent literacy process that teachers use with fluent English speakers; however, the initial activities, sequence, and the strategies may differ in order for the learning activities to be meaningful and functional. Teachers make vocabulary building, fluency building, phonics tasks, comprehension strategies, and writing tasks meaningful through concrete and engaging contexts that the learners can relate to personally.

Key Practice 11. Implementing Comprehensible Academic Content Instruction

Model and teach academic content using language just above ELLs' current English language proficiency levels, making new information comprehensible using appropriate instructional supports.

Providing comprehensible academic instruction and assessment essentially means that classroom processes, tasks, and assessments are differentiated according to students' varying levels of English language proficiency. When ELLs receive instruction in English, their teachers must adapt or "shelter" their instruction and assessment in order for learning activities to be comprehensible for the learners. In the language education field, the term *sheltered instruction* is used to describe how general education and content teachers teach ELLs (in any subject) using comprehensible language and instructional supports. According to Wright (2010), the word *sheltered* is a metaphor for simplifying the language without watering down the content, thus protecting ELLs from the language demands of mainstream instruction that may be beyond their comprehension.

In this book, we use the term *sheltered instruction* to describe the adapted instruction in content areas where learning academic content is the goal. Some of the methods that teachers use to shelter instruction are adjusting their speech, increasing student interaction, providing multiple background information experiences, and using demonstrations, hands-on examples, and visuals to make new information comprehensible. Teachers also shelter ESL by differentiating instruction according to their students' English language proficiency levels. For example, teachers working with ELP level 1 and level 2 ELLs routinely introduce new lessons with pictures, graphics, and modeling. "The ultimate goal of sheltered instruction is accessibility for ELLs to grade-level content standards and concepts while they continue to improve their English language proficiency" (Wright

2010, p. 223). Although sheltered instruction is designed to be used with ELLs, many of their English-speaking peers also struggle to develop academic language. When general education and content teachers implement sheltered instruction in their classrooms, all students benefit.

Organizing the Key Practices into Effective Program Configurations (Practice 12)

In our work, we have seen that the fine instructional efforts of highly qualified teachers are often thwarted when they are constrained to work with ELLs in poorly developed programs. A well-planned language education program is instrumental in implementing effective instruction for ELLs. We suggest that teachers and administrators who read this book share the twelve key practices with their supervisors. They can suggest that the school district establish a PLC that can be coordinated by a district-wide language education committee. As the language education committee proceeds with their tasks, they can communicate and discuss their progress with the other professional learning community teams at the school and classroom levels. Hord and Sommers (2007) point out that a PLC is not just a set of dedicated groups working together on selected tasks. Rather, PLC members are collaborators who share the same goals and support their work through careful study of and reflection on relevant research and information that relates to the needs of students. All of the teams need to spend some time learning about how the ESL, literacy, and academic content instructional components are implemented effectively. As the team members become familiar with the twelve key practices, the PLC can meet together to discuss what they have learned. Members of the various teams will want to present their ideas and make some general recommendations to the language education committee, which is charged with the task of putting all of the practices in place in program configurations that meet the needs of the district's ELL student populations.

Key Practice 12. Structuring the Language Education Program

Organize the instructional program for ELLs to effectively meet the literacy, academic, and language needs of the district's ELL population.

During the first year, the district language education committee can work as a task force to review, refine, and/or restructure the school district's instructional programs for ELLs. Representatives from various stakeholder groups can participate in this decision-making process that will lead to locally appropriate language education programs that are grounded in research. The committee should be made up of educators with different responsibilities and should be large enough to represent various stakeholder groups—but small enough for members to have purposeful conversations. Specifically, we suggest a mix of two district administrators, the ESL/bilingual program coordinator, two principals (one elementary, one secondary), two or more ESL/bilingual teachers, two mainstream teachers, a special education teacher, a member of the board of education, a language-minority community member, and a parent representative.

Before the committee members can undertake the task of restructuring the language education program, they must study relevant research in the language education field and become familiar with effective practices. The committee can use this book as a study guide to learn the twelve key practices that can improve instruction for ELLs in any program configuration. They can use the core instructional key practices as a reference tool as they plan and/or restructure the district's ESL, literacy, and academic content instructional components. They can use the reading lists at the end of each chapter to locate research findings and helpful implementation information. In this way, the committee can gain the knowledge and the skills needed to develop comprehensive language education programs.

As the language education committee learns how instruction for ELLs is effectively implemented using the twelve key practices, they must also review various forms of student data (e.g., student demographics, standardized test scores, home language and cultural background surveys). In this way, they are learning information about the specific language, literacy, and academic needs of the district's ELL student population. At this point, the committee members will be keen observers as they review the research and prepare to use the Twelve Key Practices Checklist to evaluate their current program practices. These initial processes will give the team a knowledge base from which to systematically plan research-based and locally appropriate comprehensive language education programs that match the needs of their ELL student population. In this book, we use the term *comprehensive* (as in *comprehensive* ESL or bilingual education programs) to describe instructional program configurations that have been carefully designed by a team of educators that take into consideration the literacy, academic, and English language needs of the district's ELL student populations. After the restructuring tasks are completed and decisions are made, the committee remains as a standing district-wide committee that oversees the implementation of the changes to the language education program, arranges professional development initiatives, and coordinates the collaborative efforts of the PLC network.

Using the twelve key practices handbook as an implementation guide can be initiated by school collaborative teams as well as by the language education committee. For example, language education teachers may be the first educators to read this handbook. As they become familiar with the twelve key practices, the teachers will want to convene a study team to read and discuss the information and suggestions about content-based ESL, meaning-based literacy, and sheltered instruction. The study teams can use the twelve key practices to increase ways to provide meaningful, comprehensible instruction and assessment in equitable, language-rich classrooms. By working with the teachers with whom they share their ELL students, they can use the twelve key practices to develop common instruction and assessment strategies so that the ELLs can more fully understand directions and complete tasks as they move from classroom to classroom. The teacher teams will want to share what they learn with the school leadership teams and suggest some school-wide common classroom practices.

All of the key practices are incorporated into the Twelve Key Practices Checklist following this chapter. The checklist is written using measurable statements that can be used to evaluate and monitor language education programs and instruction at the district, school, and classroom levels. Each key practice general statement is followed by implementation guidepost statements that represent the tasks, processes, practices, and/or strategies of research-based teaching practices that occur in effective language education programs. The language education committee and school leadership teams can use the checklist as a diagnostic tool to identify the areas that represent the biggest challenges during the restructuring process. The teams can use the results of the checklist as a starting point to determine the professional development that educators need to know in order to successfully implement the practices. For example, the results on the checklist may indicate that mainstream teachers need training in sheltered instruction. Results may indicate that teachers and administrators need professional development to understand how to use the ELLs' primary language to support instruction. Also, when individual teachers use the checklist to evaluate their own teaching practices, they can recognize ways in which they can immediately make instructional improvements.

In this chapter, we have shared twelve key practices that help educators work toward the common goal of school success for ELLs. We have provided brief overviews of all of the practices and have pointed out that the practices are most effective when collaborative teams at the district-wide, school-wide, and classroom levels work and learn together to meet this goal. In the next chapter, we more fully discuss the first key practice, structuring equitable school and classroom learning environments that affirm diversity and value bilingualism.

QUESTIONS FOR REFLECTION AND ACTION

1. Use the Twelve Key Practices Checklist to take note of the practices that are implemented at your school. These are strengths that can be built

upon. Make a list of practices that have not been addressed. What steps can be taken to bring attention to these needs?

2. Highlight the practices that were rated as in progress or in place in some classrooms. Then, identify three highlighted practices that you think could be addressed in order to move that practice into the implemented column. Compare your list with others in your study group.

Recommended Readings

Center for Equity and Excellence in Education. (2005). *Promoting excellence series: Guiding principles*. Arlington: George Washington University.

DeJong, E. (2011). *Foundations for multilingualism in education: From principles to practice*. Philadelphia: Caslon Publishing.

WIDA Consortium. (2010). *World-class instructional design and assessment's guiding principles of language development*. Available at http://www.wida.us/AcademicLanguage/index.aspx.

Wright, W. (2010). *Foundations for teaching English language learners: Research, theory, policy, and practice*. Philadelphia: Caslon Publishing.

Zemelman, S. et al. (2005). *Best practice: Today's standards for teaching and learning in America's schools*. Portsmouth: Heinemann.

TWELVE KEY PRACTICES CHECKLIST

The checklist is written using measurable statements that can be used to evaluate and monitor language education programs and instruction at the district, school, and classroom levels. The district language education committee and school leadership teams can use the checklist as a diagnostic tool to identify the areas that represent the biggest challenges during the restructuring process. Various teams can use the results of the checklist as a starting point to determine the professional development that educators need to know in order to successfully implement the practices. Teacher teams can use the checklist to evaluate their own teaching practices to recognize ways in which they can immediately make instructional improvements.

SCORING DIRECTIONS:
1 = This practice IS implemented.
2 = This practice is in progress or is in place in some classrooms.
3 = This practice is NOT currently in place.

Shared Practices at the District, School, and Classroom Levels
PRACTICES 1–4

Key Practice 1.			**Structuring Equitable School and Classroom Environments:** Literacy, content, and ESL instruction is implemented in language rich, low-anxiety environments that affirm diversity and value bilingualism.
1	2	3	• On-going professional development is planned for all stakeholders that provides information, shares effective strategies, defines roles, and shapes positive attitudes about ELLs.
1	2	3	• District policies and procedures for ELLs are institutionalized and in place in all schools.
1	2	3	• All teachers who have ELLs in their classrooms have substantial training in sheltered instruction methods.
1	2	3	• School routines, events, and activities are developed to represent ELLs' languages, cultures, and experiences.
1	2	3	• Teachers plan enriching and comprehensible lessons that include multicultural examples/perspectives.
1	2	3	• Teachers display useful language on walls and provide numerous trade books about current topics around the classroom. (e.g., picture books, content books, ESL supplemental materials in English, and, when possible, in the ELLs' primary language).
1	2	3	• Classroom instruction and schedules are implemented in ways that allow ELLs to be actively engaged in learning throughout their school day.

IMPLICATIONS AND COMMENTS _____
_____
_____
_____

Key Practice 2.			**Educating ELLs through Collaboration:** The challenges of educating ELL student populations are addressed through collaborative teams who share common goals, common language, and common practices.
1	2	3	• An ELL-focused professional learning community of district-wide, school-wide, and teacher teams is established. These teams work and learn together to improve programs and instruction for ELLs.

1	2	3	• Periodic district language education committee meetings are convened to establish goals, monitor and refine programs, disseminate information, and provide support for collaborative efforts throughout the district.
1	2	3	• School leadership teams address policy issues, curriculum development, instructional practices, and socio-cultural issues that affect learning environments for diverse learners.
1	2	3	• Teacher teams who share ELL students (language education teachers and general education teachers) have structured planning time for purposeful and reflective conversations.
1	2	3	• Educators collaborate regularly with parents by implementing effective translation strategies, developing a parent advisory council, and connecting parents to classroom learning activities.
1	2	3	• Educators expand collaborative efforts by working with community organizations.

IMPLICATIONS AND COMMENTS _____

_____

_____

_____

Key Practice 3.	**Implementing a Balanced Student Assessment System:** Standardized measures, common assessments, and classroom assessments in literacy, academic achievement, and language proficiency are used to inform instructional and programmatic decisions.

1	2	3	• Administrators and teachers design and use a balanced assessment system that identifies ELL students' needs, documents student classroom performance, and evaluates program effectiveness.
1	2	3	• Entry and exit criteria and procedures are consistently established and implemented across the district.
1	2	3	• Classroom assessments are differentiated according to the ELLs' English language proficiency levels using a variety of reliable assessment strategies that incorporate visual, graphic, and interactive supports.
1	2	3	• Teachers build authentic assessments into instruction to measure ELLs' understanding of academic content and their progress in English language development.
1	2	3	• Common assessments, classroom assessments, and standardized assessment data are used to document ELLs' growth over time and monitor students' progress.
1	2	3	• Data from standardized assessments and authentic assessments are reviewed and used to evaluate language education program effectiveness.

IMPLICATIONS AND COMMENTS _____

_____

_____

_____

			Key Practice 4.	**Embracing an Additive Bilingualism Perspective:** Instructional and linguistic decisions for ELLs are based on understanding that ELLs are emerging bilingual students who use two languages for social and academic purposes.
1	2	3		• Bilingualism is valued, and bilingualism and biliteracy development is promoted to the greatest degree possible.
1	2	3		• A sequence of ESL instruction is provided over a period of several years so that ELLs can reach the high levels of English language proficiency needed for school success.
1	2	3		• Language instruction is planned so that what is learned in one language supports and reinforces what is learned in the other language.
1	2	3		• Primary language support is used to preview, explain, and clarify concepts that ELLs encounter in English-speaking classrooms.
1	2	3		• Primary language instruction is provided in bilingual classrooms to develop academic language, to develop literacy, and to teach grade-level subjects (whenever possible).

IMPLICATIONS AND COMMENTS _____

_____

_____

_____

The Common Classroom Practices for All ELL Educators
(PRACTICES 5–8)

			Key Practice 5.	**Using Big Ideas to Plan Instruction:** Curriculum and instruction are planned that specifically target the "big ideas" (statements of essential learning) that lead to core state standards.
1	2	3		• Teachers use standards to identify the big ideas that students will need to understand the key concepts in units and lessons.
1	2	3		• Teachers structure comprehensible learning activities that lead to understanding of the big ideas.
1	2	3		• Teachers use materials that explain and exemplify the big ideas (charts, visuals, tradebooks, videos).
1	2	3		• Teachers develop differentiated assessment strategies that allow ELLs to demonstrate their understanding of the big ideas and give examples.

IMPLICATIONS AND COMMENTS _____

_____

_____

_____

			Key Practice 6.	**Implementing Meaningful Vocabulary-Building Instruction:** Teachers pre-teach vocabulary words necessary to understand lessons and passages. New words in context are taught during the lessons/passages, and practice is provided for students to use the words in various contexts after the lessons/passages.
1	2	3		• Teachers explicitly teach new vocabulary and involve the students in definition-getting.

1	2	3	• Teachers plan oral vocabulary-building strategies to move ELLs' receptive vocabulary toward expressive language.
1	2	3	• Teachers structure oral and written activities for students to use new vocabulary.
1	2	3	• Teachers coordinate vocabulary instruction and practice in ESL, bilingual, and general education classrooms.

IMPLICATIONS AND COMMENTS _____
_____
_____
_____

Key Practice 7.	**Activating Students' Prior Knowledge:** Teachers structure activities that connect ELLs' previous knowledge and cultural experiences to current lessons and build a comprehensible context for learning.

1	2	3	• Teachers plan multiple prior knowledge activities that connect students' knowledge and cultural experiences with upcoming lessons.
1	2	3	• Teachers use instructional supports (e.g., visuals, demonstrations, and experiential activities) while implementing prior knowledge activities.
1	2	3	• Teachers ask open-ended questions to encourage English-proficient and ELL students to share their knowledge and experiences.
1	2	3	• Teachers structure pre-reading activities that build vocabulary and increase comprehension before all reading assignments.

IMPLICATIONS AND COMMENTS _____
_____
_____
_____

Key Practice 8.	**Structuring Student Interaction:** Opportunities for academic development and language practice are provided by implementing activities that require students to talk with each other about what they are learning.

1	2	3	• Program configurations and classroom schedules are organized in ways that promote meaningful interactions among ELLs and their English-speaking peers.
1	2	3	• Teachers promote learning-centered classroom talk that engages all students and requires them to share ways of thinking and problem solving.
1	2	3	• Teachers implement interactive learning tasks that ask students to use target vocabulary to talk about newly learned information.
1	2	3	• Teachers plan small-group instructional tasks that require students to work interdependently.

IMPLICATIONS AND COMMENTS _____
_____
_____
_____

The Core Instructional Practices of Every Program for ELLs
(PRACTICES 9–11)

Key Practice 9.	**Implementing English as a Second Language Instruction:** Daily ESL instruction in the four language domains (listening, speaking, reading, and writing) is planned and implemented. Instruction is focused on the academic language that ELLs need to understand and express essential grade-level concepts.
1 2 3	• Teachers coordinate academic content and language instruction with core content and language development standards.
1 2 3	• Teachers connect receptive language skills and beginning level ELLs' oral language to academic English language instruction.
1 2 3	• Teachers use a content-based ESL approach when teaching intermediate and advanced ELLs.
1 2 3	• Teachers implement common classroom practices with meaningful language learning activities for ELLs at all English language proficiency levels by using sensory, graphic, and interactive supports.

IMPLICATIONS AND COMMENTS _____

_____

_____

_____

Key Practice 10.	**Implementing Meaning-Based Literacy Instruction:** Whenever possible, initial literacy instruction is taught in the primary language; when literacy is taught in English, teachers plan and implement meaning-based literacy instruction that builds on students' oral language and uses comprehensible text at appropriate English language proficiency levels.
1 2 3	• Teachers begin instruction by finding out what ELL students already know about literacy.
1 2 3	• Teachers use ELLs' oral language as a pathway to reading and writing.
1 2 3	• Teachers integrate meaningful and functional literacy tasks within the five essential elements of reading using a balanced literacy approach.
1 2 3	• Teachers implement multiple comprehension strategies before, during, and after reading.
1 2 3	• Teachers use nonfiction text as well as fictional stories and passages to improve reading and writing across the curriculum.
1 2 3	• Teachers use appropriately leveled texts and students' knowledge of the English language to help struggling older readers improve their reading skills.
1 2 3	• Teachers document the ELLs' progress in literacy learning over time.
1 2 3	• Teachers use bilingual support staff and ELL parents strategically so they can support the literacy development of ELLs.

IMPLICATIONS AND COMMENTS _____

_____

_____

_____

			Key Practice 11.	**Implementing Comprehensible Academic Content Instruction:** Teachers model and teach academic content using language a little above the ELLs' current English proficiency levels, making new information comprehensible by using appropriate instructional supports.
1	2	3		• Instructional activities are aligned to district curriculum guides and core state standards.
1	2	3		• Teachers include language objectives as well as content objectives in sheltered instruction lesson planning.
1	2	3		• Teachers differentiate instruction according to ELLs' language proficiency levels.
1	2	3		• Teachers implement specific strategies to help older struggling ELLs learn from their textbooks.
1	2	3		• Teachers use authentic assessment strategies to evaluate ELLs' progress and fulfill grading requirements.
1	2	3		• Teachers develop strategic ways to use the ELLs' primary language to support academic instruction in English.

IMPLICATIONS AND COMMENTS _____
_____
_____
_____

Organizing the Key Practices into Effective Program Configurations
(PRACTICE 12)

			Key Practice 12.	**Structuring the Language Education Program:** Instruction is organized to effectively meet the literacy, academic, and language needs of the districts' ELL populations.
1	2	3		• A district language education committee is established to develop or restructure the language education program.
1	2	3		• The extent of the use of the ELLs' primary language is determined according to the specific academic needs of the district's ELL populations.
1	2	3		• New and restructured program configurations have been constructed by figuring out how ESL, literacy, and academic content instruction can be effectively implemented.
1	2	3		• The language education program has been developed through a collaborative process that defines the purpose of the language education program, grounds the program in standards, includes short- and long-term professional development plans, and shares information with parents and other stakeholders.
1	2	3		• The language education committee monitors the programs for ELLs by annually assessing professional development needs and reviewing student data to evaluate the ELLs' progress.

IMPLICATIONS AND COMMENTS _____
_____
_____
_____

Shared Practices at the District, School, and Classroom Levels

KEY PRACTICE 1 **Structuring Equitable School and Classroom Environments**

Implement literacy, content and ESL instruction in language-rich, low-anxiety environments that affirm diversity and value bilingualism.

KEY PRACTICE 2 **Educating English Language Learners through Collaboration**

Address the challenges of educating ELL student populations through collaborative teams who share common goals, common language, and common practices.

KEY PRACTICE 3 **Implementing a Balanced Student Assessment System**

Complement standardized measures with common and classroom assessments that yield evidence of ELL performance in literacy, academic achievement, and language proficiency, and use that assessment data to inform instructional and programmatic decisions.

KEY PRACTICE 4 **Embracing an Additive Bilingualism Perspective**

Make instructional and linguistic decisions about ELLs based on an understanding of these learners as emerging bilingual students who use two languages for social and academic purposes.

Key practices 1 through 4 ensure equitable learning environments for all diverse learners, not just English language learners (ELLs). Since they are designed to be implemented at the district, school, and classroom levels, we think of these four practices as the "big picture" key practices. Principals, school leadership teams, and grade-level teacher teams generally have the responsibility to plan, implement, and oversee effective implementation of district policies, school program structures, school-wide practices, and common classroom practices and procedures. Collaborative teams that meet regularly can use this handbook as their common focus for improving instruction and achievement for ELLs. They can take on the challenge of and responsibility for planning the implementation of the "big picture" key practices that will be shared by all educators who work with ELLs.

Structuring Equitable School and Classroom Environments

Implement literacy, content, and ESL instruction in language-rich, low-anxiety environments that affirm diversity and value bilingualism.

- Increase staff members' cultural competence by planning on-going professional development that provides information, shares effective strategies, defines roles, and shapes positive attitudes about ELLs.

- Institutionalize district policies and procedures for ELLs in all schools.

- Make certain that teachers who have ELLs in their classrooms have substantial training in sheltered instruction methods.

- Create school and classroom environments that affirm linguistic and cultural diversity by representing ELLs' languages, cultures, and experiences within school routines, events, and activities.

- Plan enriching, comprehensible instruction for all learners that includes multicultural perspectives and examples in lessons, displays useful language prompts on classroom walls, and uses comprehensible trade books about grade-level topics.

- Implement instruction, tasks, and classroom schedules in ways that allow ELLs to be actively engaged in learning throughout their school day.

THE BIG IDEAS

- Providing equitable and effective learning environments for English Language Learners (ELLs) is the responsibility of all educators.

- Structuring for equity for linguistically and culturally diverse learners involves decision-making about policies, program configurations, curriculum development, instructional activities and socio-cultural considerations.

- Collaborating teams can use the twelve key practices to guide their decision-making at the district, school, and classroom levels.

Diversity in educational settings is the norm. First, the number of *language-minority students* who speak a language other than English at home doubled between 1979 and 2005 (Center for Great Public Schools, 2008) and many—but not all—of these language-minority students are officially designated by schools as ELLs. Some of these ELLs may be new arrivals with strong educational backgrounds in their home countries who have developed literacy in their first language. Others may be long-term ELLs who have been in U.S. schools for years and speak conversational English but are struggling with grade-level reading and writing in English. Still others may be refugees with limited or interrupted formal schooling who have not developed school literacies in any language. Some of these ELLs may have strong support for education and literacy from their homes, while others may be struggling to survive economically and socially. How ELLs feel about their relationships with the English speakers and language-minority students in their school, the local community, and the larger society influences their orientation toward learning English and toward taking on the challenge of learning complex grade-level content in a new language (Nieto, 2000). Providing equitable learning environments for *all* students means that teachers and administrators must learn more about the needs of students who generally do not thrive in "one-size-fits-all" instructional programs designed for the language-majority student population.

Furthermore, we find tremendous diversity in the range and scope of the actual language-minority population or ELL population in any particular district or school as well as in the district and school response to the challenge of providing an equitable education to its diverse learners. Some schools and districts have small numbers of ELLs who are relatively new to the community; some have increasing numbers of ELLs from a wide range of linguistic and cultural backgrounds; and some have large numbers of students from the same linguistic and cultural background who are well-established in the local community. Some districts have been addressing the challenges of diverse learners in their schools for several decades; other districts are only beginning to take on this challenge. Some districts have significant numbers of teachers who know how to shelter and differentiate instruction for the ELLs in their classes and programs, but many administrators and teachers today are just beginning to really embrace the notion that they are ELL educators too if they have ELLs in their classes or schools.

Key Practice 1 discusses creating equitable school and classroom environments for all students, particularly ELLs, in any district or school context. We share ways that teachers can implement instruction in environments that affirm diversity, value bilingualism, and foster integration. We provide information for administrators and leadership teams to help them arrange sheltered ESL training and on-going professional development that provides information, shares effective strategies, defines roles, and shapes positive attitudes about ELLs. We discuss how administrators and teachers can integrate the ELLs' languages, cultures, and experiences within school routines, activities, and events. We provide suggestions for including multicultural perspectives and examples that can enrich classroom instruction. Finally, we discuss the importance of actively engaging ELLs in learning throughout their school day.

Developing Cultural Competence among Staff Members

Learning environments for linguistically and culturally diverse learners are more equitable when administrators, teachers, and school staff members make decisions about school policies, program structures, curriculum development, and instructional activities that are informed by their understanding of how socio-cultural issues influence learning and teaching. One of the often-stated goals that we educators have for our students is that they become culturally competent to be successful in a global society. Commins (2010) points out that "if students are to become culturally competent, so must educators." In educational settings, *cultural competence* generally describes the ability of educators to successfully teach students who come from cultures other than their own. Staff members can become culturally competent educators through on-going professional development that provides information, shares effective strategies, defines roles, and shapes positive attitudes about ELLs.

Nieto suggests three steps to help educators learn how to become more competent to teach culturally diverse students: "First, we simply need to learn more. Second, we need to confront our own racism and biases. Third, becoming a multicultural person means learning to see reality from a variety of perspectives" (Nieto, 2000, pp. 338–339). Furthermore, Diller and Moule (2005) describe the process of becoming culturally competent as developing certain personal and interpersonal awareness and sensitivities, developing certain bodies of cultural knowledge, and mastering a set of skills that provide a foundation for effective cross-cultural teaching. The authors suggest that there are four basic cultural competence skill areas that apply to individual educators, to the schools where they work, and to the educational system in which they work. First, educators must accept and respect the fact that their students represent different cultural backgrounds and customs, different ways of communicating, and different traditions and values. Secondly, they must be culturally aware that their own cultures—all of their experiences, background, knowledge, skills, beliefs, values, and interests—shape their sense of who they are; where they fit into their family, school, community, and society; and how they interact with students. Next, educators need to understand the dynamics of cultural interactions and know that there are many factors that can affect relationships, interactions, and cultural experiences. Finally, educators can learn about academic considerations of their ELL's particular cultures. All of these processes can help educators adapt and affirm diversity by designing educational services and instruction to better serve diverse student populations.

It is important that the language education committee plan professional development for the committee itself as well as the teachers, administrators, teacher assistants, and other personnel who will work directly with the

ELLs. Professional development must focus on staff members' responsibilities to provide equitable, effective learning environments for ELLs. However, these stakeholders do not necessarily need the same type or amount of professional development.

In our work as educational specialists, we have participated in and presented at numerous workshops at teacher institutes, at schools on in-service days, and through multiple workshops at the Illinois Resource Center. It is clear to us that participants gain more knowledge and are more actively engaged in professional development when the training specifically relates to their educational roles and responsibilities. The *Matching Professional Development to Educators' Roles Template*, following this chapter, represents our recommendations for professional development according to the typical roles and responsibilities of various stakeholders. The topics represent the knowledge and skills that we believe are necessary to implement the twelve key practices. The chart is not meant to be an all-encompassing list of all professional development training. However, the language education committee and school leadership teams can use this comprehensive list as a well-developed starting point to design short- and long-term professional development action plans. The committee and administrators who also plan professional development may need to adapt and add specific topics to make the training locally appropriate.

The language education committee can use the professional development template along with the results from the Twelve Key Practices Checklist to plan specific training for specific groups of educators. Professional development can be arranged and presented at professional learning community (PLC) meetings, faculty meetings, study groups, workshops, and other learning opportunities offered by the school district. Many of the topics are often addressed at statewide conferences and in graduate-level courses that are designed for teachers of ELLs. The many topics on the chart can be used to develop a menu of options so that teachers and other stakeholder groups can select the topics that they are most interested in learning. Table 2.1 shows how several topics can be clustered together.

Institutionalizing District Policies and Procedures for English Language Learners

Educators who see language and cultural diversity "as resources to be developed rather than as problems to be overcome offer more positive environments for ELLs and their families and members of their households" (Freeman & Hamayan, 2006, p. 41). One of the first concepts about language learning that all educators can understand, embrace, and implement

Table 2.1 Sample Workshops for Educating ELLs

Topic 1: Becoming Culturally Competent Educators In Multicultural Schools

- Planning and implementing school-wide environments that support bilingualism and culturally diverse learners
- Understanding second language acquisition, the basics of academic language proficiency, and common myths and misconceptions about ELLs

Topic 2: Assessing ELLs in Mainstream Classrooms

- Using core state standards to develop big ideas and plan instruction and assessments
- Differentiating instruction and assessment according to the ELLs' language proficiency levels
- Creating rubrics, portfolio systems, and other common assessments to measure growth of ELLs in mainstream and language education classrooms

Topic 3: Implementing Two Common Classroom Key Practices

- Using big ideas to plan instruction and develop content and language objectives
- Developing and implementing comprehensible vocabulary activities for ELLs

is a policy that supports additive bilingualism. Just about all educators agree that being bilingual is a great human resource in social, academic, and economic settings. These educators can also easily accept the notion that learning a second language does not mean having to give up one's first language—rather, it involves adding a new language to one's repertoire (Walqui, 2000). When educators find ways to use the ELLs' first language as a tool to support learning *and* improve their first language skills, they are helping the students maintain their primary language. In this way, they are demonstrating that they value bilingualism. On the contrary, when well-meaning educators ignore the students' home language or perceive that their students' fluency in another language is a handicap, they tend to eliminate, or subtract, all signs of the students' language. This practice is characteristic of subtractive bilingualism (Richard-Amato & Snow, 2005).

At the district level, the school board, the superintendent, and other district administrators are the stakeholders that set broad policies and establish district-wide guidelines that affect language education programming and services. The language education committee can work with these leaders to look at the district's mission statement in light of the twelve key practices. They can use the Twelve Key Practices Checklist to help them determine if current staffing, programming, and daily instruction enable diverse learners (and, in particular, ELLs) to have ample opportunities to reach the goals set forth in the district's mission statement. Results from the use of the checklist will most likely indicate that professional development is needed and program configurations need to be adjusted. For example, the district administrators may want to hire additional English as a Second Language (ESL) teachers in order to facilitate the coordination of ESL instruction with content instruction in mainstream classrooms. Furthermore, they may decide to hire certified bilingual teachers or bilingual noncertified staff to provide meaningful primary language instruction and/or support. As attrition occurs naturally, the policy makers will want to hire teachers with diverse cultural backgrounds to more closely resemble the diversity of their student populations in all classrooms. Examples of these and other district-wide policies that can be adapted to more closely meet the needs of ELLs are described in Table 2.2.

Table 2.2 Institutionalizing Policies to Improve School and Classroom Environments for Linguistically and Culturally Diverse Learners

POLICIES AND DISTRICT-WIDE PRACTICES	
Mission Statements, Philosophy, and/or Purpose Statements	• goal statements recognize and value diverse learners. • school district policies and practices state how diverse learners are able to reach the goals set forth in goal statements.
Educators' Goals for English Language Learners	• administrators and teachers share the goal of providing instruction and programming for ELLs to be active, engaged learners who meet core state standards and English language proficiency standards. • secondary ELLs have full opportunities to meet graduation requirements. • the language education program configurations allow enough time to provide comprehensible literacy and academic instruction as well as ESL instruction.
Diversity of Teachers and Other Educators	• efforts are made to hire linguistically and culturally diverse administrators, teachers, and classified staff members. • efforts are made to place bilingual and culturally diverse teachers in general education classrooms as well as in language education classrooms.
Language Education Teachers' Schedules and Classroom Space	• the class size and/or case load of language education teachers does not exceed the number of students assigned to general education and content teachers. • the schedule of the language education teacher is based on the ELLs' needs rather than the logistics of an itinerant teacher's schedule. • the space designated for language education teachers has equivalent resources, materials, and status of classrooms of mainstream teachers.
Professional Development	• the districts' professional development initiatives provide training for all educators about educating ELLs and other diverse learners. • substantial sheltered instruction training is provided for all teachers who have ELLs in their classrooms.
Views Toward Bilingualism and Multiculturalism	• policy makers and program planners adopt the perspective of additive bilingualism as they develop language education program configurations.
Duration of ELLs' Participation in Language Education Program	• program configurations allow 5–7 years for ELLs to reach the academic English language proficiency needed to successfully learn complex academic concepts in the mainstream classrooms. • there are substantial course offerings at the secondary level (required and elective courses) that are designated for ELL students.

Providing Substantial Training in Sheltered Instruction

Classroom environments are most safe and positive for ELLs when instruction is comprehensible and students believe that they can be successful learners. When mainstream teachers receive substantial training in sheltered methods, they can significantly increase the amount of time that the ELLs are actively engaged in their classrooms. We define *substantial* sheltered instruction training as training that is similar to a graduate course, consisting of more than five all-day sessions at least one week apart so that between sessions participants can practice what they have learned. In this way, they can reflect about what works and what does not and bring these issues back to the training classroom for discussion. The training should include the typical components of sheltered instruction: implementing multiple vocabulary-building strategies; using graphic, sensory, and interactive supports to make information comprehensible; and utilizing ELLs' languages, cultures, and experiences to support learning. In addition, the sheltered instruction training must also teach how to adapt literacy instruction for ELLs and how to differentiate classroom tasks and assessments according to the ELLs' diverse needs and English proficiency levels.

Two widely known sheltered instruction training models, the Sheltered Instruction Observation Protocol (SIOP) (Echevarria et al., 2004) and Content and Language Integration as a Means of Bridging Success (CLIMBS) (WIDA Consortium, 2009) are research-based ESL methodologies that help ESL and mainstream teachers plan comprehensible instruction for ELLs. Information about these training models can easily be accessed via internet searches; in addition, many education professors, consultants, and specialists have developed sheltered instruction training programs based on SIOP and CLIMBS principles. A common outcome of the training is that elementary and secondary teachers who have received training in sheltered instruction training say that the training benefits all their students, not just their ELLs.

General education and secondary content teachers with sheltered instruction training can more effectively work with the certified language education teachers at their grade level and cluster level (primary, intermediate, secondary) and at the school level. Together, the teachers can share ideas, develop common instruction and assessment strategies, and coordinate units and lessons. All of these collaborative efforts help ELLs become actively engaged in all classrooms.

Creating School and Classroom Environments That Affirm Diversity

At the school level, principals and leadership teams can discuss ways that the entire school staff can create environments that convey respect for the immigrants' cultures and languages. Even minor physical conditions can determine whether or not the school is inviting to ELLs and their parents. For example, visitors and parents who arrive at the school's entrance usually find the door locked. Visitors from the majority culture group generally understand that locking school doors is a security precaution to ensure that students are safe; they know that there is a doorbell at a specific main entrance. Parents from other cultures may not make this assumption. To them, the locked doors may indicate that parents and visitors are not welcome. Creating student-made, welcoming signs at the school entrance in several languages is a great way to demonstrate that administrators, teachers, and other staff members affirm the diversity of the families, students, and the diverse community. And, of course, these signs should also point out where the doorbell is.

When ELLs enter new schools and classrooms, they are likely to experience frustration, anxiety, and embarrassment. Griego-Jones (1993) states that children's own attitudes and perceptions are at the core of their motivation to learn. When these learners perceive that their teachers respect them, try to get to know them, and value what they already know in their first language, they are more willing to take the risk to speak up and participate in classroom activities. Furthermore, when teachers and other school staff members understand the challenges that ELLs face, they can counteract negative messages the language-minority children may be experiencing in other areas of their lives (Nieto, 2000).

Adolescents in middle and high school are often characterized as students who especially need to find ways to gain a sense of belonging. Reacting to peer pressures, some students have met the need to belong by taking a negative path, such as joining gangs or taking part in other harmful activities (Nieto, 2000). The best way for teens to feel like they "belong" at school is to have positive, successful school experiences. In many schools, teachers have responded to minority-language students' social needs by sponsoring student clubs. For example, at one Illinois high school, the school soccer team's coach actively recruits students from the language education program. A Latino service club undertakes various service projects in the community and plans an annual senior recognition banquet. Another club of Asian students provides tutoring support at a

REFLECTIONS FROM THE FIELD

Structuring Opportunities for Meaningful Cross-Cultural Experiences

Sue Wagner

My colleague Barb Bonner and I thought that there were very few structured opportunities for students to develop friendships with students outside of their own ethnic and cultural groups at our high school. So we proposed the development of a student cross-cultural committee. The principal loved the idea and thought that the committee should be a human-relations task force that could also address issues of racial tensions that occasionally occurred at school. With his help, Barb and I established the Cross-Culture Committee (CCC). We targeted 50 or more students who had leadership qualities and were willing to make cross cultural friends. English teachers and guidance counselors helped us select White, African American, Latino, Asian, and other diverse students for this important student committee.

The CCC met once a month. Topics for the meetings varied; we had guest speakers, pertinent videos, and student panels that discussed various cross-cultural issues. One year, the committee performed at the annual Prejudice Reduction Conference sponsored by the Chicago Anti-Defamation League. The students presented funny skits that showed incidents of racial tension or cross-cultural conflicts that happen in high schools (e.g., inter-racial dating, excluding others by switching to another language). The skits were a resounding success; the CCC got a standing ovation from students from across the Chicagoland area. I will always remember Jill, the homecoming queen, turning around and saying to me, "Oh, Mrs. Wagner, I loved today—just think, I never would have become friends with my Latino and Laotian friends if it wasn't for the CCC!

middle school. These targeted clubs provide a sense of belonging and purpose for the students in their cultural group as well as in the school.

Principals and school leadership teams can take the responsibility to ensure that all school staff members (administrators, teachers, teacher assistants, secretaries, lunch room staff, etc.) understand their roles in providing equitable school and classroom environments where all learners feel secure and can have self-confidence that they can succeed. They can make sure that staff members understand the research and rationale of the key practices. For example, as the teachers learn appropriate ways to utilize the ELLs' primary language (e.g., encouraging them to process information in their own language with a bilingual tutor), they will also want to make sure that other staff members do not reprimand ELLs for using the primary language in the lunch room or on the playground.

As the principal and leadership team learn about research in the field and discuss the key practices, they will want to use the Twelve Key Practices Checklist to see how many of these essential practices are currently in place in school settings and classrooms. As the team uses the checklist to guide their discussions and decision-making, they are learning ways to improve learning environments for ELLs. The team will want to review the checklist results to identify the practices, strategies, tasks, and processes that can be focused on and implemented more consistently to improve learning environments. The results can be discussed at a faculty meeting where administrators and teachers can share ideas and suggest ways to make sure that school environments support learning for diverse learners.

Planning Enriching, Comprehensible Instruction for Diverse Learners

When teachers make efforts to develop and implement multicultural curriculum units, their students learn and respect their own cultures as well as the cultures of the broader society. Clarissa Adams-Fletcher, the 2011 Foreign Language Teacher of the Year, points out that "students who can communicate effectively, collaborate, think critically, be creative and innovative, and have an open-minded disposition toward cultural differences will become the backbone of our society" (Adams-Fletcher, 2011).

As teacher teams design curriculum units and themes, they can develop topics, themes, and objectives to help students know themselves, understand each other, and explore world views. They can create learning activities that provide multiple perspectives about various issues in the community, country, and world. At the same time, they can plan learning activities that recognize and value the diversity of the students within their classrooms. Bilingual and ESL teachers can take the lead by sharing information about their ELLs' cultures, experiences, and background knowledge with their collaborating teacher teams. Teachers can ask their ELLs to share their meaningful experiences (e.g., farming in drought conditions, wartime problems, political and immigration issues). Information about the ELLs' home countries and previous experiences can then be connected to instruction. Older ELLs are often part of family discussions about many issues and often want to share their views. The curriculum is enhanced when teachers integrate the cultural contributions and perspectives of the diverse groups represented in their classrooms, at the school, and in society (Hamayan & Freeman, 2012).

There are multiple multilingual resources on the world-wide web that English-speaking teachers can use to strategically employ primary language support for classroom instruction as well as to find resources to include their ELL students' languages in class activities (Sanchez-Lopez & Young, 2011). For example, one website offers songs, rhymes, and information from all over the world in English and in other languages. A few of these websites are listed in the Recommended Readings at the end of this chapter. When teachers extend curriculum topics by infusing multicultural examples and perspectives into their themes and topics, they are planning meaningful learning activities for ELLs and their English-proficient peers.

ELL students thrive when they are comfortable enough to speak up and take the risks that accompany second language learning. Jeannette Gordon, one of our colleagues at the Illinois Resource Center, suggests a quick tip to make lessons more multicultural. She suggests that teachers routinely add the phrase "from around the world" to lesson plans and content objectives. For example, during a health unit, a graphic of the food pyramid can include foods "from around the world." As a language arts project, the students can develop family histories by writing to grandparents

REFLECTIONS FROM THE FIELD

Using ELL Students as Classroom Resources

Sue Wagner

One of my student pages (helpers), Quang, was a Vietnamese student who was an English-proficient, high-achieving junior, fully exited from the language education program. One day, Quang came into my office when the sixth period bell rang, as usual. Something was bothering him so I asked him what was up. He told me that he just took his history test about the Viet Nam War. He said he did well on the test but the textbook didn't accurately describe the war. He said that the teacher never asked him, the only Vietnamese student in the class, if he wanted to share his insider's view. I was surprised. Quang would have been an excellent resource! I highly respected his history teacher. I told Quang that perhaps the teacher didn't even know that he was from Viet Nam, since there were many Asians at our school. Or, perhaps, if he knew that Quang and his family fled Viet Nam, maybe he thought it would be improper or too personal to ask him to share his views of the war. I said that I would be happy to suggest to the teacher that he ask Quang to share some thoughts and experiences. (For example, Quang's father was just released from a "re-education camp" after many years.) "Oh, no," he insisted. "It's too late now." I respected Quang's wishes so I didn't talk with the teacher. However, I asked him and several of my advanced ELL students (from several language groups) to help make a list of ways that their experiences could be used as resources in various courses. They enthusiastically came up with some great ideas. As I recall, they suggested life in countries where residents are not free, immigration and refugee issues, monarchies, coups, caste systems, and other societal structures. I shared their ideas at the next faculty meeting.

and sharing perspectives on issues in their home countries. The family history and research products can be showcased and shared with other students in English (and in the primary language, when possible).

Secondary teachers generally have over 100 students in their various classes. These large student numbers make it difficult to get to know students individually. Even so, secondary teachers can adapt course curriculum and instruction to take into account the interests and experiences of diverse learners. The language education teachers can share general information with their colleagues about their ELL students' backgrounds, jobs, experiences, talents, and interests. These discussions can help teachers in all departments find ways to include and connect the ELLs' experiences to course curricula. Using ELL students as resources, social studies department teachers can incorporate wartime events, natural disasters, cultural conflicts, and historical information about the ELLs' home countries into their units and themes. The world language department teachers can provide course offerings beyond traditional foreign language courses. They can design heritage language courses designed to help students improve their first language skills in order to become fully bilingual and bicultural in oral and written expression.

There are several typical ways that teachers can make their classroom environments engaging and user-friendly for ELLs. They can display useful language on classroom walls (current vocabulary words, big ideas of curriculum topics, writing prompts, student writing samples, greetings in many languages, etc.) In addition, they can identify and use engaging visuals and video clips, standards-based picture books, content books, and

ESL supplemental materials (in English and primary language) about current classroom topics. These user-friendly learning prompts and materials help all learners.

Ensuring That English Language Learners Are Actively Engaged in Classroom Instruction

It is extremely important that teachers implement instruction, tasks, and classroom schedules in ways that allow ELLs to be actively engaged in learning throughout their school day. ELLs are "actively engaged" in their learning when language demands are reduced and instruction is appropriately adapted for them. We define ELLs as active and engaged learners when they are able to:

- understand and respond to speech that is directed to them;
- be engaged in meaningful tasks which allow them to connect what they already know with new information;
- comprehend many oral class presentations and follow most directions;
- answer questions and orally participate in classroom activities;
- understand and use some academic language; and
- understand the cultural norms of the classroom and school.

Active, engaged ELLs who can do the preceding classroom tasks will certainly continue to struggle with English grammar, vocabulary, and syntax both orally and in their written products. However, when they cannot exhibit the characteristics of active and engaged learners, they are typically not being provided with comprehensible instruction appropriate for their English language proficiency (ELP) levels. Admittedly, meeting these needs is a huge demand, especially for teachers who have little training and limited experience working with children who are not yet fluent in English.

Coordinating the school subject area teaching schedule is a must so that ELLs are actively engaged when they move from one classroom to another subject in a different classroom. For example, at the elementary level, a specific two-hour time period (usually called the literacy block) is scheduled when all children at a specific grade level are engaged in literacy. Time schedules for general education, bilingual, or ESL classroom content area instruction must also be coordinated so that ELLs with intermediate ELP levels (levels 4 and 5) can begin the transition into general education classrooms through increased amounts of time learning subject matter in the mainstream classrooms. When teachers establish specific time periods for literacy blocks and content area instruction, ELLs and children in other special programs can be actively engaged in meaningful instruction in all school subjects as they move between general education classrooms to language education and other specialized classrooms.

In this chapter, we have shown how developing equitable instructional programs for ELLs involves collaborative decision-making about policies, program configurations, curriculum development, instructional activities, and socio-cultural considerations. We have discussed the organization and roles of PLC teams at the district, school, and classroom levels. These teams can take on the challenge to create effective school and classroom environments so that ELLs are actively engaged in learning grade-level concepts. In the next chapter, we discuss how these teams can work and learn together to meet the goal of school success for all learners and, in particular, ELLs.

QUESTIONS FOR REFLECTION AND ACTION

1. Nieto suggests three steps to help educators learn how to become culturally competent to teach diverse students: "First, we simply need to learn more. Second, we need to confront our own racism and biases. Third, becoming a multicultural person means learning to see reality from a variety of perspectives." As a group, discuss what these steps mean to each of you.

2. How do administrators, teachers, and support staff create equitable environments for language learners at your school? Place the responses in these four categories: (1) school policies and program structures; (2) curriculum development; (3) instructional activities, and (4) socio-cultural considerations. Which areas need to be addressed to improve school settings and classroom environments for diverse learners?

Recommended Readings

BBC Languages. (2011). News and analysis in your language. Available at http://www.bbc.co.uk/worldservice/languages/.

Commins, N., & Miramontes, O. (2005). *Linguistic diversity and teaching.* Mahwah, NJ: Lawrence Erlbaum Associates.

eGlossary. (2012). Math concepts translated into various languages. Glencoe, IL: McGraw Hill. Available at http://www.glencoe.com/sec/math/mlg/mlg.php

Freeman, R. (2004). *Building on community bilingualism.* Philadelphia: Caslon Publishing.

International Children's Digital Library. (2011). Multilingual books online. Manchester, MA, available at http://www.icdlbooks.org/.

Nieto, S. (2000). *Affirming diversity: The sociopolitical context of multicultural education.* New York: Addison Wesley Longman.

WIDA Consortium (2009). CLIMBS professional development training program. Madison, WI: Wisconsin Center for Educational Research.

Yannucci, L. (2011). Mama Lisa's world of children and international culture, a place for songs, rhymes and traditions from across the globe. Available at http://www.mamalisa.com/.

The checklist is written using measurable statements that can be used to evaluate and monitor language education programs and instruction at the district, school, and classroom levels. The district language education committee and school leadership teams can use the checklist as a diagnostic tool to identify the areas that represent the biggest challenges during the restructuring process. Various teams can use the results of the checklist as a starting point to determine the professional development that educators need to know in order to successfully implement the practices. Teacher teams can use the checklist to evaluate their own teaching practices to recognize ways in which they can immediately make instructional improvements.

SCORING DIRECTIONS:
1 = This practice IS implemented.
2 = This practice is in progress or is in place in some classrooms.
3 = This practice is NOT currently in place.

			Shared Practices at the District, School, and Classroom Levels
			Structuring Equitable School and Classroom Environments: Literacy, content, and ESL instruction is implemented in language rich, low-anxiety environments that affirm diversity and value bilingualism.
1	2	3	• On-going professional development is planned for all stakeholders that provides information, shares effective strategies, defines roles, and shapes positive attitudes about ELLs.
1	2	3	• District policies and procedures for ELLs are institutionalized and in place in all schools.
1	2	3	• All teachers who have ELLs in their classrooms have substantial training in sheltered instruction methods.
1	2	3	• School routines, events, and activities are developed to represent ELLs' languages, cultures, and experiences.
1	2	3	• Teachers plan enriching and comprehensible lessons that include multicultural examples/perspectives.
1	2	3	• Teachers display useful language on walls and provide numerous trade books about current topics around the classroom. (e.g., picture books, content books, ESL supplemental materials in English and, when possible, in the ELLs' primary language).
1	2	3	• Classroom instruction and schedules are implemented in ways that allow ELLs to be actively engaged in learning throughout their school day.

IMPLICATIONS AND COMMENTS _____

_____

_____

_____

Matching Professional Development to Educators' Roles Template

H = This is a high priority area of professional development for this stakeholder group.

H* = This stakeholder group is likely to have previous training in this area. However, ongoing professional development is highly recommended.

✓ = This topic is not a high priority for this stakeholder group; however general knowledge of this topic is recommended. For example, administrators don't need to know specific teaching strategies; however, they do need to know how to look for evidence of these strategies when evaluating and providing feedback to teachers of ELLs.

✱ = This is a high priority area for teachers or other educators who have assigned responsibilities for implementing this practice to ELLs (e.g., formal literacy instruction, parent education coordinator).

NA = This topic is not applicable for this group.

THE BIG PICTURE: Shared Practices at the District, School, and Classroom Levels

	General Education Teachers, Specialists (art, music, etc.)	Secondary Content Teachers	ESL Teachers & ESL assistants	Bilingual Teachers & Bilingual Assistants	Principals	Language Education Program Coordinator	Superintendent	Language Education Committee	Secretaries, Nurses, Bus Drivers, Cafeteria Staff, etc.
Working within professional learning communities	H	H	H	H	H	H	H	H	✓
Planning and implementing school-wide environments that support bilingualism and culturally diverse learners	H	H	H	H	H	H	✓	H	✓
Understanding the basics of additive bilingualism, second language acquisition process, and how ELLs develop academic language proficiency,	H	H	H*	H*	H	H*	✓	H	✓
Becoming culturally competent educators/individuals and common myths and misconceptions about ELLs	H	H	H*	H*	H	H*	H	H	H
Using authentic entry-level assessment procedures (e.g. home language surveys, writing samples, gathering background information, informal reading inventories)	✱	✱	H	H	✓	H	✓	✓	NA
Creating rubrics, portfolio systems, and other common assessments to measure growth of ELLs in mainstream and language education classrooms	H	H	H	H	✓	✓	NA	NA	NA
Developing multicultural curricular themes and topics across grade levels	H	H	H	H	✓	✓	NA	NA	NA
Developing language-rich school and classroom environments	H	H	H	H	✓	H*	✓	✓	NA
Developing and implementing effective parent involvement strategies (learning activities at home, how to support children's literacy development, etc.)	H	✱	H	H	✓	H*	NA	✓	NA
Working with language minority community and developing a parent advisory committee	✱	NA	H*	H*	H	H*	✓	✓	NA
Using primary language support effectively in English-speaking classrooms	H	H	H	H*	✓	✓	✓	NA	NA
Understanding when student use of the primary language is appropriate and when it is inappropriate	H	H	H	H	H	H	✓	H	H
Implementing effective translating and interpreting strategies (working with translators and interpreters as well as translating and interpreting skills)	✓	✓	H	H*	H	H	✓	✓	✓
Teaching ELLs with limited prior schooling and ELLs with special needs	✱	✱	✱	✱	✓	H	✓	✓	✓

Matching Professional Development to Educators' Roles Template
(Continued)

	General Education Teachers, Specialists (art, music, etc.)	Secondary Content Teachers	ESL Teachers & ESL assistants	Bilingual Teachers & Bilingual Assistants	Principals	Language Education Program Coordinator	Superintendent	Language Education Committee	Secretaries, Nurses, Bus Drivers, Cafeteria Staff, etc.
THE COMMON CLASSROOM PRACTICES FOR TEACHERS WHO SHARE ELLs									
Using big ideas to plan instruction and develop language and content objectives **SUGGESTED STRATEGIES:** anticipation guides, learning logs, exit slips, Venn diagrams	H	H	H	H	✓	H	NA	NA	NA
Effective vocabulary building activities for teaching ELLs **SUGGESTED STRATEGIES:** word sorts, connect-twos, word walls, cognate walls, concept maps	H	H	H	H	✓	✓	NA	NA	NA
Activating and building upon prior knowledge **SUGGESTED STRATEGIES:** KWLs, word sorts, picture walks, using text structure clues	H	H	H	H	✓	✓	NA	NA	NA
Implementing cooperative learning strategies with a focus on enhancing oral language development and student interaction **SUGGESTED STRATEGIES:** retellings, jigsaw, say something, T-charts	H	H	H	H	✓	✓	NA	NA	NA
Teaching, explaining and clarifying newly learned concepts **SUGGESTED STRATEGIES:** graphic organizers, sentence/ paragraph frames, connect-twos, LEA,	H	H	H	H	✓	✓	NA	NA	NA
Using the primary language to improve reading and writing in both first and second languages **SUGGESTED STRATEGIES:** read-alouds, dictations, echo reading, LEA	H	H	H*	H*	✓	✓	NA	NA	NA
Using instructional strategies to develop classroom assessments **SUGGESTED STRATEGIES:** Venn diagrams, sentence strips, concept maps, T-charts, and other graphic organizers	H	H	H	H	✓	✓	NA	NA	NA

	General Education Teachers, Specialists (art, music, etc.)	Secondary Content Teachers	ESL Teachers & ESL assistants	Bilingual Teachers & Bilingual Assistants	Principals	Language Education Program Coordinator	Superintendent	Language Education Committee	Secretaries, Nurses, Bus Drivers, Cafeteria Staff, etc.
THE CORE INSTRUCTIONAL PRACTICES FOR TEACHERS WHO SHARE ELLs									
Substantial training in sheltered instruction, including the use of sensory, graphic, and interactive supports appropriate to students' ELP levels	H	H	H*	H*	✓	H*	NA	✓	NA
Meaning-based literacy and essential components of reading instruction for ELLs	H	✼	H	H	H	✓	✓	✓	NA
Implementing effective strategies: before, during, and/or after reading SUGGESTED STRATEGIES: anticipation guides, DRTA, marking a text, exit slips, learning logs	H	H	H	H	✓	✓	NA	NA	NA
Co-planning, curriculum coordination, and fostering student integration	H	✓	H	H	H	H	NA	✓	NA
Differentiating instruction and assessment according to the ELLs' language proficiency levels	H	H	H	H	✓	H*	NA	NA	NA
Using core state standards to plan instruction and assessments for ELLs	H	H	H	H	H	H	NA	NA	NA
Using ELD standards to plan instruction	H	H	H	H	✓	H	NA	NA	NA
Effective content-based ESL instructional strategies in four language domains (listening, speaking, reading, and writing)	✓	✓	H*	H*	✓	H*	NA	✓	NA
THE PROGRAMMING PRACTICE: Organizing all of the key practices into effective language education program configurations									
Understanding legal requirements and local policies that affect the education of ELLs	✓	✓	H*	H*	H	H*	H	H	✓
Planning program configurations that effectively use the primary language and sheltered instruction (in English) across the grade levels	✓	✓	H	H	H	H	✓	H	NA
Using data (including standardized, state, local and classroom assessments) to improve the education of ELLs	H	H	H	H	H	H	✓	H	NA

Educating English Language Learners through Collaboration

Address the challenges of educating ELL student populations through collaborative teams who share common goals, common language, and common practices.

- Establish an ELL-focused professional learning community of district-wide, school-wide, and teacher teams that work and learn together to improve programs and instruction for ELLs.

- Convene periodic district language education committee meetings to establish goals, monitor and refine programs, disseminate information, and provide support for collaborative efforts throughout the district.

- Establish school leadership teams that address school policy issues, curriculum development, instructional practices, and socio-cultural issues that affect learning environments for diverse learners.

- Structure time for general education, bilingual, and ESL teachers who share ELLs to have regular time for planning and for purposeful, reflective conversations.

- Connect the home and school by collaborating regularly with parents, implementing effective translation strategies, developing a parent advisory council, and connecting parents to classroom learning activities.

- Link the school and community by expanding collaborative efforts to include working with community organizations.

THE BIG IDEAS

- Collaborative teams at the district-wide level, school-wide level, and classroom level that share the common goal of school success for all learners, including English language learners (ELLs), can coordinate their efforts and share responsibilities.

- The most important working relationship that can improve instruction for elementary and middle school ELLs is collaboration among general education teachers and language education teachers who teach the same ELLs every day.

- Collaborative efforts of educators, parents, and leaders in community organizations support student learning.

Structuring equitable school and classroom environments that enable ELLs to achieve all program goals, including core state content and English language proficiency standards, is indeed challenging. Effectively addressing this challenge will not happen simply as a result of good intentions and good planning by individual educators working in isolation. However, when educators share a common goal and sincerely believe that effective changes can be realized when they work and learn together as a professional learning community (PLC), they are able to take on these challenges (Hord & Sommers, 2007).

Key Practice 2 outlines how collaborative teams of educators working at the classroom, school, and district levels who share common goals, common language, and common practices can in fact improve instruction and achievement for all students, particularly ELLs. District and school administrators can establish and initiate an ELL-focused PLC. They can convene periodic district language education committee meetings to establish goals, monitor and refine programs, disseminate information, and provide support for collaborative efforts throughout the district. They can establish school leadership teams that address school policy issues, curriculum development, instructional practices, and socio-cultural issues that affect learning environments for diverse learners, and they can structure time for general education, bilingual, and ESL teachers who share ELLs to have regular time for planning and for purposeful, reflective conversations. Effective PLCs can connect the home and school by collaborating regularly with parents, implementing effective translation strategies, developing a parent advisory council, and connecting parents to classroom learning activities. These PLCs also expand their collaborative efforts to include working with community organizations.

Establishing an English Language Learner–Focused Professional Learning Community

The term *professional learning community* is often used to describe a group of collaborative teams that work and learn interdependently to achieve a common goal. (DuFour & Ecker, 1998; DuFour et al., 2006). As its name implies, successful PLC teams are a community of *learners* as well as collaborators. When an ELL-focused language education PLC at the district, school-wide, and classroom levels learns, shares responsibilities and resources, solves problems, and makes decisions together, it can substantially improve language education programs and instruction. In this chapter, we describe how PLC teams can work as an interactive system to divide tasks, collaborate with each other, and support each other's work.

The first step toward meeting the goal of academic success for ELLs is for the district, school-wide, and teacher PLC teams to study relevant research and gather information about meeting the needs of the district's ELL populations. The Recommended Readings list at the end of each chapter in this book can help the teams find research-based information pertaining to each team's particular focus. For example, the district language education committee will want to review the research about federal laws and state regulations that affect language education programs. They will want to learn about effective policies and overarching principles that guide programmatic decisions. They will want to learn what the research says about various program approaches and second language instructional approaches designed to educate ELLs. These learning processes will help the language education team work with the school leadership teams to design, restructure, and implement the district's language education programs according to the needs of each school's specific ELL student populations.

The school leadership team will want to learn how to improve school-wide environments for diverse learners, how to develop school-wide assessment practices, and how to appropriately use and value the ELLs' languages and cultures. At the classroom level, teacher PLC teams will want to learn about meaning-based literacy instruction and how to adapt academic instruction for ELLs (sheltered instruction). They will also want to learn how to create common classroom assessments and learn how the ELLs' primary language can be used effectively to support learning.

As the PLC network members have purposeful, reflective conversations about educating ELLs and implementing the twelve key practices, they can begin to clarify each team's roles and responsibilities in meeting their goal. For example, although all of the teams will address the four "big picture" key practices, each committee will focus their attention on the practices in different ways. Table 3.1 shares how members of the PLC might divide tasks and coordinate their efforts as they all work towards implementing the four "big picture" key practices.

Convening Periodic District Language Education Committee Meetings

During the planning phase (year 1), as the various collaborative teams get started toward meeting their collective goal, the language education committee can coordinate and share information about the work of the PLC subgroups. The language education committee (under the direction of the superintendent) can initiate the PLC network by explaining the proposed goal, the tasks, and the processes of the PLC teams' work to principals and school leadership teams. The committee can provide research information and arrange professional development to help school leadership and teacher teams address school environment issues and the socio-cultural needs of ELLs. They can gather, synthesize, and report the results after the various committees have used the Twelve Key Practices Checklist to evaluate the current instructional program for ELLs. They can establish

Table 3.1   How a Language Education Professional Learning Community Shares Responsibilities for the Big Picture Key Practices

THE BIG PICTURE	**District Level:** The language education committee
Shared Practices at the District, School, and Classroom Levels:	**Focus of BIG PICTURE Key Practices:**
1. Develop **school and classroom environments** that support diversity	1. Foster positive **school environments** for ELLs across the district by providing professional development for various stakeholders.
2. Address challenges through **collaboration**	2. Support **collaboration** of PLC teams across district.
3. Utilize a balanced student **assessment** system	3. Develop comprehensive district **assessment** plan and oversee standardized assessment procedures.
4. Embrace an **additive bilingualism perspective**	4. Communicate an **additive bilingualism** perspective with district staff members and determine use of the **primary language** in program configurations.
The PLC network ensures that the four big picture key practices are addressed at all levels (district, school, and classroom).	**School-wide Level:** School leadership team
	Focus of BIG PICTURE Key Practices:
	1. Develop school-wide guidelines and practices that value diversity and support the development of language rich, low-anxiety **school and classroom environments.**
	2. **Collaborate** with district language education committee, staff development coordinator, teacher teams.
	3. Support development and implementation of common classroom **assessment** procedures.
	4. Learn how to value and support **additive bilingualism** and provide professional development about effective use of the **primary language** in school and classroom settings and program configurations (primary language support and instruction, student use of primary language).
	Classroom Level: Grade-level teams, teams of teachers who share ELLs
	Focus of BIG PICTURE Key Practices:
	1. Implement **classroom environments** that value bilingualism, utilize the ELLs' background knowledge and experiences, and display language prompts and other instructional supports.
	2. **Collaborate** with school leadership team, principal and other PLC teams.
	3. Create and implement common classroom **assessments** and manage portfolio system.
	4. Implement effective use of the **primary language** in classrooms (primary language support and/or instruction, student use of primary language).

goals, monitor and refine programs, disseminate information, and provide support for collaborative efforts throughout the district.

The district committee and the school-wide collaborative teams can meet quarterly to discuss and coordinate their work. For example, if the checklist results show that assessment of ELLs is often not adapted, which committee should be responsible to design and utilize a balanced assessment system? When results show that teachers do not have training in sheltered instruction methods, how can the language education committee and the principals plan and arrange substantial training in sheltered instruction? At the end of the year, these teams can share and discuss their progress and recommendations. These collaborative efforts ensure district-wide input to the members of the language education team as they prepare their recommendations about program development and restructuring to the school board.

During the implementation phase (year 2), the language education committee can share information about the PLC's goal, processes, and decisions at the district's principals meetings and other district-wide committee meetings. Committee members and the district language education coordinator can also share current research and information about effective practices for ELLs. If the district has an instructional council that makes curricular decisions and oversees textbook adoptions, the language education committee can provide information to identify effective materials for ELLs that are compatible with district benchmarks, English language proficiency standards, and core state standards.

All staff members who interact with diverse student populations inadvertently send messages that make children feel valued—or not. Bus drivers, secretaries, teacher assistants, librarians, security personnel, lunchroom workers—or any staff members who interact with ELLs—have the potential to play a part in creating welcoming school and classroom environments for all diverse language-minority children. Noncertified staff members rarely have professional development opportunities with certified school personnel. Therefore, the district's language education committee must find ways to provide professional development and share positive and important information about the language education program with all district employees. The professional development chart can be used to identify high-priority topics for noncertified staff members (see Matching Professional Development to Educators' Roles Template following the previous chapter). For example, a language education committee representative can request to be put on the agenda at a particular group's (e.g., bus drivers, lunchroom workers) meeting to present the rationale for language education program changes and purposes. A brief question and answer session about the district's culturally diverse students can be conducted. Providing short informational articles for the school district's newsletter is also a good way to share information.

Establishing School Leadership Teams

Leadership teams address many issues including school policy issues, instructional practices, and socio-cultural issues that affect learning environments for diverse learners. The principal can take the lead in ensuring that the environmental, instructional, and socio-cultural needs of ELLs are

REFLECTIONS FROM THE FIELD

How Administrators and Teachers Collaborated with My Students

Megan Salgado, Teacher

In May of 2006, there was a lot of negative talk about "illegal aliens." Across the country, several Latino students were planning walk-outs at their schools. The students in my Spanish for Native Speakers class said they wanted to walk out, too. Many were ELLs and about half were undocumented. I was worried so I shared my concerns with the principal. The next day, the superintendent, assistant superintendent, and the principal came to my classroom to encourage the students not to walk out. The students said they wanted to do something to make a statement and present a united front. The superintendent listened and suggested a "walk-in." The students reluctantly agreed. They decided to hold an immigration forum, suggesting that it should be a serious day. The administrators agreed, set a date, and found speakers. Several social studies teachers helped the students plan the event. The students made posters to adver-

tise the immigration forum that said "Be respectful, unite, be heard."

Out of 1800 students, 900 participated. The speakers talked about immigration policy issues and about the responsibilities of citizens. Then the students were assigned to groups to discuss what immigrants must do to be successful residents. The groups agreed that immigrants need to learn English, stay out of trouble, stay in school or work, and pay taxes. I will always appreciate the administrators' quick action to come into my classroom, show respect, listen to my students, and help them create a school-wide, meaningful discussion about immigration. The immigration forum was very successful, especially for my Spanish for Native Speakers class. One of the parents told me, "What you allowed our children to do changed their lives."

addressed by the school's leadership team made up of administrators, teachers, and representative ancillary certified personnel. Principals are instrumental in fostering collaborative efforts that will create and maintain successful instructional environments for ELLs. The principal's perceptions of the goals and status of the language education programs, the language education teachers, and the immigrant families have an impact on how other teachers and noncertified school staff members view the program and respect the ELLs (Wagner, 2001). When principals show an interest in teachers' collaborative efforts and projects, they are fostering environments where teachers and other staff members know they have the freedom to learn and try out new practices (Wagner, 2001).

The principal and the school leadership team can share the twelve key practices system with teachers and suggest that they all work together toward the goal of success for diverse learners. In many schools, the situation may be reversed—it will be teacher teams who share the key practices with the principal and school leadership team and suggest a school-wide effort. In either case, principals and the leadership team can help solve problems and make accommodations that the teachers may not be able to do themselves. For example, the principal and leadership team might be able to reassign classrooms so that collaborating general education and language education teaching teams can be near one another.

After reviewing the research and using the Twelve Key Practices Checklist, the principals, the school leadership team, and teacher teams can share what they have learned and discuss the challenges they face. In many cases, the teams will suggest immediate changes that will improve instruction for ELLs. For example, the teams may want to adjust classroom time schedules, develop school-wide policies to value and support bilingualism, and start developing common assessment practices.

Structuring Planning Time for General Education and English as a Second Language/Bilingual Teachers

The most important working relationship that can improve instruction for elementary and middle school ELLs is the collaboration among the general education teachers and the language education teachers who teach the same group of ELLs every day. These collaborative efforts are most effective when the language education teachers share their students with no more than three to four general education teachers. Clustering the ELLs into specific classrooms at each grade level minimizes the number of general education teachers with whom the language education teacher needs to collaborate. General education and ESL/bilingual teachers who share ELL students need structured time to have purposeful and reflective conversations.

Structured planning time is the optimal way for teachers to work and learn together. The school leadership team can take on the challenge to increase the time that mainstream teachers, language education teachers, and bilingual assistants can work together. The team may be able to help clear the obstacles that often prevent regular teacher collaboration. For example, with the principal's help, they might be able to schedule art, music, computer education, and/or physical education lessons in ways that the teachers have time to meet together while their students are attending these specialized lessons. In some schools, principals and the school leadership teams have figured out ways that they can use substitute teachers once a month for a half day to enable various collaborating teams to work together. In addition, the principal may be able to help teachers schedule their individual planning times in ways that accommodate their current collaborative efforts, or the principal may be able to set aside planning time during monthly staff meetings. The reality in many schools, however, is that there is never enough set-aside time to collaborate. In these cases, the principal and teachers need to be creative in order to find time for collaboration. By coordinating the scheduling of subject areas, lunch, and shared recesses, teachers may be able to squeeze in time to work together. Meeting outside of the school setting may enhance the collaborative process.

The initial purpose of the collaborative efforts between language education and general education teachers is how to divide assessment responsibilities. In other words, which teacher is responsible for teaching and evaluating student performance in the various subjects, how can they monitor student growth in separate classrooms, and how can they all contribute to and manage the portfolio assessment system. However, when language education and general education teachers are responsible for teaching the same group of ELLs, their students' learning is the center of their relationship. Therefore, as they begin to collaborate regularly, discussions about particular students usually enter the conversation. These conversations provide student-centered reasons to work together. The teachers will want to make sure that the ELL students will be engaged in learning activities that lead to core state standards and language standards in both classrooms, so they will want to find ways that concepts and vocabulary learned in one classroom setting can be reinforced and practiced in the other classroom. For example, an ESL teacher who teaches the vocabulary of scientific investigation in the ESL classroom will want to work with his/her general education colleagues to help them find ways that the ELLs can practice their new words in the mainstream science lessons. As teachers learn more about the importance of coordinating ESL and academic content instruction, they will want to do some long-range curriculum planning to develop big ideas for their themes and units (as discussed in Key Practices 9–11).

As the teachers work together, they will find that they can talk about implementing all twelve key practices. For example, they will realize that they can improve all classroom environments for ELLs by implementing the same management strategies. Spending time in different classrooms with different rules and procedures is challenging for all learners. In one class, a student can get up and sharpen a pencil without asking; in another classroom, the student must raise a hand and ask permission to get out of his/her seat. For intermediate and older ELLs with English language proficiency (ELP) levels 1 to 2, classroom rules and expected behaviors may be very different from their experiences in the classrooms in their home countries. When teachers meet regularly, they can agree on common classroom procedures (e.g., lining up, turning in work, chewing gum, bathroom breaks). Primary, intermediate, and middle school grade-level meetings are a good time to establish consensus on classroom management and discipline procedures. The ESL and bilingual teachers can then clarify the rules and consequences to the ELL students.

The purposes of teacher collaboration may differ depending on the children's grade level and how the school's language education program model is structured. For example, in a school that has a primary bilingual program, the focus is usually on how to integrate the ELLs and the general education students for meaningful social and academic learning experiences. At the intermediate and secondary levels, bilingual and/or ESL classroom teachers and general education teachers may also be interested in integrating students, but the purpose of the integrated learning activities is often how to ensure a smooth pathway for the ELLs who are transitioning into general education classrooms.

General education teachers, content teachers, ESL teachers, and bilingual teachers all have different knowledge, perspectives, and resources. These teachers can all benefit by exploring ways that their varied strengths can benefit their students and help each other in the process. Mainstream teachers who have ELLs in their classroom for part of the day can observe and identify gaps and problems that the students are encountering in the mainstream classrooms. In turn, ESL and bilingual teachers can suggest sheltered instructional strategies to support learning in those areas and help locate appropriate materials. Together, they can plan effective strategies and discuss ways to differentiate instruction for all learners, not just the ELLs.

There are academic and social reasons for language education teachers to establish collaborative relationships with teachers or specialists who are not part of their grade-level teams. They may want to work with teachers who show an interest in developing multicultural lessons or in combining students for an integrated unit. Other teachers may want to initiate a cross-age tutoring project. Reading teachers and librarians are wonderful resources for language education teachers—these specialists love books and are often knowledgeable about children's literature, content books, and other trade books that may be written at appropriate literacy levels for ELLs. Secondary content teachers from different departments may want to collaborate so that their students can work together on a service project for the school or community. Gonzalez and Darling-Hammond (1997) point out that teachers learn and benefit from collaboration with staff members with different roles or from other programs. The authors state that cross-role participation can contribute to a common sense of purpose rather than reinforce the separations that often exist across programs. Furthermore, reflective deliberations among teachers in different grades and programs can help all teachers get a clearer picture of language and cultural conflicts that may exist at school and help them figure out ways to address such problems.

Brisk (1991) states that there is evidence that meaningful daily contact between minority-language children and their majority-language peers is crucial to the success of any language education program. She points out that segregated programs do not prepare language-minority children—or the majority-language children—to live in harmony with one another. She suggests that general education teachers and language education teachers find ways to integrate their students regularly for social activities as well as academic learning activities. Secondary teachers may choose to collaborate to initiate class exchanges and cross-cultural activities which can foster friendships and mutual respect among the ethnic groups repre-

REFLECTIONS FROM THE FIELD

The Value of Integrated Learning Activities   *Sue Wagner*

Wilma Torres and Linda Simpson often created integrated learning activities for Wilma's students in her bilingual resource classroom and Linda's multi-age, looped third and fourth grade general education classroom. For example, they planned a poetry fest as a culminating event for a poetry unit. While I was visiting their classrooms, the third and fourth grade bilingual students were sent to the gym for the dress rehearsal. I tagged along with Yolanda. The students were part of four-member groups also comprised of Linda's third or fourth grade mainstream students. Each group had learned a poem about the life cycles of insect groups—honeybees, water boatmen, water striders, crickets, wasps, or grasshoppers. They had made costumes, memorized their lines, and were ready to perform for other third and fourth grade classrooms, parents, and guests. Yolanda and three

girls from the general education classroom were honeybees. As soon as Yolanda arrived in the gym, three ten-year old girls clustered around her. All three of them helped her get into her wings. "Let's practice," said the queen bee. The girls rehearsed their poem in a corner of the gym. All of them knew their lines. The queen bee started, "I am loved. I am loved by everyone." Yolanda's solo line was, "I build some new cells, slaving every day."

Linda Simpson said that the integrated learning activities had really been great for the bilingual and general education students and the children formed new friendships. She commented about Yolanda's poetry group, "She was shy at first but the girls really scooped her right up—there was a real investment in each other. It is one of the best things we do to get them into teams like that."

sented in the student body. Collaborative efforts at all school levels should also include discussions of how the ELLs can have access to the many exciting things happening at school like clubs, after-school programs, sports, and technology opportunities.

Connecting Home and School

Parents of ELLs often lament that they do not feel qualified to support their children's learning since they do not know English. However, most immigrant parents have strong commitments to education (Rodriguez-Brown, 2008). When immigrant parents understand that they are welcome, respected, and needed in their children's education, they are more likely to be involved in their children's learning. In order for the ELLs' parents to be able to collaborate with teachers and support their children's learning, they need information to know what is expected of them and to learn how to support and reinforce learning. Collaborating regularly with parents involves implementing effective translation strategies, developing a parent advisory council, and connecting parents to classroom activities.

Implementing Effective Translation Strategies

Using bilingual/bicultural staff members (e.g., home/school liaisons, tutors, parent educators, teacher assistants) to translate and interpret home-school communications is a positive step toward keeping the parents informed. These bilingual adults are often asked to translate and interpret school communications and intuitively know a lot about translating and interpreting. However, they may not know how to explain the complexities of translating to their English-speaking colleagues. Likewise, administrators and teachers may not know how effective interpretation is implemented and what is involved in translating documents. Teachers and administrators who initiate translations and interpretations need to discuss their priorities and concerns about these processes with their translators. The guidelines in Table 3.2 can be used to facilitate a discussion and help establish translation and interpreting procedures. The guidelines can be shared and discussed with teachers and bilingual support staff at staff meetings and/or during professional development sessions.

Developing a District-Level Parent Advisory Committee

Another important step that administrators and teachers can undertake to initiate collaborative relationships with non–English-speaking parents is to establish a language education parent advisory committee. Developing a district-level parent advisory committee is an effective way to establish a leadership group of parents of ELLs. This group, along with the language education program coordinator and teachers, can convene quarterly general meetings for all parents of ELLs. Administrators and language education teachers should not simply start a committee on their own and choose specific parents to be on the committee. Rather, they can identify specific parents who they already know to help plan the initial parent council meeting. A letter providing information about the group's intent to start an advisory committee should be sent to the parents of all of the ELLs. The letter can encourage parents to be a part of this process and invite them to come to a planning meeting at a designated time. Parents on the planning committee as well as the administrator of the language education program can sign the letter. This sequence of events helps ensure that the committee will be established for parents by parents. In addition, the parents on the committee may want to phone other parents to remind them about the meeting. Although making reminder phone calls to parents can be time consuming, it is often worth the effort. Many educators that we have worked with have seen an increase in parent participation at meetings because of the phone calls.

After getting to know the parents at the first meeting, administrators and teachers can explain that they should work with their children in the language they know best—their primary language. Unfortunately, well-meaning educators sometimes think that parents should switch to English at home in order to help their children learn. This advice is quite simply wrong; telling immigrant parents to use English in the home can lower the quality of communication between parents and children (Cummins, 2000). The parents will be pleased to know that by using the home language,

Table 3.2 The DOs and DON'Ts of Translating and Interpreting

DO use bilingual teachers to screen prospective teacher assistants, parent educators, home-school liaisons, and/or others who will serve as translators and interpreters for school personnel. Conduct the interview in primary language and in English to determine oral fluency. To determine the ability to do written translations, ask candidates to (1) translate sample notes from parents in primary language to English and (2) translate home/school communication from English to primary language.	**DON'T** assume that a person who "knows" the primary language is a good interpreter and an accurate and acceptable translator.
DO ask interpreters to translate the exact message of the speaker. However, ask them to tell the speaker (before or after conference or meeting) when additional information will be needed or if the message is culturally inappropriate.	**DON'T** allow interpreters to "go on and on" in the primary language after you have said only a short sentence or two.
DO introduce yourself, interpreter, and family members and make sure that you establish rapport with the parent or other family member before "getting down to business." The interpreter should also introduce the family members to school personnel at the meeting/conference. The North American culture is often perceived as a task-oriented culture whereas many other cultures, including Hispanic cultures, are perceived as more relationship-oriented cultures.	**DON'T** use an interpreter without extending a warm welcome and conducting appropriate introductions.
DO stress the importance of confidentiality to the interpreter. Furthermore, establish if the interpreter knows the family, relatives, or situation before the meeting. If the interpreter knows the family, decide if this topic or issue is too sensitive for this individual to serve as the translator.	**DON'T** use an interpreter who knows the parent/family member for discussing sensitive health, social, or behavioral issues. Parents may be embarrassed or worried about confidentiality.
DO pause for interpretation after approximately a "paragraph" of information.	**DON'T** ask an interpreter to remember very long orations before pausing for the interpretation. On the other hand, stopping at the end of each sentence is choppy and may inhibit understanding.
DO make every effort to use certified bilingual personnel to translate and interpret important and sensitive issues such as learning problems, special education referrals, pregnancies, and serious behavior problems.	**DON'T** use support staff such as the custodian, cafeteria helper, or other employees to interpret sensitive issues.
DO use translators and interpreters to share information about what their children are currently learning in the classroom. In frequent brief notes or classroom newsletters, write questions that parents can ask their children about lessons in various content areas (e.g., tell me about the layers in rocks). Share news and suggest ways that parents can help with projects and assignments. Parents can do this even when they have limited schooling themselves.	**DON'T** use translators and interpreters only for global school information and issues. Parents need to know what's happening in the classroom if they are going to support their children's learning.

Table 3.2   (*continued*)

DO make the effort to learn about cultural traditions, assumptions, norms, and expectations of the language group of the target parents. Use your translators and/or interpreters to help you understand cross-cultural issues. Effective home/school communication requires that educators be good listeners as well as good speakers.	**DON'T** assume that because something has been translated that the parents have full understanding of the communication. Background knowledge and cultural expectations and assumptions often differ between messenger and recipient, and these differences may cloud communication.
DO have procedures in place to have one person draft the translation and another to edit to make sure the document is correct in form and understandable to the target population, especially for mass mailings. It is especially useful if one of the translators is familiar with the nuances of the language and culture of the target population. Of course, this procedure may be too cumbersome for brief written communications to one or two families.	**DON'T** send unedited translated school forms and newsletters. As educators, we don't assume that the first draft of any communication is perfect. Poor translations may not be understood and may be perceived negatively by the recipients.
DO attempt to translate and/or communicate all of the information that general education parents receive. Of course, this may be impossible for low-incidence language groups; phone calls from an interpreter to the families may suffice.	**DON'T** only translate forms (e.g., immunization, emergency cards, home surveys), portions of newsletters, and urgent announcements.
DO send translations with back-to-back English originals.	**DON'T** assume parents with Hispanic or other ethnic surnames should automatically receive the translated version. Parents who are bilingual are often insulted when schools make this assumption.

they will help their children become proficient in two languages—their primary language and English. Educators can further explain that it is important for children to retell newly learned information, and that when parents ask their children questions about classroom subjects, they are helping their children develop academic language in the home language.

Connecting Parents to Classroom Activities

Attendance at school events and participation in parent meetings are common forms of parent involvement. However, getting parents involved in their children's learning can be a more effective parent involvement strategy. Language education and general education teachers can encourage parent involvement by frequently communicating with parents about what their children are studying and by suggesting learning activities at home. Below, we present two effective ways for teachers to get the ELLs' parents involved in their children's learning.

1. The Apple Letter. In many elementary classrooms across the U.S., weekly letters are sent home to parents on Fridays. These important communications let parents know how to support their children's learning. It

Dear Parents,

Next week we are going to be learning more about China. Enclosed is a world map. Ask your child to show you where China is. We will be talking about the people, places, food, and jobs in China. We will eat rice with chopsticks on Wednesday. We will be making the Great Wall of China in the hall. Ask your child to tell you about the Great Wall of China. We need large pieces of cardboard. Please let me know if you have some.

Thank you.

FIGURE 3.1   The "Apple" Letter.

is ideal that these weekly letters be translated into the language of the home. However, in schools where this is not possible, at the beginning of the school year, through an interpreter, the general education teacher can explain to the ELLs' parents that their children will be bringing home a lot of student work, school communications, and homework in their backpacks. The teacher can tell the parents that important communications about learning will have a graphic apple drawn around the information. These "apple letters" always tell parents something about what their child is learning in the classroom and suggest a task or suggest questions that the parents can ask their children. When the parents see the apple letters in the backpacks, they know that they are receiving important information to ask the family interpreter (e.g., an older child or a family member or friend who comes by regularly) about. Figure 3.1 depicts a sample of an informal apple letter.

2. Parent/Teacher Classroom Meetings. Immigrant parents may be hesitant to participate in large-group parent/teacher activities because of their lack of familiarity with the U.S. culture, unfamiliarity with U.S. educational practices, and, sometimes, their own limited educational experiences (Rodriguez-Brown, 2008). However, parents are almost always interested in meeting their children's teachers. In addition, they often want to meet the parents of the children that their own sons and daughters talk about. General education and language education teachers can capitalize on this interest by inviting the parents (and their children) to come to the classroom for *short* quarterly meetings. The meeting should be held early enough for parents to get home for their children's bedtimes. At the first meeting, after getting acquainted, teachers should specifically point out that parents should work with their children in the language that they know best, the home language. Then, while the children do an art project or watch a video, the teacher and parents can briefly discuss a topic that will help the parents support their children's learning. Here are some ideas for the meetings.

- At the preschool and primary level, model reading a story to the children and suggest books that they can read at home. Show how to make everyday tasks into learning activities, e.g., sorting socks, playing with cards, recognizing store signs, "I Spy" games. Suggest ways that families can have literacy experiences in the community (reading signs in the car, reading information at the zoo, reading bus maps, etc.) Provide maps of the local community that show locations of the library, zoo, parks, museums, etc.

- At the intermediate level, show the parents what the students are currently working on. Ask the students to talk about something that they are learning about and have them show their parents some of their written work. Suggest questions that the parents should ask their children at home during the upcoming week.

- At the secondary level, explain the system of course credits and graduation requirements.

- At all levels, tell the parents about their children's daily classroom schedule and about the subjects that they study. At the end of the meeting, ask the students to tell their parents about their favorite subjects, their favorite classroom activities, and their favorite books.

Linking School and Community

Expand collaborative efforts to include working with community organizations. In culturally diverse communities across the U.S., there are community organizations, churches, and social service agencies that have programs that serve the immigrant families in the school district. For example, some agencies provide social services; other organizations may offer programs such as teaching adult ESL classes, sponsoring recreational activities, providing short courses that teach various skills, or providing summer programs. The language education committee can take the lead to iden-tify and learn more about the community resources that are available for ELL students and their families. This information should be shared with principals, teachers, social workers, librarians, and other staff members who can help make ELL students and their parents aware of these services.

Members of the district's language education committee can get in touch with representatives of the community organizations to discuss goals, clarify information, and initiate collaborative efforts that will be mu-tually beneficial to the school district and the agencies. Perhaps teachers can suggest ways that their students might support the agencies' work through community service projects (e.g., collecting pennies, recycling, cleaning up a park).

Many public libraries have story hours in Spanish and/or other lan-guages. Bilingual and ESL teachers can offer to send notes home to parents to remind them about the story hours and other library events. In a differ-ent scenario, if a local public library is reluctant to provide story hours or provide library materials in languages other than English, teachers and/or school librarians can meet with the public library staff to explain the im-portant role that parents play in developing literacy and suggest titles of books for the library to purchase. They can emphasize that when parents talk and share books with their children in any language, they are help-ing develop their children's language skills and literacy skills, even when parents have limited schooling themselves. All of these joint collaborative efforts of district educators and community organizations can help the language-minority parents support their children's learning as well as help the families feel more welcome in the community and schools.

In this chapter, we have described how collaborative teams at the district-wide level, school-wide level, and classroom level can work as a PLC to-ward the common goal of school success for ELLs. We have shown how they can use the Key Practice 2 to share responsibilities, coordinate their efforts, develop common practices, and collaborate with parents and community organizations. In the next chapter, we address how various teams at the district and school levels can develop a balanced assessment system to evaluate ELL student learning.

QUESTIONS FOR REFLECTION AND ACTION

1. Make a list of the major on-going committees at the district and school levels. How do these committees address the diverse needs of ELLs and share information with other standing committees?

2. How could a language education PLC be initiated to encourage collab-orative discussions that can improve instruction for ELLs across the district?

3. How do teachers currently help non–English-speaking parents support their children's learning? How does the district work with community organizations that serve immigrant families? How can these efforts be expanded?

Recommended Readings

DuFour, R. et al. (2006). *Learning by doing: A handbook for professional learning communities at work.* Bloomington, IN: Solution Tree.

Echevarria, J. (2012). "How do you ensure that the general education teachers and English as a second language teachers collaborate to address the content and language needs of English language learners?" In E. Hamayan & R. Freeman (Eds), *English language learners in school: A guide for administrators.* Philadelphia: Caslon Publishing.

Hord, S., & Sommers, W. (2007). *Leading professional learning communities: Voices from research and practice.* Thousand Oaks, CA : Corwin Press.

Rodriguez-Brown, F. (2008). *The home-school connection.* New York: Routledge.

Ruebling, C. (2006). *Redesigning schools for success: Implementing small learning communities and teacher collaboration.* Longville, MN: AuthorHouse.

Waterman, R., & Harry, B. (2008). *Building collaboration between schools and parents of English language learners: Transcending barriers, creating opportunities.* National Center for Culturally Responsive Educational Systems (nccrest). Available at http://www.nccrest.org/Briefs/Practitioner Brief_BuildingCollaboration.pdf.

The checklist is written using measurable statements that can be used to evaluate and monitor language education programs and instruction at the district, school, and classroom levels. The district language education committee and school leadership teams can use the checklist as a diagnostic tool to identify the areas that represent the biggest challenges during the restructuring process. Various teams can use the results of the checklist as a starting point to determine the professional development that educators need to know in order to successfully implement the practices. Teacher teams can use the checklist to evaluate their own teaching practices to recognize ways in which they can immediately make instructional improvements.

SCORING DIRECTIONS:
1 = This practice IS implemented.
2 = This practice is in progress or is in place in some classrooms.
3 = This practice is NOT currently in place.

			Shared Practices at the District, School, and Classroom Levels
			Educating ELLs through Collaboration: The challenges of educating ELL student populations are addressed through collaborative teams who share common goals, common language, and common practices.
1	2	3	• An ELL-focused professional learning community of district-wide, school-wide, and teacher teams is established. These teams work and learn together to improve programs and instruction for ELLs.
1	2	3	• Periodic district language education committee meetings are convened to establish goals, monitor and refine programs, disseminate information, and provide support for collaborative efforts throughout the district.
1	2	3	• School leadership teams address policy issues, curriculum development, instructional practices, and socio-cultural issues that affect learning environments for diverse learners.
1	2	3	• Teacher teams who share ELL students (language education teachers and general education teachers) have structured planning time for purposeful and reflective conversations.
1	2	3	• Educators collaborate regularly with parents by implementing effective translation strategies, developing a parent advisory council, and connecting parents to classroom learning activities.
1	2	3	• Educators expand collaborative efforts by working with community organizations.

IMPLICATIONS AND COMMENTS _____

_____

_____

_____

Implementing a Balanced Student Assessment System

Complement standardized measures with common and classroom assessments that yield evidence of ELL performance in literacy, academic achievement, and language proficiency, and use that assessment data to inform instructional and programmatic decisions.

- Design and use a balanced assessment system that identifies ELL students' needs, documents student classroom performance, and evaluates program effectiveness.

- Institutionalize consistent entry criteria and procedures across the district.

- Differentiate classroom assessments according to the ELLs' English language proficiency levels by using a variety of reliable assessment strategies that incorporate visual, graphic and interactive supports.

- Build authentic assessments into instruction to measure ELLs' understanding of academic content and their progress in English language development.

- Complement standardized measures with common assessments and classroom assessments to document ELLs' growth over time and monitor student progress.

- Institutionalize consistent exit criteria and procedures across the district.

- Review assessment data to evaluate language education program effectiveness.

THE BIG IDEAS

- On-going common classroom assessments are essential to monitor growth in literacy, academic achievement, and language development.

- Assessment of English language learners (ELLs) is ongoing and best done in conjunction with instruction that is appropriate for the students' language proficiency levels.

- Reviewing ELL students' assessment data over time helps educators plan appropriate instruction, understand the effectiveness of the program for ELLs, and plan professional development opportunities for all stakeholders.

Developing and using a balanced student assessment system for ELLs includes identifying ELL students' needs, documenting student classroom performance in literacy, academic achievement, and language proficiency, and evaluating program effectiveness. District and school leadership teams need to establish and implement consistent entry criteria and procedures for ELLs across the district, differentiate classroom assessments according to the ELLs' English language proficiency (ELP) levels by visual, graphic and interactive supports, build authentic assessments into instruction to measure ELLs' academic content learning and English language development, complement standardized measures with common assessments and classroom assessments, institutionalize consistent exit criteria and procedures across the district, and use assessment data to evaluate program effectiveness.

Key Practice 3 focuses less on statewide standardized testing and legal accountability requirements and more on district and school common assessments and classroom-based measures. We present authentic, student-centered procedures for appropriately identifying ELLs and discuss entry and exit criteria to and from language education programs. We also share ways to help teacher teams plan and coordinate authentic classroom assessments that measure the ELLs' language growth and academic knowledge.

Designing and Using a Balanced Student Assessment System for English Language Learners

The assessment of ELLs is an on-going, cyclical process. Finding out what ELLs already know and can do is the essential first step to providing appropriate, effective instruction. Once the ELLs are enrolled in a language education program, on-going classroom assessments are essential to monitor growth in literacy, academic achievement, and language development. Assessment for ELLs also includes criteria and measures to determine transition and exit into the general education program. The cycle is complete when student data help district educators inform instruction, plan professional development, and improve language education programs. All of these measures contribute to a balanced assessment system.

What is different about assessing ELLs is that according to federal law, two different aspects of their learning must be constantly taken into consideration—their proficiency in English and their knowledge about academic content. School districts administer standardized assessments to ELLs for English language proficiency and also for academic achievement. These standardized tests are part of the balanced assessment system but they are not the entire assessment system for ELLs. In other words, educators must find ways to assess ELLs that show what they know in light of their developing language skills.

In order to maximize effective implementation of a balanced assessment system, the language education committee or an assessment subcommittee can develop a comprehensive assessment plan that is aligned with core state standards, program goals, and district benchmarks. The plan will clarify common assessment procedures for all teachers and administrators who work with ELLs. The term *common assessment* refers to student assessments that are developed collaboratively by a team of teachers responsible for the same curriculum or grade level. These teachers implement these common assessments in their classrooms and report and use the data in the same way. The district assessment plan can serve as a guide to help teachers collect and use data to monitor students' progress. The plan can include ways to gather data that provide useful information for making day-to-day instructional decisions as well as identify data that informs administrators about long-range student achievement (Gottlieb & Nguyen, 2007). It can describe how teachers develop and use portfolio systems effectively and create common assessments that consistently collect and measure student work according to predetermined criteria. All teachers working with ELLs need to know their role in assessing their students; the district assessment plan will help teachers compile the data they need to make instructional decisions.

Institutionalizing Consistent Entry Criteria and Procedures Across the District

Federal law and the Office for Civil Rights guidelines have required districts to identify and appropriately educate ELLs since the 1970s. However, many districts have yet to establish uniform screening measures. The most identifiable ELLs in a school district are recently arrived immigrants with little understanding of the English language. Identifying ELLs with higher levels of English proficiency is more difficult. As educators learn more about the complexities of academic English and the backgrounds and needs of their language-minority students, they recognize that there are socially fluent students who are still developing academic English language proficiency but are not receiving any special services. These language-minority students are considered ELLs, regardless of what country they were born in or how long they have lived in the U.S. The language education committee (or a subcommittee of committee members and language education teachers) must make sure that home language screening procedures are implemented consistently in all school buildings in order to appropriately identify all ELL students in the district.

Establishing Consistent Entry Criteria

There are two basic criteria that identify a student as being an ELL. First, the student comes from a home where a language other than English is spoken regularly or the student understands or speaks a language other than English. (For example, many districts receive internationally adopted students who have a primary language other than English but the adoptive

REFLECTIONS FROM THE FIELD

The Importance of Appropriately Identifying ELLs   *Tammy King*

Imagine a school district tripling its ELL population during the course of one school year—but not because of the most likely reasons! That is exactly what happened a few years ago in a small Midwestern city. I was asked to facilitate monthly meetings in the district. My task was to facilitate the district-wide committee that would create a new language education program to better educate the district's ELLs. In October the district reported that they had 27 ELLs split between two schools. By May of that same school year, a total of 83 ELLs had been identified in four schools. This boom was not a result of an influx of immigrants. Rather, this population jump resulted directly from implementing uniform screening procedures for ELLs across the district. When the committee was convened, it became obvious that district staff were not administering a home language survey to every new enrollee, despite the state's legal mandate to do so. The school secretaries only passed out the survey to some families. By distributing the survey to all enrolled students that year and then assessing the English language proficiency of those students who had a home language other than English, the committee was able to correct the oversight. Ultimately, 56 additional students were identified as ELLs. The newly identified ELLs all had various levels of social proficiency in English. However, they were weak in academic English language proficiency and were struggling academically. Consistent implementation of entry assessment procedures that appropriately identify all ELLs is critical in order to provide the instructional support that incoming ELLs need to be successful learners.

parents only speak English.) Second, the ELL student has not yet attained grade-level proficiency in academic English.

A home language survey typically addresses the first criterion by asking parents a few questions at the time of registration. The survey usually asks two important questions. (1) Is a language other than English spoken in the home? If the answer is yes, the parent is asked to identify what language is spoken. (2) Does the child speak a language other than English? If the answer is yes, the parent is asked to identify what language the child speaks. In many states, if the answer is yes to either of these questions, the district is required to administer a state-approved English language proficiency measure. (Samples of home language surveys in several languages can be found at the Illinois State Board of Education website listed in the Recommended Readings at the end of this chapter.) District assessment teams may include additional questions; for example, some home language surveys ask about the language use of the siblings or caretakers of the ELLs. In order to avoid misidentifying any students, the home language survey should be filled out for each student the first time she/he enrolls in the district.

The second criterion is addressed by assessing the English language proficiency of students who come from a language-minority background (Gottlieb, 2006; Abedi, 2007). All states have adopted standards-based English language proficiency assessments in order to identify ELLs in their school systems. However, in most schools, it is not feasible or appropriate to administer the state's English language proficiency test at the time of the new ELL students' enrollment. The new ELL students already experi-

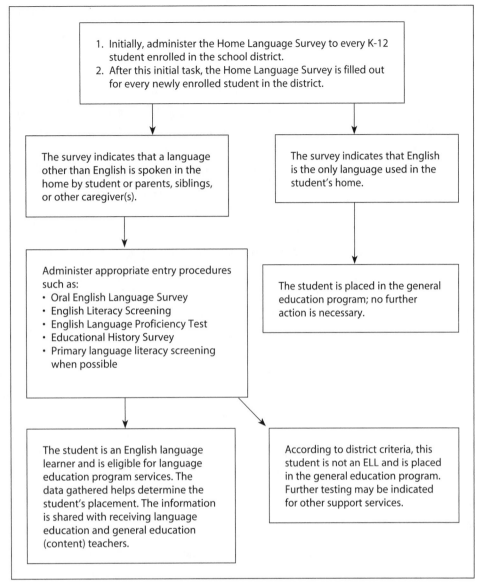

1. Initially, administer the Home Language Survey to every K-12 student enrolled in the school district.
2. After this initial task, the Home Language Survey is filled out for every newly enrolled student in the district.

The survey indicates that a language other than English is spoken in the home by student or parents, siblings, or other caregiver(s).

The survey indicates that English is the only language used in the student's home.

Administer appropriate entry procedures such as:
• Oral English Language Survey
• English Literacy Screening
• English Language Proficiency Test
• Educational History Survey
• Primary language literacy screening when possible

The student is placed in the general education program; no further action is necessary.

The student is an English language learner and is eligible for language education program services. The data gathered helps determine the student's placement. The information is shared with receiving language education and general education (content) teachers.

According to district criteria, this student is not an ELL and is placed in the general education program. Further testing may be indicated for other support services.

FIGURE 4.1   Identification of English Language Learners (ELLs)

ence high anxiety on the first day of school in a new culture. Results from the state-approved language proficiency test may not accurately measure the students' English proficiency. Instead, an authentic oral English language survey and/or a literacy screening measure can be administered. These brief measures can provide immediate, useful information for the receiving teacher(s) until the new students can be further evaluated. Figure 4.1 suggests appropriate entry procedures for the identification and placement of newly arrived ELLs.

A score from an English proficiency test is a great start but is not designed to relate the depth of school knowledge, primary language literacy development, and cultural information of new ELLs. More information is needed in order to decide what type of support a student needs. Many administrator/teacher teams have developed an education history process for their new ELL students, especially for those ELLs who have recently immigrated to the U.S. The education history survey becomes a part of the district's entry procedures for ELLs. The goal is to screen the ELLs' literacy skills and find out if the newly arrived students have had academic experiences comparable to their grade-level peers. The interview also ascertains if the students attended school regularly and provides a glimpse into their previous school experiences. More importantly, the process enables receiving teachers of the new ELLs to learn useful information to connect new content with what the students already know.

The educational history process can begin on the day a new ELL arrives at the school. In most cases, the student and the parents are often accompanied by an interpreter, who can be a family member, neighbor, or friend. This fortunate circumstance provides an opportunity to conduct a significant and useful interview through a dialog that respects the families, their experiences, and their home cultures. Table 4.1 shares an example of a survey which includes a primary language literacy screening activity for recent immigrant students at the intermediate and secondary levels.

The authentic information gathered through this educational history process, although subjective, is a common assessment that provides information that helps determine placement decisions. It is important to remember that literacy skills and school knowledge in the primary language serve as a strong foundation for students to learn English and to continue learning academic knowledge in the U.S. ELLs who are already academically behind their grade-level peers will need more time with the bilingual and/or ESL teacher than students who come with literacy and knowledge at their grade level. Furthermore, knowing about students' previous school experiences (or lack of formal school experiences) can help teachers plan the type of instruction students will need to be successful. For this reason, the responses to the questions should be summarized on the Anecdotal Notes section of the *Entry Information Checklist and Annotations Template* following this chapter.

Some of the questions on the education history survey may not be appropriate to identify language-minority students who have been in the district for two or more years and are socially fluent in English. These students have often been inappropriately placed in general education classrooms and may not have been identified previously as ELLs. Previous school records, parent interviews, and classroom-level performance-based assessments will provide useful information and effectively take the place of the educational history survey. Gottlieb (2006) offers several sample surveys (home language, oral language, and literacy screening) along with a decision tree flowchart that can be used for initial identification and placement of ELLs.

Whether using published assessment tools or locally created common assessments, it is important to gather and record the assessment data

Table 4.1   Educational History Survey

STEP 1

For ELLs in Pre-K thru primary grades: use an interpreter to have a "getting to know you" conversation with the parents and the new ELLs.

- Ask the parents background questions about their region, their community, and the schools their children attended previously (U.S. and/or in the home country.)
- Be interested in the family, culture, what kind of work they did, and why they came to this area.
- Be sensitive to parents who may choose not to answer questions that they deem to be too personal to share with someone outside their family.
- Ask the parents if the child attended school regularly before arriving in this country.
- Ask them if the child learned to read (in his/her first language).

For ELLs in intermediate and secondary grades: conduct an interview using an interpreter, talking directly with the students.

- Tell me about your town in your country.
- Tell me about the school you attended in your home country.
- What was it like? What grade were you in?
- How often did you have math class? Science?
- What was your favorite school subject? (What subject were you "good" at?)
- What was your hardest school subject?
- Do you like to read?
- Did you miss a lot of days of school? Why?
- Is there something special you hope to learn at this school?
- Will you be e-mailing or writing to friends back home?

STEP 2   *Literacy Screening for ELLs in grades 2–12*

Writing in the Primary language

- Ask the new ELL to complete a writing sample in his/her primary language.
  Sample topic: Tell me about your family (or school).
- Ask the student to tell you what he/she wrote (through interpreter).

  Look at the fine motor ability of the writing. Look for long sentences, punctuation and/or diacritical marks. Even if you don't know the language, does the writing sample appear to be age appropriate? If not, the student may have had irregular school attendance.

Reading in the Primary language

- Using a children's book or story in student's primary language that is at or below his/her age or grade level, ask the new ELL student to orally read a page or paragraph.
- Ask him/her to retell the story or information to the interpreter.

  Listen for fluent reading, intonations, obvious miscues, or a struggle for words. Observe what the student does when coming across an unfamiliar word. Does he/she slow down, reread the sentence, etc.? Even if you don't know the language, does the student appear to be reading adequately? Is the student able to retell the information? (Ask the interpreter.) If not, this may be an indication that the student may not have grade-level literacy skills.

about the literacy skills, academic knowledge, and English language proficiency of each student who has been identified as potentially needing language education services. The *Entry Information Checklist and Annotations Template* provides a format for recording the student data and the sources of that information. This form can serve as a summary of the various entry assessments. Once complete, it can be copied and distributed to all teachers that will be working with the new student. The original should be placed in the student's permanent file. It can serve as the cover sheet for the packet of entry assessments for the student (home language survey, educational history survey notes, and any other entry assessments that were administered).

Evaluating Entry Information to Determine Student Placement

Some ELLs were born in the U.S.; other ELLs arrive from their home countries at various ages. Some come with age-appropriate schooling in their native countries and others do not. Analyzing and evaluating the information gathered during the entry process helps administrators, language education teachers, and general education teachers place the child appropriately.

In school districts with bilingual education programs, early childhood teachers and bilingual/ESL teachers have a difficult task when making placement decisions. Research supports that whenever possible, preschool programs for ELLs should provide strong primary language and pre-literacy components that build a strong foundation in the primary language (Snow, 1992; Genesee et al., 2011; Tabors, 2008). However, in school districts across the U.S., teachers and administrators, with good intentions, submerse ELL children who do not speak English in English-speaking preschool programs without any ESL support or primary language instruction. In the all-English preschool classrooms, the children interact with native English speakers and begin speaking English socially. They often learn to identify numbers, colors, and shapes in English. For immigrant families, seeing their children learn English in preschool is a joy. However, the children's apparent grasp of two languages becomes problematic when parents enroll their children in kindergarten or first grade. The home language survey clearly shows that the family speaks a language other than English at home. The standardized English proficiency test, educational history survey, and local school readiness tests (many of which measure the very language skills children typically learn in preschool) show oral fluency in English. Does the child qualify for the language education classroom (bilingual or ESL) or does his/her English-speaking ability suggest that a regular education classroom is the appropriate placement?

The tendency is to enroll ELLs in English-speaking kindergarten classrooms if they have attended preschool in English. However, we suggest

REFLECTIONS FROM THE FIELD

Correcting an Inappropriate Placement Decision

Magali Williams, Bilingual Teacher

When I was six years old and in first grade in Puerto Rico my family moved to New York. At the time, there were no entry level procedures at the school; they simply placed me in a general education kindergarten classroom with no support. They put me back in KINDERGARTEN! It was awful! The teacher ignored me. It was the worst thing that could happen. I was so ignored that I even acted up occasionally, just to see if they noticed—and, no, *nada*. I knew everything a first grader should know. I already knew how to read, I could write, I knew how to add and subtract, and they put me back in kindergarten with my little sister.

Horrendous. I became very quiet and reserved. I was the kind of student who needed to work in school so one day, I decided to do math by myself, to keep myself busy. The kindergarten teacher saw what I was working on and realized that I *could* do a lot of school tasks—that's when I started getting instructional support. The next year, the first grade teacher really worked with me, especially in literacy. Soon I was reading better than some of the English speakers. When we moved to the Bronx at the beginning of second grade, they moved me back up to third grade with my age group.

that decision makers consider the language development and usage in the preschoolers' lives. Five-year-old ELLs who have attended one year in an English-speaking preschool program have spent 180 days, approximately four hours each day, in an English-speaking school environment. That adds up to 720 hours. (Admittedly, the children may also have experienced several hours per week playing with English-speaking siblings and other neighborhood children.) Yet by the age of five, the children have also spent more than 17,000 hours interacting with family members in the home language. The students' experiences and knowledge in the primary language need to be part of the placement discussion, since a strong foundation in the primary language enhances literacy instruction.

Ideally, initial literacy instruction can be provided in the child's primary language in school districts with primary bilingual education classrooms taught by certified bilingual teachers. However, in districts where formal literacy instruction in the home language is not possible, teachers must not ignore the fact that these little learners are already bilingual. The English-speaking teachers (with whom the children are placed) can use bilingual assistants, tutors, and parent volunteers to help value and utilize the primary language to support learning.

In many districts, there are increasing numbers of another subgroup: older ELLs who arrive with limited formal schooling in their native countries (Center for Applied Linguistics, 2008). It is important to gather as much background information as possible on these students so that instruction can be tailored to their unique strengths and considerable needs. Students who have had limited formal schooling will not perform as well in school as immigrant students who arrive with age-appropriate schooling (Freeman et al., 2002). They have gaps in their knowledge foundation and desperately need content area and literacy instruction through their home language while they are learning English. These students can be appropriately served in secondary newcomer programs.

Older ELLs who have been in the U.S. and attended school for seven years or more and continue to qualify for language education services are referred to as long-term ELLs (LTELLs) (Freeman et al., 2002; Menken et al., 2007). Often these students have various levels of English language proficiency, primary language proficiency, and literacy skills in both of their languages. Frequently, these students speak both the primary language and English with their siblings and in the neighborhood and are often "stuck" at intermediate ELP levels. Appropriate placement and services for these students is challenging. Menken et al. suggest analyzing a student's educational history, recording year-by-year information such as the country the student lived in and where he/she attended school and the language of instruction (2007). This information can be gathered during the educational history survey process. The amount and duration of primary language instruction or support that the student has received will impact the decision to provide primary language support in the future. Primary language support may not be appropriate if these students have had all their previous schooling in English; some ELLs might reject this late offer of primary language support. Even so, they can be afforded the opportunity to strengthen their first language and literacy skills in courses designed for native speakers offered through the secondary world language course offerings.

At the secondary level, these LTELLs often have great difficulty thriving in linguistically challenging coursework in English. For example, high school language arts course offerings are designed for native English-speaking students who have spoken English for at least thirteen years and have already studied English language arts for eight or more years. With this in mind, it is clear to see that high school English language arts courses do not match the language needs of intermediate ELLs who are not native speakers of English and have not previously had appropriately adapted English instruction. In school districts where several ELLs from this group are identified for the first time, secondary program planners need to develop and implement long-term, sustained content-based ESL instruction that matches the needs of these socially fluent ELLs.

Once ELLs are evaluated for placement in a bilingual or ESL program, the parents need to be informed. On occasion, parents may refuse language education program services for their child. With good intentions, they may think that submersing their children in the general education English-speaking classroom is the best way for them to learn English quickly. Although it may be wise to accept the parents' decision, it is essential that they receive information about how the language education program is designed to help their children learn English, how the program will help them learn to read and write, and how instruction is adapted so that their children will learn grade-level academic content. In our experience, well-informed parents make appropriate decisions about their children's education. When the parents continue to refuse services, their children must be assessed in academic achievement and English language proficiency. The parents need to be regularly informed of their students' progress and be given the opportunity to accept services for their child at a later time.

Differentiating Classroom Assessments by English Language Proficiency Levels

When teachers document students' performance in instructional activities, they are gathering useful, authentic data that can be saved and recorded regularly from classroom observations, assignments, and projects. Charts, running records, rubrics, and student writing samples can be collected in student portfolios for future reference and be used to chart students' growth over time. The key is to differentiate assessments for ELL students by ELP level using visual, graphic and interactive scaffolds and supports.

During classroom instruction, many teachers have learned to provide sensory supports (i.e., images, realia, illustrations, physical activities), graphic supports (i.e., charts, tables, diagrams), and interactive supports (i.e., working in pairs, cooperative groups, primary language support) to enable ELLs to learn key concepts. Unfortunately, teachers who have learned to differentiate *instruction* for ELLs have not always differentiated their *assessments*. Making assessments comprehensible to ELLs is extremely important; otherwise, the resulting assessments may end up measuring a student's lack of English proficiency or lack of familiarity with American culture rather than showing what they know about the subject area.

Differentiating assessments provides a fair and equitable way for ELLs to demonstrate what they know about the big ideas and objectives of a lesson using the amount of English they are able to produce. This typically means adding visual, graphic, or interactive supports to an existing assessment. In this way, teachers are building performance-based assessment into the lesson. To get started, teachers use the big ideas and objectives along with the WIDA CAN DO Descriptors as they differentiate the lesson to meet their students' needs. The CAN DO Descriptors provide guidance on what students at different ELP levels can understand and produce in English. Next, the teachers plan how to assess students at each level of English proficiency on the same topics, varying the visual, graphic, and interactive supports and the amount of English the students need to understand and produce. Table 4.2 shows how the CAN DO Descriptors

Table 4.2   Differentiating Assessments by English Language Proficiency Level

ELP Level	6–8 Grade-Level Cluster CAN DO Descriptor*	Assessment options to assess the type of work that archeologists do
Level 1	• *Produce high frequency words* • *Label pictures and graphs*	With teacher guidance, sort archeology pictures into categories and label the pictures with single words or short phrases using a word bank.
Level 2	• *Complete pattern sentences* • *Extend "sentence starters" with original ideas*	Write a caption for several pictures of archeologists using word banks and "sentence starters." (e.g., Archeologists use technology to _____. At digs, archeologists _____.)
Level 3	• *Produce short paragraphs with main ideas and some details (e.g., column notes)*	Using sentence frames, fill in the missing words in a (fill in the blank) paragraph about archeologists' work. (e.g., Archeologists are scientists who _____. They work in different settings, for example, _____.) Ask students to write three more sentences with supporting details.
Level 4	• *Use details/examples to support ideas* • *Compose intro/body/conclusion*	Using a word bank, write three paragraphs describing the type of work that archeologists do.
Level 5	• *Produce research reports using multiple sources/citations*	Write a short essay about the work of archeologists.

*WIDA CAN DO Descriptors from http://www.wida.us/standards/CAN_DOs/Booklet6-8.pdf. Courtesy of the WIDA Consortium, Madison, Wisconsin.

can lead to differentiated assessments for ELLs who are studying a middle school archeology unit. As shown in the chart, all students can be assessed using the same objective that focuses on the type of work that archeologists do by demonstrating their understanding of the different types of work. The differentiation is in the amount of support provided and the amount of language the students are expected to write.

Building Authentic Assessments into Instruction

Educators must be able to measure ELLs' academic content learning and their English language development. By adding criteria and evidence to common instructional activities, teachers can create appropriate assessment measures for ELLs as well as general education students. The criteria are the elements of the assignment that the teacher is looking for that tie back to the objective. The evidence is the "proof"—way that the teacher knows that the student has learned the concept. Starting with the standards-based big ideas of the lessons, teachers can determine what knowledge, skills, performances, or information can be used as criteria and evidence to assess the learning that results from the activity. They will realize that some of their most-used instructional strategies can be converted into assessment measures. For example, teachers often give students a set of

10 to 15 words and phrases to sort into categories that make sense to the learners. This strategy is called an open word sort and is often used as a prereading or during-reading strategy (see caslonpublishing.com/pd-resources/twelve-key-practices for word sorts and other teaching strategies). Using the same set of words, the teacher can create a connect-two activity, which asks the students to show the relationships among the words and phrases. At the end of the unit, the teacher can (1) use a closed word sort to assess their understanding of the words or phrases, asking the students to correctly sort the words into predetermined categories and (2) ask the students to write sentences using the words in a final connect-two task. The evidence of student learning is documented with the correct placement of the words (into the predetermined word sort categories) and appropriate sentences showing the words' relationships (in the connect-two activity). Adding criteria and evidence to a learning activity can be done in any classroom. Bilingual teachers should match classroom assessment procedures to the language of instruction. That is, if the students learn content in Spanish, the assessments should also be conducted in Spanish. If the lesson was taught in English using sheltered instruction, the assessment should be given in English, using instructional supports.

Graphic organizers are ideal for collecting evidence of students' learning. For example, after the teacher has determined what the ELLs should have learned from a classroom activity, he/she can ask the students to complete the L portion of a KWL chart. Similarly, ELLs can be asked to sort or categorize words, pictures, objects, or concepts on a T-chart, or fill out a cause and effect diagram. As their English improves, the ELL students can be asked to convert their graphic charts to sentences and paragraphs; using sentence and paragraph frames helps them write academically correct statements.

Rubrics, checklists, and anecdotal notes are effective tools for organizing criteria and documenting student work. Supplying students with modeling and/or examples of the finished assignment helps clarify expectations and allows students to better understand the goal of the project. For example, a middle school social studies teacher shows her students an online video of two students sharing their slides on the three branches of government in the U.S. (posted on the SchoolTube website http://got.im/YXr). As an alternative to a paper/pencil test, ELP level 3 and 4 ELLs are paired with general education students and are asked to create their own slide presentations about the three branches, using information and notes that they have written on previously assigned graphic organizers. In advance, the teacher shares a checklist or rubric that will be used to evaluate the students' projects. The students orally present their slideshow and the teacher and/or adult guests use the rubric to evaluate the students' work. All students are evaluated on the criteria identified on the checklist/rubric that measures their knowledge of the three branches of government.

Complementing Standardized Measures with Common Assessments and Classroom Assessments

District-level and school-level decision makers need to use authentic data to monitor all students' progress and achievement, including ELLs. An effective way to chart growth over time is through student portfolios. A successful and useful portfolio system links the assignments stored in a portfolio to core state standards and language proficiency standards. O'Malley and Valdez Pierce (1996) explain that a portfolio system includes various scoring guides, rubrics, checklists, and rating scales. For example, portfolios can be designed to include checklists to measure observable literacy skills (e.g., running records) or oral language skills (e.g., retelling a short story). Writing samples that illustrate different genres (book reports, stories), solutions to math problems (that show problem solving ability), and written reports (that show use of multiple sources) are other examples of how students' written work can be used to show skills that students have learned (Gomez, 2000). Student samples along with the rubrics or checklists that are used to evaluate them typically form the bulk of a student's portfolio. In addition to monitoring the ELLs' growth over time, teacher teams can analyze student work in the portfolios to inform instruction. There are several published texts that provide detailed information about using portfolios with ELLs. Some of these are listed at the end of this chapter.

Many district and/or school assessment teams have developed common rubrics and checklists that show growth and performance in English language development, literacy improvement, and academic achievement. By developing and providing common rubrics and checklists that match district benchmarks, individual teachers do not have to make unique rubrics or checklists for many assignments and assessments. For example, a single checklist can be created and used with all science experiments; another rubric can be used for all narrative essays. Using the same rubrics makes it easy to monitor students' progress in language proficiency and content knowledge over a period of time. Creating student-friendly versions of the rubric or checklist allows ELLs to engage in self-assessment and peer assessment. Charting their own growth can be very rewarding for students. When teachers attach exemplary work samples with these rubrics, the samples demonstrate and clarify expectations and help students understand the scope of the assignment. Comparing their own work to the sample helps the learners understand their own strengths and challenges.

Creating a balanced assessment plan that is appropriate for ELLs can be a daunting task, especially when the ELLs spend time in a mainstream classroom, an ESL and/or bilingual classroom, and various specialists' classrooms. As the teachers monitor and evaluate the ELL students' progress in their respective classrooms, assessment responsibilities sometimes get confused, especially when it is time to record grades and identify strengths and weaknesses on report cards. Meeting regularly to discuss the ELLs' progress, planning and using common assessment procedures, and creating a mutual assessment plan can help eliminate many problems. The teachers can begin by creating a list of the various subject areas that are taught and how they will be assessed. Next, the teachers can list who will be responsible for teaching each area and decide who will be responsible for assessment and assigning grades. They can record their decisions and make sure that each teacher has a copy of the plan. The *Teacher Assessment Responsibilities and Planning Template* can facilitate this discussion.

Near the end of each marking period, all teachers who share the responsibility of teaching the same ELLs should arrange a time to meet and review the portfolio contents together. They can discuss the students' progress and grades in each subject area in order to complete the bottom half of the planning template. By talking about and recording the ELL students' areas of growth and improvement, the teachers are using classroom assessments to plan future instruction. Over time, student growth becomes apparent and well-documented. When it becomes clear that the student needs fewer instructional supports in the English-speaking classrooms, the teachers can use the portfolio data to determine if the student is ready to exit the language education program.

Institutionalizing Consistent Exit Criteria and Procedures across the District

Each state has adopted English language development/proficiency standards and has determined a specific English language proficiency test that must be used to measure ELLs' English development. Reviewing the scores within all four domains of English language proficiency (listening, speaking, reading, and writing) on the yearly proficiency test can provide insight about what ELLs are capable of understanding and producing in English-speaking classrooms without support. Although English language proficiency is a major indicator for readiness to transition ELLs into mainstream classrooms, teachers also need to examine how the ELLs utilize their academic English proficiency, literacy skills, and academic knowledge to complete classrooms tasks successfully.

Administrators and teacher teams who develop district-wide exit criteria should recognize that beyond test scores, the mainstream and language education teachers are all valuable resources in the exit decision. In addition to using a designated score on the language proficiency test to make decisions about exiting ELLs out of the language education program, teachers can balance evidence in the student portfolios with classroom observations of the literacy skills and academic tasks that the ELLs execute every day. The teachers know the work effort, personal responsibility, literacy skills, and English language proficiency of their students. The *Class-*

room-Based Observation Scale to Support Exiting Decisions Template lists authentic observable skills that can be documented with student work samples, rubrics, or checklists already collected in portfolios. In this way, authentic criteria are used in conjunction with standardized measures to determine the ELLs' readiness to exit language education programs.

The descriptors in the scale represent the complex skills and behaviors that intermediate-level English-speaking students are expected to do in mainstream classrooms with minimal or no support. Therefore, the descriptors represent skills that exiting ELLs would be able to execute consistently in general education classrooms with grade-level materials where they would not receive support from an ESL or bilingual teacher. Arguably, it can be said that fluent English-speaking students do not always exhibit the skills, tasks, and behaviors on the observation scale—at any grade level. However, the scale can be used as a tool to systematically observe learning behaviors of the ELLs who are at the cusp of spending all of their instructional time in the general education classroom where they will not receive regular support from the language education teacher. ELL students who do not consistently exhibit most of the listed skills may need a more gradual transitioning process. On the contrary, children who are active, engaged learners who stay on task, accept responsibility, and complete assignments in their language education classroom will generally perform well on these tasks in the mainstream classroom, providing their English language proficiency is sufficiently well developed. Likewise, ELLs who read and write well in their primary language will transfer these skills into English (Hakuta, 1986; Escamilla, 1999, 2000; Escamilla & Coady, 2001; Freeman & Freeman, 2007).

We suggest that at the elementary and middle school levels, the sending language education teachers and the receiving mainstream teachers conduct periodic transition/exit meetings to discuss exiting decisions for the ELLs who may be eligible for transitioning. Together, the teachers can review the student's language proficiency scores, look through the student's portfolio, and use the authentic observation scale to discuss the student's readiness. They can also take note of the student's potential challenges in the mainstream classroom. If at all possible, it is respectful and useful to include the student's parents in this meeting. The meeting time and location may need to be adjusted to accommodate the parents' schedule. The teachers can answer parents' questions and suggest ways for the parents to continue to support their child's overall learning when all instruction is shifted to the general education classroom. The *Exit Information Checklist and Anecdotal Record Template* can be used as a summary sheet of all the data supporting the decision to exit the ELL students.

Secondary English language learners have courses with many teachers who have not gathered data in portfolios. Therefore, making exit decisions at the secondary level requires some different strategies. A transition team, led by the counselor who serves the school's ELLs, that includes the ESL and/or bilingual teachers and a general education content teacher (who teaches a designated section for ELLs) can use several criteria to determine readiness for transition. In addition to the exit criteria set by the state according to language proficiency test scores, the committee can use the classroom-based observation scale and the student's cumulative folder (containing test scores, progress reports, and report cards) to determine the student's achievement in previous courses. The team can look at the student's grades in bilingual and ESL courses as well as review his/her successes and challenges while enrolled in mainstream courses.

After students have been exited out of a language education program, their progress should be monitored for at least two years. Although this is a commonly recommended practice, the reality is that the process of monitoring ELLs who have already transitioned out of a language education program is often neglected. Understandably, the teachers involved in the exit decision are actively focusing on the needs of their currently enrolled ELLs. However, during the quarterly or semiannual transition/exit meetings, the agenda should include discussions of ELLs who have been exited from the language education program within the past two years. The students' files with the *Exit Information Checklist and Anecdotal Record* can be pulled to refer to the areas of concern that were previously identified. An additional template, the *Monitoring Sheet for Exited Students Template*, can be used to monitor and take notes about the exited students' current performance in mainstream classrooms. Both templates will help the transition team suggest ideas and discuss ways to provide support for the students who may still be struggling in the mainstream classrooms.

Using Assessment Data to Evaluate Program Effectiveness

Standardized tests, authentic assessments, and portfolio data can all be used to track student growth. While this data can be instrumental in shaping future instruction, it can be just as important in evaluating and improving the district's language education program. We recommend that the language education committee initiate a cyclical process by looking at student data according to how the ELLs in the district are currently receiving literacy instruction and how they are currently learning content area material and developing academic English. This baseline data can be used for comparisons with future annual student data. After the language education instructional approaches have been reconfigured to implement ESL, literacy, and academic content instruction according to the twelve key practices, professional development must be provided to teachers of ELLs in order to align instruction with the core instructional practices (meaning-based literacy, sheltered instruction, and content-based ESL) and the four essential common classroom practices. Then, the committee can analyze annual student data and identify trends across classrooms and across schools. The district language education committee can work with school improvement teams to monitor student progress in each content area, discuss what seems to be working effectively, provide on-going professional development, and adjust configurations in order to address areas for improvement.

In this chapter, we have provided suggestions, processes, and templates for accurately identifying the ELLs in the school district. We have suggested ways to collect student data and have shown how standardized and authentic assessments can monitor ELL student performance and evaluate program effectiveness. In the next chapter, we explain how educators can use an additive bilingual perspective to address the needs of ELLs.

QUESTIONS FOR REFLECTION AND ACTION

1. How do teachers of newly arrived ELLs currently find out about the language, literacy, and academic knowledge that the children already know in their primary language and in English? What are the implications for the future?

2. Compare your district's entry and exit procedures to the procedures outlined in this chapter. List the strengths and areas for improvement in the district's procedures. How can teachers and administrators initiate changes to entry/exit procedures?

3. Working with your study group, use the CAN DO Descriptors to brainstorm assessment options on the topic of the U.S. Constitution for ELLs at ELP levels 2, 3, and 4 (see Table 4.2).

Recommended Readings

Gomez, E. (2000). *Assessment Portfolios: Including English language learners in large-scale assessments*. Washington D.C.: ERIC Digest, EDO-FL-00-10.

Gottlieb, M. (2006). *Assessing English language learners: Bridges from language proficiency to academic achievement*. Thousand Oaks, CA: Corwin Press.

Gottlieb, M. (2011). *Common language assessment for English learners*. Bloomington, IN: Solution Tree.

Gottlieb, M., & Nguyen, D. (2007). *Assessment and accountability in language education programs: A guide for teachers and administrators*. Philadelphia: Caslon Publishing.

Hamayan, E. et al. (2007). *Special education considerations for English language learners: Delivering a Continuum of Services*. Philadelphia: Caslon Publishing.

Illinois State Board of Education. Home Language Survey. Available at http://www.isbe.net/bilingual/htmls/tbe_tpi.htm.

O'Malley, M., & Valdez-Pierce, L. (1996). *Authentic assessment for English language learners: Practical approaches for teachers*. Reading, MA: Addison-Wesley.

Tabors, P. (2008). *One child, two languages: A guide for early childhood educators of children learning English as a second language*. Baltimore: Paul H. Brooks Publishing Co.

Valdez-Pierce, L. Assessment of English language learners. Webcast available at http://www.readingrockets.org/webcasts/ondemand/1003.

CHECKLIST FOR KEY PRACTICE 3

The checklist is written using measurable statements that can be used to evaluate and monitor language education programs and instruction at the district, school, and classroom levels. The district language education committee and school leadership teams can use the checklist as a diagnostic tool to identify the areas that represent the biggest challenges during the restructuring process. Various teams can use the results of the checklist as a starting point to determine the professional development that educators need to know in order to successfully implement the practices. Teacher teams can use the checklist to evaluate their own teaching practices to recognize ways in which they can immediately make instructional improvements.

SCORING DIRECTIONS:
1 = This practice IS implemented.
2 = This practice is in progress or is in place in some classrooms.
3 = This practice is NOT currently in place.

			Shared Practices at the District, School, and Classroom Levels
			Implementing a Balanced Student Assessment System: Standardized measures, common assessments, and classroom assessments in literacy, academic achievement, and language proficiency are used to inform instructional and programmatic decisions.
1	2	3	• Administrators and teachers design and use a balanced assessment system that identifies ELL students' needs, documents student classroom performance, and evaluates program effectiveness.
1	2	3	• Entry and exit criteria and procedures are consistently established and implemented across the district.
1	2	3	• Classroom assessments are differentiated according to the ELLs' English language proficiency levels using a variety of reliable assessment strategies that incorporate visual, graphic, and interactive supports.
1	2	3	• Teachers build authentic assessments into instruction to measure ELLs' understanding of academic content and their progress in English language development.
1	2	3	• Common assessments, classroom assessments, and standardized assessment data are used to document ELLs' growth over time and monitor students' progress.
1	2	3	• Data from standardized assessments and authentic assessments are reviewed and used to evaluate language education program effectiveness.

IMPLICATIONS AND COMMENTS _____

_____

_____

_____

Entry Information Checklist and Annotations Template

Student Name: _____   Grade: _____

Date: _____   Teacher: _____

Sources of Information Checklist

Parent interview _____
Educational History Survey_____ (completed with parent / child / interpreter)
Oral English Language Survey_____
English Literacy Screening _____
English Language Proficiency Test _____
Primary language literacy screening _____
Home visit _____
Previous school records ___
Classroom based assessments _____
Standardized achievement test score _____

Record actual tests and scores in appropriate areas in Anecdotal Notes section

---

Anecdotal Notes

Literacy	Content Area Knowledge	English Language Proficiency
Notes:	Notes:	Notes:

Areas of Interests of New Student

Possible Strengths and Challenges

Qualifies for ESL/bilingual services: Yes   or   No

Describe type of service needed:

Teacher Assessment Responsibilities and Planning Template

ELL Student Name: _____ Grade: _____ Date: _____

Subject Areas	Teacher for instruction	Teacher for assessment	Who assigns the grade
Math			
English Reading and Language Arts			
Science			
Social Studies			
Primary Language Literacy			
Fine Arts			
Physical Education			
Health			

Additional Notes

Areas of growth:

Areas of strength:

Areas to target for improvement:

Classroom-Based Observation Scale to Support Exiting Decisions Template

Name of Student: _____ Grade _____

Indicate how the student is functioning in your classroom at this time, using the following scale:

1 Not at all
2 Sometimes
3 About half of the time
4 Most of the time
5 Always

					English Language Proficiency Skills
1	2	3	4	5	Comprehends class presentations and directions
1	2	3	4	5	Identifies cause and effect from oral discourse*
1	2	3	4	5	Discusses stories, issues, and concepts*
1	2	3	4	5	Gives speeches and oral reports*
1	2	3	4	5	Offers creative solutions to issues and problems*
1	2	3	4	5	Draws conclusions from oral information**
1	2	3	4	5	Makes connections from oral discourse**
1	2	3	4	5	Expresses and defends points of view**
					English Literacy Skills
1	2	3	4	5	Interprets information or data*
1	2	3	4	5	Identifies word families, figures of speech*
1	2	3	4	5	Writes using original ideas or detailed responses*
1	2	3	4	5	Edits and revises writing*
1	2	3	4	5	Conducts research gleaning info from multiple sources**
1	2	3	4	5	Draws conclusions from explicit and implicit text**
1	2	3	4	5	Applies information to new contexts**
1	2	3	4	5	Reacts to multiple genres and discourses**
1	2	3	4	5	Authors multiple forms/genres of writing**
					Academic Behaviors
1	2	3	4	5	Participates in class discussions
1	2	3	4	5	Follows complex directions
1	2	3	4	5	Uses academic vocabulary with few gaps
1	2	3	4	5	Reads independently with little guidance
1	2	3	4	5	Identifies main ideas and key concepts
1	2	3	4	5	Finds details that support main ideas*
1	2	3	4	5	Summarizes information from graphics or notes*
1	2	3	4	5	Routinely completes written assignments

* Tasks ELLs can do *with support*. Aligned to WIDA Pre K–12 CAN DO Descriptors, ELP level 4.
** Tasks ELLs can do *with grade-level material and minimal support*. Aligned to WIDA Pre K–12 CAN DO Descriptors, ELP level 5.

Exit Information Checklist and Anecdotal Record Template

Student Name: _____ Grade: _____

Date: _____ Teacher: _____

Sources of Information Checklist

English language proficiency test _____
Standardized academic achievement _____
Classroom based assessments ESL/bilingual class _____ General ed. Class _____
Observation Scale _____ Portfolio of student work _____ Parent interview _____
Student interview _____ Report card grades _____ Other: _____

Record actual tests and scores in appropriate areas in Anecdotal Notes section

---

Anecdotal Notes

Literacy (First Language and English)	Content Area Knowledge	English Language Proficiency
Notes:	Notes:	Notes:

Possible Challenges in General Education Classroom

Monitoring Sheet for Exited Students Template

Student Name: _____ Grade: _____

Date: _____ Teacher: _____

Sources of Information Checklist

Report card grades _____
Standardized tests in academic achievement _____
Classroom-based assessments _____ Classroom observations _____
Portfolio of student work _____ Other:

Record actual tests and scores in appropriate areas in Anecdotal Notes section

Anecdotal Notes

Subject Areas	Strengths	Challenges
Literacy		
Content Area Knowledge		
English Language Proficiency		

Follow-up needed (include date and responsible person)

Embracing an Additive Bilingualism Perspective

Make instructional and linguistic decisions about ELLs based on an understanding of these learners as emerging bilingual students who use two languages for social and academic purposes.

- Value bilingualism and promote bilingualism and biliteracy development to the greatest degree possible.

- Provide a sequence of ESL instruction over a period of several years so that ELLs can reach the high levels of English language proficiency that are necessary for school success.

- Plan language instruction so that what is learned in one language supports and reinforces learning in the other.

- Use primary language support to preview, explain, and clarify concepts that ELLs encounter in English-speaking classrooms.

- Whenever possible, provide primary language instruction in bilingual classrooms to develop academic language and literacy and to teach grade-level subjects.

THE BIG IDEAS

- Additive bilingual environments are associated with higher levels of academic achievement than subtractive bilingual environments.

- It takes several years for English Language Learners (ELLs) to learn the academic English language necessary to understand and express complex concepts in English-speaking classrooms.

- Primary language support and/or instruction is most successful when teachers strategically plan language use so that instruction in one language supports and reinforces learning in the other.

Educators who are concerned about the educational achievement of ELLs want to know what the most effective kinds of programs are for ELLs. In response to this question, Kathryn Lindholm-Leary writes:

> In a recent comprehensive synthesis of the empirically based research on the achievement of ELLs (Genesee et al., 2006; Lindholm-Leary & Genesee, 2010) there was strong convergent evidence that the educational success of ELLs is positively related to sustained instruction through the student's first language.... Students who participated in an assortment of different programs and those

who received no educational intervention (that is, they were put into mainstream English classes with no additional assistance) performed at the lowest achievement levels and had the highest dropout rates. The studies reviewed in various syntheses of research on the education of English language learners also indicate that students who achieved full oral and literate (reading and writing) proficiency in both languages had higher achievement scores, GPAs, and educational expectations than their monolingual English-speaking peers (Genesee et al., 2006; Lindholm-Leary & Genesee, 2010; Lindholm-Leary & Hernandez, 2009).... These results suggest that educational programs for ELLs should seek to develop their full bilingual and biliterate competencies in order to take advantage of these interdependencies across languages. (Hamayan & Field, 2012, pp. 105–106).

In short, additive bilingual environments are associated with higher levels of academic achievement than subtractive bilingual environments.

Most schools, however, cannot offer full developmental bilingual programs that enable their students to develop their full bilingual and biliteracy competencies. Key Practice 4 explains what an additive bilingualism perspective looks like in practice in any linguistically and culturally diverse educational context including English-medium programs as well as different types of bilingual education programs. Embracing an additive bilingualism perspective means seeing ELLs as emerging bilingual students who use two languages for social and academic purposes. Educators working in districts and schools with additive bilingualism perspectives implement instruction in ways that affirm bilingual, bicultural, and biliterate students as integral parts of the classroom and the community. They utilize the languages that their ELLs speak as well as their cultural funds of knowledge as resources that enrich all students' learning experiences. These educators provide a well-articulated sequence of English as a Second Language (ESL) instruction over a period of several years so that ELLs can reach the high levels of English language proficiency that are necessary for school success and they plan language instruction so that what is learned in one language supports and reinforces learning in the other. They also use primary language support to preview, explain, and clarify concepts that ELLs encounter in English-speaking classrooms. Most importantly, wherever possible, these educators organize bilingual classes and programs that provide primary language instruction so that emergent bilinguals learn grade-level content area concepts and skills and develop academic language and literacy in two languages.

Valuing Bilingualism

ELLs, who generally speak their primary language at home (at least in the early years of second language acquisition), learn social English naturally by talking with siblings and friends, by watching TV and videos, and by interacting with English-speaking peers in the neighborhood and at school. They are emerging bilinguals with various levels of fluency in two languages. While the ELLs are learning in their classrooms, they draw on their metacognitive skills in two languages to process the information that they are learning (Cloud et al., 2009). Educators can use all of the ELLs' linguistic skills and their experiences in their bilingual and bicultural worlds to help them learn the complex academic language and content area knowledge they encounter at school. Research supports this notion. A report of a five-year longitudinal study of elementary Spanish-speaking ELLs found that children are better served when teachers capitalize on all of the students' linguistic resources and teach with a conceptual framework that includes accelerated growth in both the primary language and English literacy (Escamilla et al., 2010). This study affirms previous research that finds that ELLs are most successful when they learn in an additive bilingual environment where their first language and culture are valued by their schools and by the wider society (Lambert, 1975; Genessee, 1987; Cummins, 1994).

In an additive bilingual environment, the students' knowledge in both languages is used to facilitate learning, and the goal is for students to become fully bilingual, biliterate, and bicultural. In general education and content classrooms where bilingualism is valued and the home language of English language learners is considered a valuable resource, teachers can plan ways to use the students' primary language to help them learn. Appropriate use of primary language *support* in mainstream classrooms can substantially improve ELLs' access to grade-level literacy development, content knowledge, and academic skills. Even greater access to effective literacy development and academic success can be provided in school districts that have enough ELLs from a single language group to implement primary language *instruction* in bilingual classrooms, taught by certified bilingual teachers.

Educators who embrace an additive bilingualism perspective implement language and content instruction in ways that affirm bilingual, bicultural, and biliterate students and the linguistic and cultural resources they bring with them to school. Adopting such a perspective coherently at school and throughout the district can be challenging, however, because administrators, principals, mainstream teachers, and language education teachers often have various preconceived notions about the use of the primary language in schools and classrooms. Some of these perceptions are negative. As the language education committee and school leadership teams learn how the primary language is a valuable academic and community resource, committee members must actively share what they have learned. Administrators, teachers, and ancillary school staff members need to know that when bilingual assistants or tutors explain classroom expectations and tasks in the ELLs' primary language, they are providing information necessary to negotiate the new English-speaking classroom's culture and learning environment. They need to know that learning in the primary language allows ELLs to talk about a wide range of academic topics. These important skills transfer into English as the students improve their English proficiency. "When learners exchange ideas in their first language and participate in various ways of knowing, they can more easily discuss and write about what they learn in their new language, English" (Faltis & Hudelson, 1997, p. 102). Furthermore, educators need to know that there are socio-cultural reasons to utilize the ELLs' primary language. When teachers, other adults, and children speak the new students' language and show positive regard for the ELLs' home culture, children are more likely to acquire a sense of belonging in the school. When ELLs see their own language represented and used in the classroom, they themselves are indirectly valued (Lucas & Katz, 1993).

Providing a Long-Term Sequence of English as a Second Language Instruction

Educators who share an additive bilingualism perspective make decisions based on the understanding that language learning is a developmental process, and they provide a sequence of ESL instruction over a period of several years so that ELLs can reach the high levels of English language proficiency that are necessary for school success. Adopting such a perspective can be challenging because many believe (incorrectly) that once an ELL is conversationally fluent in English, the student is ready to be placed in the general education classroom without additional support (NCTE, 2008). Yet, when ELL children appear to be socially fluent, they often lag behind in performance in English in comparison with their monolingual English classmates. The explanation for this lag often lies in the distinction between the two types of language proficiency: social language proficiency and academic language proficiency. Social language proficiency, referred to by Cummins in 1980 as Basic Interpersonal Communication Skills (BICS), describes the social language used in oral conversations. This type of communication offers many cues to the listener and uses context-embedded language. Usually it takes about two years for students from different linguistic backgrounds to comprehend social language readily and begin to use complex grammar when speaking in English (Hakuta et al., 2000).

Becoming proficient in academic language takes much longer. Cummins (1980) coined the term Cognitive Academic Language Proficiency (CALP) to describe the context-reduced academic language of the classroom. He states that while most ELL students learn sufficient English to engage in social communication (BICS) in about two years, they typically need a minimum of five years to acquire the type of academic language skills needed for successful participation in content classrooms.

Other researchers state that it typically takes ELLs from five to ten years to become fully proficient in all aspects of academic English (Cummins 2006; Hakuta et al., 2000; Thomas & Collier, 2002; TESOL 2006; NCTE, 2008). Sadly, without instruction that is appropriately modified, ELLs may never fully attain academic proficiency in English (Scarcella, 2009). Yet educators still have a tendency to misjudge ELL students who speak fluently in social situations. It cannot be assumed that students who converse fluently in English have also acquired enough academic English proficiency to meet the challenging demands of the English-speaking general education and content classrooms without support. ELL students move up to the intermediate ELP levels within 2 to 3 years but often have difficulties at the intermediate and advanced levels for several years (Wright, 2010).

Scarcella and Rumberger (2000) identify five ways that academic language is different from everyday English: (1) more use of reading and writing; (2) higher standards of accuracy; (3) more demanding linguistic functions, such as persuading, analyzing, interpreting, hypothesizing, etc.; (4) fewer contextual clues; and (5) a larger lexicon and grammar base, which is needed for proficiency in written academic language. Scarcella (2003) adds the point that academic language proficiency also includes the ability to understand and use higher-order thinking skills such as conceptualizing and making inferences. Functional language analysis has shown that the language of one content area is different than the language of another. For example, science texts are tightly organized with a focus on making a convincing argument as to why a particular scientific theory is correct or incorrect; historical writings typically recount a series of events from a particular person (or group of people's) perspective (Fang & Schleppegrell, 2008). Not only do students need to read these texts differently, they need to learn how to write and speak in the appropriate manner for that subject area. Furthermore, Cummins points out that the ELLs have to catch up to a moving target: fluent English-speaking students are continuing to expand their linguistic repertoire; they are not standing still waiting for ELLs to catch up. "Native English speakers continue to make significant progress in academic skills (e.g., vocabulary knowledge, reading and writing skills, etc.) year after year" (Cummins, 1989, p. 27).

The good news is that teachers can use the ELLs' oral social language as a first step toward teaching academic language. Gottlieb (2006) points out that academic language proficiency links social language proficiency to academic content. When teachers teach the unique vocabulary and language structures of each content area, they are providing a helpful connection from social language proficiency to academic language proficiency and academic achievement. Hakuta et al. (2000) suggest that program planners set a policy that sets aside the entire spectrum of the elementary grades as the realistic range within which academic English acquisition is accomplished.

Planning and Coordinating Instruction in Two Languages

Educators who see ELLs as emerging bilinguals plan instruction so that what is learned in one language supports and reinforces learning in the other. During the time that ELLs are in the process of learning academic language and struggling to learn the complex, context-reduced content taught in their English-speaking classrooms, teachers can find ways to use the children's primary language to help them learn. Wright (2010) succinctly describes the difference between ineffective and effective use of primary language support. He points out that primary language support "is ineffective when it inhibits rather than supports the students' efforts to obtain comprehensible input from oral or written English" (p. 272). On the contrary, primary language support is effective when its use prepares the ELLs to understand instruction or readings in English. For example, when teachers ask their bilingual assistants to activate the ELLs' prior knowledge of a subject and preview information to be learned, they are providing scaffolds that help the ELLs make sense of the English lessons and readings that follow.

Wright suggests that primary language support is also effective after lessons when the strategy allows the ELLs to grasp a concept that was inaccessible when taught or explained only in English. Freeman and Freeman (2000) extend these two strategies into a lesson sequence that they call the "preview-view-review" strategy. In the preview stage, the key concepts are introduced in the ELLs' primary language. In the view stage, the students work with those concepts through a sheltered instruction approach in English. In the review stage, the ELLs have opportunities to review, clarify, and talk about concepts in the primary language.

When bilingual adults work with ELLs, they help the students learn complex academic skills that are difficult to demonstrate in English, even when modeled with visuals and other instructional supports. For example, with guidance from certified teachers, the bilingual assistants can work with ELLs in small groups where they can model and explain how to analyze information, identify problems and solutions, draw conclusions, make appropriate inferences, and give oral arguments for their positions.

When mainstream teachers ask bilingual assistants to reinforce the big ideas and explain major concepts that the ELLs are learning in their English-speaking classrooms, the assistants are not just teaching and clarifying information. They are modeling and using pertinent academic language in the primary language. When they get their students talking (in L1) about what they have learned (in L2), they are helping the ELLs learn and improve academic language skills in the primary language. Furthermore, the students recognize that their home language is valued as a language of learning. These discussions about school topics in the primary language also help the students gain confidence to talk about the same topics in English when they are asked to work in small groups with their English-speaking peers. As Wright points out, an important way that primary language support is effective is "when the strategies enable greater interaction between the ELLs and other students in the classroom for social and academic purposes" (2010, p. 272).

Using the Primary Language to Support Learning in English-Speaking Classrooms

It is not unusual for educators to think that translation is the main function of the primary language. However, translation may be the least effective use. Bilingual adults who try to translate as mainstream teachers teach find that they can rarely fully translate what is to be learned. "What passes for translation is more accurately described as partial explanation, the paraphrasing of large chunks of information, and short-hand explanations of complex ideas. Isolated facts rather than whole ideas and concepts tend to be communicated. . . . As a result, students accumulate slightly wrong facts, half-analyzed information, and bits and pieces of whole concepts." (Miramontes et al., 2011, p. 104).

There are many effective ways in which bilingual adults can support learning in English-speaking classrooms. These noncertified adults are usually called bilingual assistants, tutors, or aides. Primary language support is most effective when the assistants or tutors help the ELLs on a daily basis and are familiar with teacher expectations and the big ideas of the current grade-level topics. The bilingual assistants and tutors must work closely with a small number of teachers and not be responsible for the content knowledge of multiple grade levels. When ELLs are pulled out to work with bilingual assistants or tutors in the hall or library, the tutorial help is often seen as remedial in nature. Therefore, we suggest that the bilingual assistants work with small groups in the mainstream classrooms. This practice shows all learners that learning in two languages is normal and useful and that both languages have equal status.

General education and content teachers need to model and teach the bilingual assistants the four common instructional practices in this book and how to use specific strategies that they most often use (e.g., KWLs, word sorts, concept maps, sentence strips, paragraph frames, T-charts, Venn diagrams, preview-view-review). Teachers can assign the bilingual assistants to work with a small group of ELLs, giving them a specific task using these strategies. This will help the ELLs fully understand how to complete tasks using these strategies. Then, they will be prepared to use the same strategies on different topics in English when the assistant is not present. Bilingual assistants can also facilitate home/school communication. They can regularly send notes home telling parents what their children are learn-

Table 5.1   Effective Use of Primary Language Support In English-Speaking Classrooms

Using the ELLs' primary language (L1) teacher assistants, assistants, tutors, and parent volunteers can:

- Provide diagnostic information for newly arrived students by conducting informal assessment procedures (educational history information, L1 writing samples, L1 informal reading inventories).
- Connect the students' prior experiences and knowledge to new information.
- Pre-teach, explain, and give examples of new concepts, connecting them to the big ideas that are related to the daily lessons and readings.
- Clarify concepts and content knowledge that the students missed while learning in English.
- Write the big ideas of lessons and units in primary language on chart paper for classroom display (when children are literate in home language).
- Develop students' primary language academic proficiency by asking students to retell newly learned information or asking them open-ended questions (e.g., tell me about…).
- Read content books aloud in the primary language that reinforce concepts that have been taught in English.
- Help students learn cognitive strategies by asking them how they made inferences, how they solved a problem, why they supported a hypothesis, etc.
- Read stories to children in the home language, asking them comprehension questions, asking them to predict what will happen next, and asking them to connect the stories to their own lives.
- Support English vocabulary development by defining new words, clarifying usage, and providing examples in the primary language; then, the assistants can model English sentences using the new words.
- Ask questions to determine if students have understood lessons that they have learned in English.
- Develop L1 social and academic language proficiency by encouraging student interaction and peer tutoring in the primary language.
- Talk about geography, current events, and history of home countries.
- Facilitate classroom assessments by clarifying instructions in the primary language and model test-taking strategies.
- Work with cooperative groups that are clustered by primary language.
- Write weekly letters to parents to explain what the students are studying in the classroom so that parents can ask their children questions and reinforce learning.
- Promote students' self-esteem by talking about the benefits of being bilingual and maintaining their home language.
- Help ELL students conduct internet searches in their primary language to find information on classroom topics, study skills, and current events.

ing and suggest parent-child activities that can reinforce learning. Table 5.1 suggests several effective ways that bilingual adults can support learning in English-speaking classrooms.

Many school districts have a large number of ELLs from a single language group (e.g., Spanish) and small numbers of ELL students from several language groups. It is economically impossible to hire bilingual teacher assistants to provide primary language support for all of the ELLs. School administrators have often addressed this challenge by hiring an assistant who is bilingual in the most represented language group and then asking him/her to help other ELLs in English. We suggest an alternative approach. The administrators can ask language-minority community leaders to identify bilingual adults who might want to work as part-time primary language tutors. For example, in a school where there are five Spanish-speaking, three Polish-speaking, two Serbian-speaking, and two Farsi-speaking ELLs with ELP levels 1–3, an administrator may be able to locate four qualified bilingual adults who would consider tutoring 8 to 10 hours a week under the supervision of certified teachers. Sometimes English-proficient bilingual college students are willing to work with children for a few hours per week. The ESL teacher can provide initial training for the bilingual tutors so that the tutors learn the four common key practices and other strategies that are effective ways to preview, clarify, and explain classroom concepts without simultaneous classroom translation. The general education and the ESL teacher can arrange a mutually agreed upon schedule and share the supervision of the tutors. The ELLs will receive much needed help, improve language skills in both languages, and benefit from the positive adult role models who share their language and culture.

Some staff members may argue that if all of the ELLs cannot have primary language support, then none of them should. Research does not support this notion. Miramontes et al. say it best: "It may not be possible to provide the same kind of primary language support to all groups in the school population. The inability to serve all language groups fully, however, should not be the criterion for deciding not to serve particular groups at the maximum level resources allow" (2011, p. 40).

Providing Primary Language Instruction in Bilingual Classrooms

Research demonstrates that students in well-implemented additive bilingual programs achieve academically at or above grade level and develop high levels of bilingualism and biliteracy. Thus, whenever possible, educators should provide primary language instruction in coherent, developmental bilingual programs.

School districts with large numbers of ELLs from one language group can establish bilingual education programs in which primary language instruction is provided in bilingual classrooms taught by certified bilingual teachers. There is a wide misconception that bilingual teachers teach only in the primary language in their classrooms, excluding the use of English. Escamilla (2000) points out that the word bilingual means two languages. Learning English is always a primary goal of bilingual education programs. There are two huge advantages of bilingual education programs. First, certified bilingual teachers can immediately teach literacy in the students' first language, the language in which their students can use all of their knowledge and linguistic skills to construct meaning. Second, teachers can focus on academic concepts and can connect concepts with the experiences and prior knowledge that the children bring to the classroom on the very first day that they arrive at the classroom door. This fact is especially important; several research studies show that literacy and academic skills transfer across languages (Hakuta, 1986; Collier & Thomas, 1992; Cummins, 1989; Escamilla, 1987; Krashen, 1996). In other words, literacy skills and subject matter taught in the students' primary language do not have to be retaught in the other.

The biggest challenge for bilingual teachers is how to effectively implement instruction using both the primary language (L1) and the target language (L2, English). Without many published resources that share ways to effectively implement both the primary language and English instruction in bilingual classrooms, teachers have wrestled with ways to strategically use the two languages. Some teachers, in efforts to provide a specific percentage of use of each language, have tried to develop a systematic approach, e.g., using one language for one subject and the other language for a different content area. Some teachers have even tried teaching in one language (e.g., Spanish) on Mondays, Wednesdays, and Fridays and in the other (e.g., English) on Tuesdays and Thursdays. (Imagine the poor ELL who is learning long division but is absent on Wednesday.) Some teachers have tried direct translation, translating from English to the primary language of the student/s with little or no time lapse in between. Of course, the teachers have found that translating is time consuming and students often ignore the English presentation and simply rely on the translation that follows. The problems are that the preceding structures do not make instruction more comprehensible, the students may not be actively engaged, and the methods may not allow the students to ask questions when they need clarification. Effective language planning consists of strategically deciding which language to use for specific objectives and purposes.

Strategic language use starts with finding out what academic tasks the ELLs can do in their first and second languages. The goal is to be able to plan specific ways to teach in each language to help the students meet content and language standards. At the beginning of each school year, the bilingual and general education teachers can use their standardized test results (in English and the primary language), the students' portfolios, and their observations to discuss and prepare a list of their students' language strengths and challenges in both languages. By working together, the bilingual teacher is better prepared to make decisions about which language and instructional approach he/she will use for whole classroom instruction and how he/she will use L1 and L2 with small groups and with individuals in the bilingual classroom. The general education teacher has a better understanding of the ELP levels of the ELLs who spend part of their day in his/her classrooms. Knowing what the ELLs can do in both languages helps the general education teacher plan appropriate sheltered instruction and plan how he/she will implement native language support.

Using Two Languages in Bilingual Classrooms

In grades K through 2, the primary language in a bilingual classroom will most likely be the predominant language of instruction since literacy and content instruction in the children's primary language creates a strong foundation for successful learning in both languages. Effective English instruction in kindergarten consists of using songs, chants, and brief lessons connected with content instruction. In addition, bilingual teachers focus on teaching the English language that the students need to get along socially, navigate the building, and understand classroom directions, tasks, and lessons.

As the ELLs gain English proficiency and proceed through the grades, the bilingual teacher implements ESL instruction that coordinates with content area topics that the students are learning. Even so, there are many times when bilingual teachers will want to use only the primary language, not only to teach new concepts but also to develop primary language proficiency and advance first language academic vocabulary. At other times, bilingual teachers will focus on English language development and will use the target language (English) exclusively for ESL instruction and to develop academic language through sheltered instruction. During the time periods when teachers exclusively use one language or the other, a concrete reminder helps the students focus on the designated language. Urow explains that she always puts a colorful scarf around her neck when teaching in English (Urow & Beeman, 2009).

Strategic language planning includes every-day decisions that bilingual teachers must make not only based on the students' needs but also based on the target outcome of the learning activities. Mora (1998) suggests that bilingual teachers use the children's primary language to teach new, unknown concepts. Then, as the students become familiar with concepts, they can talk and write about the known concepts in the unknown target (usually English) language. We provide some general suggestions in Table 5.2.

Beeman and Urow (2009) suggest that bilingual teachers plan instructional strategies that build bridges that connect academic language in two languages. The authors define the bridge as the period during the lessons or units where the focus is on instructing students in how to transfer what they have learned and stored in one language into the other language. The authors refer to the work of Escamilla et al. (2006) and suggest that bilingual teachers talk about the structure of the two languages with their students as they compare word order, language structures, and vocabulary words in the students' two languages. Teachers can model and correct their students' errors, compare language patterns, and teach linguistic constructions in two languages. They point out that the bridge is student centered and is *not* implemented through vocabulary lists, simultaneous translation,

Table 5.2   DOs and DON'Ts of Using Two Languages in Bilingual Classrooms

DO plan the language of instruction according to the objective of the lesson. If the objective is to teach new, complex concepts, use the primary language. If the students already understand the concepts and the objective is to develop academic English language about the concepts, use English. However, plan ways to build bridges to develop academic language in both languages.	**DON'T** simply "go with the flow" and use whichever language seems right at the moment. **DON'T** set arbitrary percentages of time to teach in each language regardless of the English language proficiency levels of the children. **DON'T** establish the practice of always following the children's lead, switching to the language that each child uses when talking to the teacher and/or the other students.
DO plan to use the primary language regularly for level 1–3 students to build a foundation for cognitive development. However, teach classroom terms, cognates, topic-related vocabulary, and other common classroom language structures in L1 and L2.	
DO strategically plan the use of L1 and L2 to help individual ELLs (levels 3–5) use both languages in the classroom. Some students will over-rely on their primary language and will need specific supports to encourage the development of L2.	**DON'T** plan one-size-fits-all practices for using one language or the other for all ELLs in the bilingual classroom.
DO make sure that you model equal status for both the primary (L1) and target (L2) languages so that children see that both languages are important languages of learning.	**DON'T** automatically switch to the home language for disciplinary reasons. **DON'T** switch to English instruction when visitors enter the bilingual classroom.
DO utilize the social English proficiency levels of students in the bilingual classroom to help them build academic proficiency in both languages.	**DON'T** ignore the social English language proficiency that children bring to the bilingual classroom.
DO read aloud to children in both languages. Select and read stories or content books (at appropriate ELP levels) in English as part of ESL lessons. However, before reading, preview the story and talk about the pictures in the primary language.	**DON'T** read books aloud in English that are not comprehensible to the children without constant explanations and translations in the primary language.
DO have books in both languages in the classroom library. Then, choose books according to instructional objectives.	**DON'T** select only "bilingual" books (having both languages on same or adjacent pages).
DO place trade books around the bilingual classroom in both languages.	**DON'T** miss opportunities to display good books in both languages.
DO encourage students to interact with each other for social purposes in either language.	**DON'T** indicate disapproval of using either language for social purposes.

or reading the same book in both languages. Bridging students from their primary language to English can occur for students at any ELP level. Students with ELP levels 3 and 4 will be more proficient at bridging what they have learned in English into their primary language. In both cases, all students will benefit from these discussions. Bilingual teachers can use classroom wall space to show examples of charts, writing prompts, and other graphics that help students build these language bridges. For example, cognate walls are very useful ways to help build the bridge. (Cognates are words that are identical or almost identical in two languages and which have the same or highly similar meaning (e.g., información, director, grupo, in Spanish). As teachers and students identify cognates, they can add them to the wall and teachers can encourage the students to use the cognates in their written work.

In secondary schools with large numbers of ELLs from one language group, primary language instruction is also provided in bilingual classrooms taught by certified bilingual teachers. The bilingual teachers teach specific required content courses in different class periods throughout the day. They generally teach the courses in the primary language since ELLs with varying levels of English proficiency are enrolled in their courses. However, the bilingual teachers can strategically teach labels of concepts, big ideas, and topic-related vocabulary in English. By doing so, they provide language bridges to sequential courses that may not be offered in the primary language. For example, algebra is a required course which is often taught by a bilingual teacher. However, the sequential course, geometry, is often not offered in the ELLs' primary language. Therefore, even though the algebra teacher uses the primary language to teach day-to-day concepts and operations, he/she also inserts math-based ESL lessons to help the ELLs comprehend labels, verbs, and the specific language of mathematical structures. In this way, the bilingual teacher is building a language bridge to help the ELLs succeed in geometry. (Access to success in geometry is further improved when the geometry teacher receives training in sheltered instruction and learns multiple ways to make math instruction in English comprehensible for ELLs.) When there are enough speakers of single language groups, the world (or foreign) language departments can offer language enrichment courses for language-minority students who speak a language other than English at home. These classes are often called "Spanish for Native Speakers" or "Heritage Language" courses. These courses are designed to improve language arts skills for the students who understand and speak a minority language.

Teaching English as a Second Language in Bilingual Classrooms

In all bilingual classrooms, there should be a specific time period set aside for ESL instruction. The bilingual teachers can use the ELLs' social language to develop academic English language proficiency through planned ESL instruction. As early as kindergarten, the ELLs can begin to receive ESL instruction in all four domains (listening, speaking, reading, and writing.) Bilingual teachers generally use a combination of (1) teacher-made materials and activities that are designed to teach the language and the big ideas of the content in the subject areas and (2) adopted ESL texts with supplemental readers and other materials.

At all grade levels, explicit ESL instruction is based on ELD standards. To encourage and systematize ESL instruction, the language education coordinator can work with the bilingual teachers to establish the length of the ESL period, starting with perhaps 20 or 30 minutes at the kindergarten level and increasing the length of the ESL time period as ELL students progress through the grades. Of course, as discussed earlier, in addition to the designated time for ESL instruction, bilingual teachers can teach and/or reinforce English terms, phrases, and language structures of specific concepts as a part of content lessons (in L1) in order to build a bridge to L2 (English).

In well-planned comprehensive bilingual programs, the general education and bilingual teachers integrate the ELLs with their English-speaking peers for special subjects (e.g., physical education, technology class, music, and art instruction) and social activities. When these students come together for social and curricular activities, the ELLs use their social English language proficiency, practice their academic English skills, and develop cross-cultural friendships.

Teaching Literacy in Bilingual Classrooms

When bilingual teachers initiate formal literacy in the primary language, the ELLs can be actively engaged while learning to read and write in the language they know best. For example, the ELLs' prior knowledge, experiences, and sense of story help them to figure out what words make sense. Their knowledge of the language structure and word patterns allows them to figure out what sounds right. They can recognize and make the sounds of the language that they can hear and pronounce. When the teacher reads aloud, they can understand the story, respond to questions, predict what is going to happen next, and talk about the story.

The challenge is that teaching literacy in a language other than English is not necessarily parallel to how the English reading curriculum is generally taught. Bilingual teachers who teach reading in a language other than English must not simply follow the school's English reading curriculum and deliver the same sequence of lessons in the primary language of the children. They will need to research reading methodology in that language and juxtapose the order and strategies of the primary language reading system with the district's reading expectations. For example, Spanish bilingual teachers teach vowel sounds before consonants in beginning Spanish language reading programs. This is the reverse of the way that English-speaking children learn their letters and letter sounds.

According to Escamilla (2000, 2010), even when Spanish-speaking ELLs have only had access to formal instruction in Spanish, they regularly use what they know in both languages within various literacy instructional situations. "This usage of both Spanish and English in literacy events is not a source of confusion, but one of support" (Escamilla, 2000, p. 4). There-

REFLECTIONS FROM THE FIELD

Using Two Languages for Literacy Instruction for Emerging Bilinguals

Sue Wagner

A language education program director from a large urban school district asked me to facilitate a meeting with the district's ESL/bilingual specialists and reading specialists about whether the Spanish-speaking ELLs who arrive in first grade with social English fluency should be placed in ESL classrooms where they would receive initial literacy instruction in English. This would be a major change from the current practice of learning literacy in Spanish in bilingual classrooms. Some of the first and second grade general education teachers had been suggesting the switch. At the meeting, I shared the primary language development chapter in *Restructuring Schools for Linguistic Diversity* (Miramontes et al., 1997) with the group. I assigned groups of 3 or 4 specialists to read a portion of the chapter. After each group had read and summarized their passage, a rich discussion ensued. They talked about what literacy tasks the orally fluent first grade ELLs were currently able to do in English. They knew a lot of vocabulary words and could sound out many words. However, many could not understand the gist and nuances of children's stories that were read to them. The specialists repeatedly stated that comprehension was what reading is all about. They agreed that these ELLs, who are raised in homes where Spanish is the predominant language, do indeed have social English fluency, which is also a foundation for learning. The specialists developed two recommendations: (1) keep the socially English-fluent first graders in the bilingual program and (2) ask the primary bilingual teachers to honor the children's English proficiency by strategically using their knowledge of English in classroom literacy and academic activities. I learned a lot from these wise educators that day.

fore, in bilingual classrooms, although the children receive formal literacy instruction in their primary language, the bilingual teacher can still engage the students in English reading and writing tasks that are appropriate for their ELP level. These learning activities are often a part of daily ESL instruction and are usually initiated using personal writing activities and sharing reading of picture books. The children also can read and write in English about the topics that they are studying in the primary language. In this way, the children are using foundational literacy skills that they are learning in L1 to begin to read and write in L2.

In research-based comprehensive bilingual programs, the ELLs usually receive formal literacy instruction in their primary language for three or more years. Bilingual teachers develop a checklist of literacy skills (e.g., phonemic awareness, phonics, word recognition, comprehension skills; writing skills; fluency; and vocabulary knowledge) to establish skill levels needed to officially switch to formal literacy and language arts instruction in English. The transition process begins in the bilingual classroom and occurs at different rates of language and literacy development for different students. The transition to formal English literacy instruction does not mean that the ELLs discontinue literacy development in their first language. After the transition, the students should still have multiple opportunities to read and write in their primary language.

The work of Escamilla et al. (2010) also suggests that rather than abruptly switching from L1 to L2 literacy instruction, teachers can provide pathways for ELLs to simultaneously learn literacy skills in both languages.

REFLECTIONS FROM THE FIELD

| Transferring Literacy Skills from L1 to L2 | *Sue Wagner* |

I was working with a school district in Michigan that had initiated a bilingual program two years previously, starting at the kindergarten level. At this point, the school had bilingual self-contained classrooms in kindergarten through second grade. One spring day, I met with two second grade bilingual teachers to discuss the use of formal English literacy instruction in their bilingual classrooms. One of the teachers, Linda, told me that, during silent sustained reading, she noticed that Lorena was reading *Little House on the Prairie*—in English! She asked Lorena if she liked the book. Lorena said, "Oh yes, my older sister loves this book. She has read this book to me—and now I can read it too." The teacher asked Lorena to read a page to her and tell her about the story. Sure enough, Lorena was reading in English with fluency and comprehension. Although the ELLs did reading and writing tasks in English as part of their daily ESL lessons, they had received formal literacy instruction in Spanish in first and second grade. Linda reflected that "when the researchers say that you only have to learn to read once—now I see that it is true." I confirmed that research states that children only learn to read once; subsequently, they transfer their skills into their second language. There are many stories of precocious second and third grade bilingual students, like Lorena, who have gone to the library and have checked out books in both their first language and in English—even before the bilingual teacher has initiated the formal literacy transition process. First language literacy skills certainly transfer into the second language; however, most ELLs make the transfer through a well-planned criteria-based process.

The "Literacy Squared Intervention," a copyrighted literacy approach developed by Escamilla and her colleagues, provides accelerated growth in both Spanish and English reading and writing toward the goal of biliteracy. In this program, primary language instruction is continued for longer than three years. At the same time, however, English literacy instruction is introduced and strategically integrated.

In this chapter, we have cited research on and shown how additive bilingual learning environments can promote student learning. We have described the complexities of academic English language development and have stressed the importance of providing a sequence of ESL instruction over a period of several years. In addition, we have provided overviews of how primary language support and primary language instruction can be effectively implemented in learning environments that support additive bilingualism. In the next chapters, we show how the common classroom key practices can be effectively planned and implemented by teachers in English-speaking and bilingual classrooms.

QUESTIONS FOR REFLECTION AND ACTION

1. Take two minutes to write a sentence or two that describes "academic English language proficiency." Share your definition with members of your study group. Using your definitions and the discussion in this chapter, revise and rewrite a broader description of the complexities of

academic English and share it with colleagues who are not in the study group.

2. Review Table 5.1, Effective Use of Primary Language Support in English-Speaking Classrooms. Check the strategies that are currently being used in your district or school. Put a star next to those strategies you would like to see implemented. Share your notations with your study group.

3. How has the information about primary language support and primary language instruction changed your perceptions about using students' native language for instruction?

Recommended Readings

Mantra lingua website: Resources in 52 languages. Available at http://www.mantralingua.com/usa/home.php

Baker, C. (2006). *Foundations of bilingual education and bilingualism*. Clevedon: Multilingualism Matters, Inc.

Beeman, K. & Urow, C. (in press). Teaching for biliteracy: Strenghthening bridges between languages. Philadelphia: Caslon Publications.

Escamilla, K. et al. (2010). *Transitions to biliteracy: Literacy squared*. Final Technical Report (2004–2009). Boulder: Bueno Center, University of Colorado. Available at http://literacysquared.org/home.htm.

Freeman, Y. & Freeman, D. (1996). *Teaching reading and writing in Spanish in the bilingual classroom*. Portsmouth: Heinemann.

Mora, J. K., (2010). Dr. Mora's cross-cultural language & academic development (CLAD) instructional models. San Diego, CA: San Diego State University. Available at http://www.moramodules.com.

CHECKLIST FOR KEY PRACTICE 4

The checklist is written using measurable statements that can be used to evaluate and monitor language education programs and instruction at the district, school, and classroom levels. The district language education committee and school leadership teams can use the checklist as a diagnostic tool to identify the areas that represent the biggest challenges during the restructuring process. Various teams can use the results of the checklist as a starting point to determine the professional development that educators need to know in order to successfully implement the practices. Teacher teams can use the checklist to evaluate their own teaching practices to recognize ways in which they can immediately make instructional improvements.

SCORING DIRECTIONS:
1 = This practice IS implemented.
2 = This practice is in progress or is in place in some classrooms.
3 = This practice is NOT currently in place.

			Shared Practices at the District, School, and Classroom Levels
			Embracing an Additive Bilingualism Perspective: Instructional and linguistic decisions for ELLs are based on understanding that ELLs are emerging bilingual students who use two languages for social and academic purposes.
1	2	3	• Bilingualism is valued, and bilingualism and biliteracy development is promoted to the greatest degree possible.
1	2	3	• A sequence of ESL instruction is provided over a period of several years so that ELLs can reach the high levels of English language proficiency needed for school success.
1	2	3	• Language instruction is planned so that what is learned in one language supports and reinforces what is learned in the other language.
1	2	3	• Primary language support is used to preview, explain, and clarify concepts that ELLs encounter in English-speaking classrooms.
1	2	3	• Primary language instruction is provided in bilingual classrooms to develop academic language, to develop literacy, and to teach grade-level subjects (whenever possible).

IMPLICATIONS AND COMMENTS _____

_____

_____

_____

PART II

Common Classroom Practices for All English Language Learner Educators

KEY PRACTICE 5 **Using Big Ideas to Plan Instruction**

Plan curriculum and instruction that specifically target the "big ideas" (statements of essential learning) that lead to core state standards.

KEY PRACTICE 6 **Implementing Meaningful Vocabulary-Building Instruction**

Pre-teach vocabulary words necessary to understand lessons and readings, teach new words in context during the lessons and readings, and provide practice for students to use the words in various contexts after the lessons and readings.

KEY PRACTICE 7 **Activating Students' Prior Knowledge**

Structure activities that connect ELLs' previous knowledge and cultural experiences to current lessons and build a comprehensible context for learning.

KEY PRACTICE 8 **Structuring Student Interaction**

Provide opportunities for academic development and language practice by implementing activities that require students to talk with each other about what they are learning.

Part II is organized around four common classroom practices which are fundamental, essential teaching practices within effective ESL, literacy, and content instruction. ELLs at the elementary level often receive their instruction in two or more classrooms. Secondary ELLs receive instruction in several classrooms taught by teachers in different departments. When teachers who share the same groups of ELLs meet to learn about and reflect on teaching strategies that are effective for ELLs, they are learning effective practices for all learners. When teachers implement these common classroom practices for diverse learners, all students have greater opportunities to be actively engaged in all of their classrooms.

Using Big Ideas to Plan Instruction

Plan curriculum and instruction that specifically target the "big ideas" (statements of essential learning) that lead to core state standards.

- Use standards to identify the big ideas and key concepts that all students, including ELLs, need to understand in units and lessons.
- Structure comprehensible learning activities that lead to understanding of the big ideas.

- Use materials that explain and exemplify the big ideas (charts, visuals, tradebooks, videos).
- Develop differentiated assessment strategies that allow ELLs to demonstrate their understanding of the big ideas and give examples.

THE BIG IDEAS

- Big ideas are broad statements of essential learning that are directly related to grade-level learning outcomes and core state standards.

- Big ideas serve as excellent starting points for planning academic content, literacy, and ESL instruction.

During the past fifteen years, expert teams of educators across the country have worked to develop state content standards that define what all students should know and be able to do as a result of their schooling. In response to the standards initiative, school district teams of administrators and teachers have used the state standards to develop learning outcomes and curriculum guides in language arts, social studies, science, and math at the primary, intermediate, and secondary levels. Teacher teams have developed learning benchmarks and curriculum plans and, in many cases, have determined the order in which the content topics are taught.

Key Practice 5 demonstrates how English as a Second Language (ESL), literacy, and mainstream teachers can use standards and content objectives to identify the big ideas that all students, including English Language Learners (ELLs), will need to understand the key concepts of the lessons. All teachers who have ELLs in their classes can plan and implement comprehensible learning activities that lead to understanding the big ideas, use materials for ELLs (e.g., charts, trade books, leveled texts) that have visuals that help explain and exemplify the big ideas, and develop assessment strategies that enable ELLs to demonstrate their understanding of the big ideas with concrete examples.

Using Standards to Identify the Big Ideas of Every Lesson

Publishers have paid close attention to the standards movement and have identified standards-based big idea statements, main concepts, guiding questions, and content objectives in educational texts, tradebooks, and supplementary teaching materials. Teachers' guides often identify standards that are addressed and include big idea statements accompanied by many teaching strategies. These lesson planning tools pave the way to making lessons relevant, interesting, and comprehensible for all learners. Even so, Tomlinson and McTighe (2006) point out that some standards are written in statements that are simply too global for the purposes of building lesson objectives and providing specific guidance for instruction and assessment. They suggest that teachers "unpack" the standards by figuring out what knowledge is truly essential and enduring. As they read a standard and its subcategories for different grade levels, teachers can pause and identify the central and organizing ideas that students will remember and understand years after they have left the classroom. For example, Illinois Social Science Standard 14 states that students should understand election processes and responsibilities of citizens. Standard 14.C.3 states that middle and junior high students should "compare historical issues involving rights, roles and status of individuals in relation to municipalities, states and the nation." A middle school social studies teacher can discern that the central and organizing idea of this standard is about the rights, roles, and status of individuals within the context of historical and current voting rights. There are several important and interesting big ideas that the teacher can use to guide instructional planning. Here are three examples.

1. *Throughout history, minority groups have typically had less access to power than majority groups.*
2. *Many individuals struggled to gain voting rights for all citizens.*
3. *State legislators can establish various requirements for the right to vote.*

There are multiple content topics, skills, information, and resources that teachers can select to teach a unit or course—and of course, they cannot address them all. Wiggins and McTighe (2005) discuss how teachers can go about determining what is worth teaching and learning amid a range of content standards and topics. According to Wiggins and McTighe, teachers must choose important knowledge (facts, concepts, and principles) and skills (processes, strategies, and methods) that they consider essential learning. They suggest that teachers focus on "the enduring understandings that will anchor the unit and establish a rationale for it." They define the term *"enduring"* to refer to the big ideas or important under-

Table 6.1   Identifying Big Ideas

MISCONCEPTIONS	INCORRECT BIG IDEA	CORRECT BIG IDEA
Big Ideas are not topics.	The characteristics of sound.	Sound is a kind of energy in the form of waves.
Big Ideas are not details.	When people talk or sing, their vocal cords vibrate.	All sounds come from objects that vibrate.
Big Ideas are not objectives that demonstrate learning, rather they are statements of essential learning.	Students will explain the relationship between pitch and the frequency (speed) of vibrations.	The frequency of sound vibrations determines pitch, higher when faster, lower when slower.
Big Ideas are not in question form.	How do people measure sound?	The intensity of sound is measured in decibels.
Big Ideas are not sentence fragments; they are complete statements.	How people hear	The parts of the ear work together with the brain to enable people to hear sounds.
Big Ideas are not value judgments or stated from one cultural perspective.	Hearing people should respect the deaf.	Perceptions of the deaf have changed through time, but prejudices still exist.

Jeanette Gordon, 2007. Used by permission of the author.

standings that we want students to "get inside of" and retain after they have forgotten many of the details. Enduring understandings go beyond discrete facts and skills; rather, they focus on larger concepts, principles, or processes (2005, p. 10). Many educators have worked to convert these enduring understanding into statements of essential learning or big ideas, which serve as excellent starting points for content-based ESL instruction and academic content (sheltered) instruction.

Our colleague at the Illinois Resource Center, Jeanette Gordon, has taught hundreds of teachers how to understand and use big ideas in their units and daily lesson plans. Gordon defines big ideas as broad statements that directly relate to grade-level learning outcomes and core state standards. She states that big ideas are statements that are either principles (always true) or generalizations (usually true). Gordon's clarification and examples of big ideas are shown in Table 6.1.

Some authors suggest that big ideas can be written in the form of essential questions. However, Gordon points out the advantage of writing big ideas as statements: it is always possible to place "*I learned that…*" before a big idea statement. For example, using one of the preceding big ideas, a student can say: "*I learned that throughout history, minority groups have typically had less access to power.*" Being able to insert "*I learned that*" as the sentence starter is a very helpful way to check if the statement that a teacher develops is really a big idea. Likewise, big ideas always summarize many examples. Therefore, another sentence starting with "*For example*" can always follow a big idea, e.g., "*For example, for many years, African Americans were not allowed to vote in the United States."* If examples are not possible, the statement may be a secondary concept or a detail, not a big idea.

Structuring Comprehensible Learning Activities That Lead to Understanding the Big Ideas

Using a simple big idea that is personally meaningful is a great way to introduce the concept of big ideas to students. For example, the first time a teacher explains big ideas to the students, he/she can write on the board: *"Life is good."* Under the statement, he/she can write:*"For example, my baby makes me laugh!"* and *"For, example, my students make me happy because they are learning new things every day."* Then, the students can all contribute a *"For example"* statement that makes them smile and understand that life is good. The teacher can write down what the students dictate as evidence that life is good. Walmsley (2010) suggests that teachers reinforce students' understanding of big ideas by infusing big ideas into daily classroom conversations. They can identify and talk about the big ideas as they read fiction and nonfiction passages with the students. They can explain that big ideas can be theories and hypotheses and that the "for example" statements can serve as evidence that the theories are correct. They can encourage children to share their own understandings of big ideas in the books and passages that they read.

Teachers can display big idea statements on chart paper to introduce a new unit. The statement provides a clear understanding of what the lesson will be about—as long as the statement is meaningful to all of the learners. A teacher might write the following on the whiteboard or chart paper:*"The Earth has renewable and nonrenewable natural resources."* The teacher and the students talk about what the terms *natural resources, renewable*, and *nonrenewable* mean. They can provide several examples of renewable and nonrenewable resources. For ELLs with ELP levels 1 and 2, teachers can provide pictures of renewable and nonrenewable resources and help the students place the pictures under the two headings. For ELLs with ELP levels 3-5, the teacher can ask the students to identify resources and use a T-chart to display their answers. This comprehensible activity will help the ELLs understand the terms as well as the big ideas.

Teachers can also incorporate big ideas within a lesson to check to see if the students are grasping the big idea. A sentence sort can be used to guide their thinking. To prepare for the activity, the teacher writes a big idea at the top of a sheet of paper, such as *"A person's lifestyle can influence his/her health in positive and negative ways."* Based on what the students have learned and read about, the teacher writes several comprehensible examples (written as sentences) that give examples of positive and negative lifestyle choices. The teacher then makes several copies of the document.

He/she cuts each paper into sentence strips, mixes them up, and puts the strips into an envelope, repeating the process until he/she has enough envelopes for the activity. The teacher gives one full envelope and a large piece of construction paper to each pair of students. First, they must read all of the strips and find the big idea statement. Then, they must orally read the other strips and organize and place the strips into two appropriate categories: positive lifestyle choices and negative lifestyle choices.

Explaining and Exemplifying the Big Ideas

ELLs with beginning levels of English language proficiency will not understand discussions of big ideas without sensory, graphic, and interactive supports. Teachers can use materials for ELLs (e.g., charts, tradebooks, leveled texts) that have visuals that help explain and exemplify the big ideas for ELLs at all ELP levels in ways that do not "water down" the curriculum for English speakers. In addition to making their own drawings and charts, teachers can use commercially made supplementary materials, posters, models, charts, and other instructional supports that are specifically designed to help ELLs understand the big ideas in many content areas. Teachers can use wall space and tables to display these visual assists. In addition, there are many educational websites that have developed videos that help students understand the big ideas and main concepts taught in multiple subjects at any grade level. Furthermore, the World Wide Web is truly *world wide*. Educational videos can be found in multiple languages—however, bilingual adults need to identify and review the websites for appropriate content.

The libraries at school and in the community generally have multiple content books available for teacher use. However, some of these materials may not be at the ELLs' instructional or independent reading levels. There are many published trade books and content materials that have been adapted to be comprehensible for ELLs and other students with low literacy skills. School libraries need to expand their holdings to include these high-interest reading materials in English and in the primary languages of the ELLs in the school. Principals, school leadership teams, and teachers can work with the librarian to acquire nonfiction content books that clarify the big ideas of content area subjects for ELLs. These differentiated reading materials are also beneficial for English speakers who are at different levels of literacy development in English.

Developing Differentiated Assessments to Demonstrate Understanding of Big Ideas

As teachers teach new information, they often ask the students to use *graphic organizers* to write facts, learn vocabulary, organize information, and understand relationships among the big ideas and main concepts. Students at ELP levels 1 and 2 may be asked to complete graphic organizers and/or cloze sentences for an assessment. For intermediate ELLs, the graphic organizers are summaries of what the students know about the topic. The teacher can assess students by asking them to retell and/or write sentences about what they have learned, using the words and brief phrases they have written on the graphic organizer as prompts for sentences and paragraphs.

Another teaching strategy that helps teachers assess the students' understanding of big ideas is an *anticipation/reaction guide*. This strategy works well for ELLs with ELP levels 3 and 4. Before learning about a topic and/or before reading a passage, the students are asked to complete an anticipation guide in pairs or small groups (as shown in discussion of Key Practice 9). The students are asked to agree or disagree with 4 to 6 statements about a topic. Most of the statements are big ideas. The students are asked why they agree or disagree but are not told if their beliefs are correct. After they have learned more about the topic and have read the passage, the teacher asks the students to return to the anticipation guide and rethink their beliefs, changing their opinions if they want to. At this point, the activity is now a *reaction guide* that can be used to evaluate their understanding of the big ideas. After the teacher has the students rethink their opinions, the teacher asks them to clarify why they now agree or disagree with the statements and state examples from the readings to explain their positions. In this way, they are retelling the big ideas and giving examples. Other teaching strategies that work well as assessment strategies to check students' understanding of the big ideas are learning logs, literature logs, converting graphic organizers into paragraphs, and poster sessions.

In this chapter, we have shown how big ideas are identified, written, and used as starting points for planning academic content, literacy, and ESL instruction. We have provided several examples of how they can be used within prior knowledge strategies and during lessons. We also have suggested ways that students can be assessed by showing their understanding of the big ideas. In the next chapter, we discuss and give many examples of how teachers can implement meaningful vocabulary-building activities.

QUESTIONS FOR REFLECTION AND ACTION

1. Look at the teachers' editions, curriculum guidelines, and resource materials that you currently use to plan instruction in a particular content area. Is it clear how the topics relate to the state core content standards? Do the introductions to the units provide big idea statements?

2. Using the samples in Table 6.1, Identifying Big Ideas, develop a big idea about a topic that your students are learning this week and write it as follows: *"My students learned that.... For example ..."*

Recommended Readings

Ellis, E. et al. (2005). Big ideas about teaching big ideas. *Teaching Exceptional Children*, 38(1), 34–40. Available at http://www.graphicorganizers.com/images/stories/pdf/Big%20Ideas%20About%20 Teaching%20Big%20Ideas.pdf.

Tomlinson, C., & McTighe, J. (2006). *Integrating differentiated instruction and understanding by design*. Alexandria, VA: Association for Supervision and Curriculum Development.

Walmsley, S. (2010). *Teaching big ideas*. University of Albany. Powerpoint presentation, available at http://www.albany.edu/reading/documents/IRABigIdea2a.pdf.

Wiggins, G., & McTighe, J. (2005). *Understanding by design*. Boston: Prentice Hall.

CHECKLIST FOR KEY PRACTICE 5

The checklist is written using measurable statements that can be used to evaluate and monitor language education programs and instruction at the district, school, and classroom levels. The district language education committee and school leadership teams can use the checklist as a diagnostic tool to identify the areas that represent the biggest challenges during the restructuring process. Various teams can use the results of the checklist as a starting point to determine the professional development that educators need to know in order to successfully implement the practices. Teacher teams can use the checklist to evaluate their own teaching practices to recognize ways in which they can immediately make instructional improvements.

SCORING DIRECTIONS:
1 = This practice IS implemented.
2 = This practice is in progress or is in place in some classrooms.
3 = This practice is NOT currently in place.

			The Common Classroom Practices for All ELL Educators
			Using Big Ideas to Plan Instruction: Curriculum and instruction are planned that specifically target the "big ideas" (statements of essential learning) that lead to core state standards.
1	2	3	• Teachers use standards to identify the big ideas that students will need to understand the key concepts in units and lessons.
1	2	3	• Teachers structure comprehensible learning activities that lead to understanding of the big ideas.
1	2	3	• Teachers use materials that explain and exemplify the big ideas (charts, visuals, tradebooks, videos).
1	2	3	• Teachers develop differentiated assessment strategies that allow ELLs to demonstrate their understanding of the big ideas and give examples.

IMPLICATIONS AND COMMENTS _____

_____

_____

_____

KEY PRACTICE 6

Implementing Meaningful Vocabulary-Building Instruction

Pre-teach vocabulary words necessary to understand lessons and readings, teach new words in context during the lessons and readings, and provide practice for students to use the words in various contexts after the lessons and readings.

- Explicitly teach new vocabulary, involving the students in definition-getting.
- Build students' oral vocabulary as a foundation for moving ELLs' receptive vocabulary toward expressive language.
- Structure oral and written activities for students to use new vocabulary.
- Coordinate vocabulary instruction and practice in ESL, bilingual, and general education classroom settings.

THE BIG IDEAS

- English Language Learners (ELLs) must see and hear vocabulary words in context many times before they can correctly use their new words in oral and written form.

- When teachers who share the same group of ELLs meet on a regular basis, they can find ways to coordinate and support each other's vocabulary instruction.

Just about all teachers actively teach vocabulary in their classrooms every day. As a result, ELLs are inundated with new words in their various classrooms. Fortunately, their increasing social fluency provides a natural bridge to academic vocabulary development. Teaching vocabulary and related word knowledge skills to ELLs is most effective when general education, English as a second language (ESL), and bilingual teachers share strategies and information about the vocabulary terms that the ELLs are learning in their respective classrooms. This information will help them find ways to model and reinforce the vocabulary words in a variety of classroom experiences. Furthermore, when these teachers use many of the same vocabulary-building strategies, the students become familiar with the tasks that they are expected to do and are more willing to raise their hands and participate in vocabulary lessons and class discussions.

Learning new words is more difficult for ELLs than it is for their English-proficient peers who may be familiar with several of the words in a new vocabulary list. When ELLs look at a new word, they may not recognize the meaning of the word, even when they can pronounce it. Similarly they may not know the word or words in that context (e.g. a student may know multiple, common, and least but not know the math term least common multiple). Meaning is the essential first step in vocabulary building: when teachers introduce the new words using visuals and examples and involve the students in writing comprehensible definitions, they are providing a clear path for the ELLs to understand the general meanings of the vocabulary words the first time that the words are introduced.

Key Practice 6 shows how general education, literacy, and ESL teachers can implement meaningful vocabulary-building instruction for all of their students as well as ELLs. We show how teachers can pre-teach vocabulary words that their students need to understand content lessons and read academic texts, teach new words in context during the lessons, and provide practice for students to use the words in various contexts after the lessons. Teachers who use common vocabulary instructional practices in their respective classrooms provide a powerful bridge for ELLs to improve their academic language and learn to read and write at grade level.

Explicitly Teaching New Vocabulary

Vocabulary-building strategies for ELLs should always include classroom talk. When introducing new words, teachers should isolate the word(s) and actively involve the students in definition-getting. They must use everyday language and lots of examples to define the words—copying dictionary definitions from the board simply will not do the job. After modeling the new words and using the words in sentences, the teacher should point to the words and ask the students to repeat the words two or three times. While introducing a new vocabulary list, the teacher can place new words among synonyms and phrases in everyday social language so that the ELLs can connect the new words to words and concepts that they already know. At the definition-getting stage, the dictionary can wait until the words have been seen and heard in context enough times for the ELLs to have receptive understanding of the vocabulary words. For ELLs with English language proficiency (ELP) levels 3–5, a thesaurus is often a more useful tool than a dictionary. Likewise, asking all students to write a complete sentence with words that they are just beginning to understand is *not* a good strategy. Students have to see and hear new words in context multiple times before they can express and write the words in authentic ways.

Determining the number of new words that can be taught at the same time depends on the age and language proficiency of the students and should be adjusted according to the difficulty of the academic vocabulary. As a general rule, teachers can focus explicit instruction on 5 to 10 words at a time at the primary level, 10 to 15 words at a time at the intermediate level, and 10 to 15 words at a time in each subject area for secondary students.

Bilingual support staff can assist the ESL and mainstream teachers with vocabulary development. According to Montgomery (2007), the selection of vocabulary words to teach ELLs can be grouped into three tiers. Tier 1 words are words that identify terms and concepts that the ELLs typically know in their primary language but do not know the label for in English (e.g., *banana, teacher, sound*). These high-frequency words can be illustrated, labeled in both languages, and taught as sight words that children must recognize and orally produce automatically. The next set, Tier 2 words, are more sophisticated words that are important and useful in understanding the students' current texts and lessons (*vibration, renewable, minority groups*). These Tier 2 words can often be demonstrated and taught using visuals. Many Tier 2 words are also known in the primary language so teachers can share their vocabulary lists with bilingual assistants who can use the primary language to help attach meaning to the words and clarify, explain, and provide examples. Tier 2 words also include words that have connections to other content words and concepts (e.g., *relate to, vary, influence, category, compare, interpret, summarize*).

Teaching Tier 3 words becomes more difficult since Tier 3 words are less concrete and are low-frequency words that are found mostly in academic content books in the upper grades (e.g., *justify, relate, isotope, procrastinate, amoeba*). Primary language support is very helpful in teaching these important, context-reduced terms (Colorin Colorado, 2007). In order to help students understand and use these abstract words, teachers can combine the use of vocabulary-building strategies (such as concept maps and synonym trees) with trade books and other materials that provide clear definitions and many examples.

Building Students' Oral Vocabulary

ELLs generally understand more than they can say. Talking about words and seeing how they are used in print enables ELLs to move from receptive vocabulary to expressive language. Teachers can purposefully implement oral vocabulary-building strategies to facilitate this developmental process.

Teachers can use classroom space to provide sentence frames (starters) and lists of words according to the words' functions. For example, to help young learners talk about classroom topics and write stories, teachers can write target vocabulary words and functional words individually on tongue depressors and place sets of these word sticks in various mugs. One mug might have several rubber-banded sets of current science vocabulary words for students to hold while they are doing oral activities in small groups. Another set of sticks might be words students can use instead of "said" (e.g., *mumbled, whispered, spoke, shouted, tattled, ranted,*

REFLECTIONS FROM THE FIELD

Using Flashcards for Older Learners
Sue Wagner

Mr. Brown, the graphic arts teacher, brought me a box full of cut-off ends of poster board and suggested that I might be able to use the print shop scraps for flashcards. Using flashcards for teenagers? I thanked him and politely said I would figure out how I can use them. The next Monday, I made flashcards for 15 new words. I placed all of the cards on the chalk tray. The students were accustomed to the Monday process of defining the new words. After we developed comprehensible English definitions, I passed the flashcards to the student groups. I told them to copy the definition and add anything else on the back of the flashcard (in English or their first language) that would help them remember the word's meaning. The students enthusiastically took on the task. Since I shared the classroom with other teachers, I had to pick up the cards, put them on the counter, and place them back on the chalk tray when I arrived to the classroom every day. I discovered that the flashcards reminded me to model and encourage students to use the words as we encountered them in the readings. On Friday, before the vocabulary quiz, I noticed a group of students looking at both sides of the cards. Nice.

As the weeks went by, the stacks of flashcards on the counter got taller and taller. When we had extra class time, I pulled out a few flashcards for review. I noticed that my students often pulled out words after they finished their work. One day, I saw Nasreen placing the flashcards in two piles. She explained that she was putting the words that she knew in one pile and the words she didn't remember in another pile. Wow! Nasreen was rating her words, an effective vocabulary-learning activity! That gave me an idea. I created a graphic organizer with three columns: words they knew and could say, words they understood but didn't use, and words they were "clueless" about (a popular teenage expression). I could quickly assess what words I needed to focus on by walking around and seeing how my students were rating their words. Mr. Brown and Nasreen helped me learn how to use flashcards for older learners.

jabbered) as they write stories. Another set of words can be math terms that the students have learned and are asked to use to explain their work.

Teachers can also reserve a prominent space to display flashcards of the academic language that the students are currently studying. The displayed flashcards serve as a reminder for the teacher to model the words in various contexts throughout the day. As the teacher uses the words in context, he/she can point to the flashcard so that the students take note of the printed words.

As students become more familiar with how the new words are used, they begin to express the new words in the correct context. This is a great time to conduct a word sort activity. In developing an open word sort, the teacher makes a list of 8 to 10 words (or phrases) derived from key concepts, big ideas, and main concepts that the students are studying. Then, the teacher looks at the list of words and figures out what logical categories he/she would use to sort the words. Next, he/she adds a few more words that will make connections to help the existing words fit into categories. These words may be common sense, logical words that simply offer clues to help the students designate categories. When implementing the word sort activity, the teacher can randomly write the words into two lists (labeled list A and list B) on the white board. He/she assigns the students to work in pairs since working in pairs (instead of small groups) will promote more involvement by each student. Student A copies each word on list A on small slips of paper (sticky notes work great) and student B does the same with list B. After the students spread their words on the desk or table, the students are asked to discuss the words and then manipulate the slips and sort them into categories that make sense to them. The teacher walks around the room to encourage student interaction and gives each pair a clean sheet of paper. As the pairs complete the task, the teacher tells the students to write their chosen categories on the paper and tape their words under their category titles. In an open word sort, the various pairs of students will have different categories. The teacher then asks the pairs to share their work with the whole group, discussing their reasons for their categories. As a follow-up activity, the teacher can prepare an exit slip that requires the students to use some of the words from the word sort in brief sentences and/or paragraphs.

All of these simple vocabulary practices provide the context to help the students use the words themselves. The words become increasingly familiar and can become part of the students' expressive vocabulary. Other vocabulary-building strategies that help move receptive vocabulary into expressive language skills are connect-twos, concept maps, synonym trees, chants, songs, word webs, graphic organizers, personal word banks, retelling, comparing and contrasting words, and sentence frames.

Structuring Oral and Written Activities to Use New Vocabulary

Teachers must provide multiple opportunities for students to see target vocabulary words in print. They also need to plan and implement specific strategies for students to use the new words in oral and written activities. In addition to the students' textbooks and the supplementary materials that the teacher is using in a unit, teachers in all grade levels can check out books from the school library and public libraries about current classroom topics. The teacher should select many books so that there are various texts that match the students' instructional and independent reading levels.

When library books about a new topic arrive in the classroom, the students are excited (even older learners). They pick up the books, look at the pictures, and often become engaged in reading about the topics. The teacher can ask them to preview the books and make lists of vocabulary words and other important words that they find. The students can share their lists and the teacher can develop oral and written activities using the word lists.

Teachers can also read aloud from some of these texts in whole group settings and can point out the vocabulary words that they find in the trade books, repeating the sentences in which the words are used. In addition to using the library books for explicit instruction, the teacher can encourage the students to use the books for silent, sustained reading and encourage them to browse through the books, look at the pictures, and read the captions whenever the students finish their assignments. When possible, the students should be able to check the library books out so they can read content books at home.

After the students have had opportunities to hear the words in context, see the words in text, and practice using the words in various oral activities, it is time to ask students to write sentences (and paragraphs, reports, and term papers, depending on the grade level of the students) using the new words. By this time, they are far more likely to use the new words correctly in the sentences they create. The teacher can dictate a big idea statement to the students. The statement serves as a topic sentence and the teacher asks the students to complete the paragraph by giving examples and elaborating on the big idea using a particular list of vocabulary terms. The students can be encouraged to write long, interesting sentences so that they can try out words and language patterns that they have seen and heard. When teachers encourage ELL students to take the risk to write long, interesting sentences, they need to evaluate the students on the content of their writing, not the correct form. Other effective writing activities for ELLs include modeled writing, making books, the L portion of KWLs, learning logs, cloze activities, sentence frames, using information from graphic organizers to write paragraphs/reports, literature logs, and peer editing activities.

Coordinating Vocabulary Instruction in English as a Second Language, Literacy, and Content Classrooms

Children learn vocabulary most effectively when ESL, literacy, and content teachers coordinate their respective vocabulary instruction. By meeting together on a quarterly basis, teachers can preview the next quarter's curriculum topics, discuss the big ideas that they will focus on, and talk about the key vocabulary words and language structures that they will be using in their lessons. They can talk about the vocabulary-building teaching strategies they plan to use. The bilingual teacher, aide, or tutor can identify words that are cognates so that they can use this natural bridge to English vocabulary development. This leads to a discussion about other ways to effectively use the bilingual support staff to support instruction. Also, since the teachers share the same ELL students, they can decide how many words can be taught at a time and figure out how they can support each other's vocabulary lessons.

In this chapter we have shown how teachers can implement oral vocabulary-building strategies to move ELLs' receptive vocabulary toward expressive language. We have discussed teaching strategies for introducing new words and helping students to use their new words in oral and written activities. We have stressed the importance of coordinating vocabulary instruction and practice in ESL, bilingual, and general education classroom settings. In the next chapter, we discuss how implementing comprehensible prior knowledge activities can help ELLs understand classroom lessons and increase reading comprehension.

QUESTIONS FOR REFLECTION AND ACTION

1. Ask the teachers with whom you share your ELL students about the vocabulary words that they are currently focusing on in their classrooms. Then, figure out ways in which each of you can model and use some of each other's words.

2. With your study group, discuss how you can increase the use of classroom space to display flashcards and other sets of functional vocabulary words. Then, brainstorm various ways to encourage your students to use these helpful prompts.

Recommended Readings

Allen, J. (1999). *Words, words, words: Teaching vocabulary in grades 4-12.* Portland, ME: Stenhouse Publishers.

August, D. et al. (2005). The critical role of vocabulary development for English language learners. *Learning Disabilities Research & Practice,* 20 (1), 50–57.

Calderón, M. et al. (2009) Expediting comprehension for English language learners (ExC-ELL). Powerpoint presentation about vocabulary building. Available at margaritacalderon.org/index .php?option=com_docman&task=doc_download&gid=20.

Marzano, R., & Pickering, D. (2005). *Building academic vocabulary: Teacher's manual.* Alexandria, VA: Association for Supervision & Curriculum Development (ASCD) Publications.

CHECKLIST FOR KEY PRACTICE 6

The checklist is written using measurable statements that can be used to evaluate and monitor language education programs and instruction at the district, school, and classroom levels. The district language education committee and school leadership teams can use the checklist as a diagnostic tool to identify the areas that represent the biggest challenges during the restructuring process. Various teams can use the results of the checklist as a starting point to determine the professional development that educators need to know in order to successfully implement the practices. Teacher teams can use the checklist to evaluate their own teaching practices to recognize ways in which they can immediately make instructional improvements.

SCORING DIRECTIONS:
1 = This practice IS implemented.
2 = This practice is in progress or is in place in some classrooms.
3 = This practice is NOT currently in place.

			The Common Classroom Practices for All ELL Educators
			Implementing Meaningful Vocabulary Building Instruction: Teachers pre-teach vocabulary words necessary to understand lessons and passages. New words in context are taught during the lessons/passages, and practice is provided for students to use the words in various contexts after the lessons/passages.
1	2	3	• Teachers explicitly teach new vocabulary and involve the students in definition-getting.
1	2	3	• Teachers plan oral vocabulary-building strategies to move ELLs' receptive vocabulary toward expressive language.
1	2	3	• Teachers structure oral and written activities for students to use new vocabulary.
1	2	3	• Teachers coordinate vocabulary instruction and practice in ESL, bilingual, and general education classrooms.

IMPLICATIONS AND COMMENTS _____

_____

_____

_____

Activating Students' Prior Knowledge

Structure activities that connect ELLs' previous knowledge and cultural experiences to current lessons and build a comprehensible context for learning.

- Plan multiple prior knowledge activities that connect and build upon students' knowledge and experiences to upcoming lessons.
- Use instructional supports (e.g., visuals, demonstrations, and experiential activities) to make prior knowledge activities comprehensible.
- Ask open-ended questions so all students can share prior knowledge and experiences.
- Structure pre-reading activities that build vocabulary and increase comprehension before all reading assignments.

THE BIG IDEAS

- English language learners (ELLs) need multiple prior knowledge activities to be ready to learn complex information and comprehend unfamiliar text.

- Prior knowledge activities using sensory, graphic, and interactive instructional supports ensure that the ELLs experience a comprehensible introduction to the complex concepts and language that they will encounter in upcoming lessons and readings.

Before starting a lesson or reading an expository or narrative text, teachers routinely set the context by talking about the topic and asking their students questions that will connect their knowledge and experiences to the lesson/reading passage. What is different for ELLs is that a quick discussion that reminds the children of previously learned information about the topic is not enough background-building information. ELLs need multiple prior knowledge activities to be prepared to tackle new text. They are just beginning to have enough knowledge of the English language to use their linguistic and literacy skills to comprehend text. Their school and cultural experiences may be very different from the experiences of their English-speaking peers and they usually do not have the requisite vocabulary about the subject that their English-speaking classmates already know. Teachers can address these challenges by implementing prior knowledge activities that explicitly link the students' background and experiences to classroom concepts. Effective prior knowledge strategies can also build upon the students' existing knowledge and develop their vocabulary skills.

Key Practice 6 shows teachers how to structure classroom activities that activate students' prior knowledge and create shared experiences to build a meaningful context for learning for all students. We show how teachers can plan multiple prior knowledge activities that connect ELL students' diverse knowledge and cultural experiences with upcoming lessons and how they can use instructional supports (e.g., visuals, demonstrations, and experiential activities) while implementing prior knowledge activities. We discuss why asking open-ended questions is important for ELLs and why it is so important for teachers to implement pre-reading activities before all reading assignments.

Planning Multiple Prior Knowledge Activities

Teachers of ELLs need to plan multiple prior knowledge activities that connect students' knowledge and cultural experiences with upcoming lessons. Prior knowledge activities, such as demonstrations, KWLs, anticipation guides, prediction activities, vocabulary-building activities, videos, experiments, and other experiential activities, are a great way to introduce a unit or lesson. For example, field trips, traditionally saved until the end of a unit, can be planned for the beginning of the unit's lessons in order to set the context and connect upcoming lessons with real world experiences. Bilingual assistants can also help access the ELLs' prior knowledge by previewing a story or content passage in the primary language and connecting what the students already know about the subject to the lesson.

Before a second grade science unit on magnetism, for example, a teacher might typically implement a brief KWL about the new lesson by asking the students to tell what they already know about magnets and what they want to learn about magnets. ELLs (and other children) who do not know what the word *magnet* means will have trouble being engaged in this prior knowledge activity. However, a KWL is an excellent prior knowledge strategy, especially when it is used after a cooperative learning activity in which the students are introduced to the topic. A teacher can plan an activity which introduces the following big idea: *Magnetism is a force that can be used for many things*. He/she plans to introduce the following vocabulary words during the cooperative activity: *magnets, magnetism, attract, repel, poles*. The children are asked to manipulate various types of magnets and see if classroom objects (that the teacher provides each group) are attracted, repelled, or experience no effect when the magnets are placed near the objects. The teacher prepares questions for the students to ensure that the group talks and shares information as they work: What happens to magnets when you change the direction of the ends (poles)? Which items are attracted to a magnet? Why do magnets attract some things but not others? Can you think of some good uses of magnets? Next, the students might watch a video that answers these questions using real life examples. In this way, the teacher is building upon the students' prior knowledge about magnets. Next, the teacher can implement a KWL

REFLECTIONS FROM THE FIELD

Planning Field Trips as Prior Knowledge Activities

Cristina Sanchez Lopez, Education Specialist

I was doing a workshop for elementary ESL and general education teachers about sheltered instruction. I was talking about the importance of building background knowledge and I suggested that they engage in experiential activities and field trips in the early stages of a unit rather than waiting until the end. A kindergarten teacher really identified with this information and wanted to share her story about a field trip to a farm. She said that she thought she had set the context for the farm unit by previewing the vocabulary, then reading a story, and having the children play with a toy farm set. The class went to the farm at the end of the unit as a culminating experience. She remembered walking around the farmyard with the children asking them what they saw, all along reinforcing the things they had done in the classroom prior to the trip. One ELL child was a little

disappointed because he had not found a silo like the one he had played with in the classroom. He was looking all around, clearly showing that he was looking at eye level. He had no experience with farms, much less a silo. So the teacher pointed up at the silo. The boy said, *"That's* the silo?" He was very surprised—he couldn't believe how enormous the structure really was. The teacher realized that he had lived in an urban area in his home country and must have never been to the countryside. She reflected on the fact that using the toy farm set was a good idea, but if they had taken the field trip earlier in the unit, the information about cutting the corn and storing the silage would have made more sense to him. She said that the following year they still looked at pictures of farms and played with the farm toys. However, they took the children to the farm much earlier in the unit of study.

activity in which the students talk about what they know about magnets, trying out the vocabulary words and telling what they learned in the activity and the video. As the students share their knowledge, the teacher writes useful vocabulary words and phrases on the board. At this point all of the children are ready to express what else they want to learn about magnets. Note that these activities are implemented *before* the learners are asked to read and write about magnetism. Even though increasing the number of prior knowledge experiences takes additional time, the time spent will help all the children (and most certainly the ELLs) be more prepared to comprehend the upcoming lessons, read the text with increased comprehension and fluency; and provide the information, academic vocabulary, and language skills that the students will need to talk and write about magnets.

Using Instructional Supports to Activate Prior Knowledge

Prior knowledge activities using visuals, demonstrations, and experiential activities are effective for all learners and are essential for ELLs with English language proficiency (ELP) levels 1–3. Prior knowledge activities using sensory, graphic, and interactive instructional supports give the ELLs a comprehensible introduction to the concepts and language that they will encounter in the upcoming lessons and readings. Prior knowledge activities are especially important when the following tasks require students to read independently, even when teachers differentiate reading passages according to the ELP levels of the students. Without pre-reading activities, ELLs and other struggling readers are likely to have difficulty understanding the text, especially if the vocabulary is unfamiliar. Richard-Amato and Snow (2005) point out that young readers have a tendency to give up in this situation. Pre-reading strategies get students ready for the new content both affectively as well as cognitively. In other words, by participating in prior knowledge activities, the ELLs believe that they can understand what they will be reading and they are more willing to give it a go.

Asking Open-Ended Questions So All Students Can Share Prior Knowledge and Experiences

Comprehensible classroom discussions should always be a part of prior knowledge activities. As teachers plan an introductory activity, they include opportunities for interaction between teacher and students and also interaction among the students. Teachers can ask questions that encourage English-proficient and ELL students to share their knowledge and experiences. As the students respond and talk about what they already know, teachers can explicitly link students' learning the big ideas of previous lessons to the new lesson. Teachers can also state some big ideas that summarize the students' information and ask questions that lead, step-by-step, to the new topic. Teachers can vary the length and difficulty of the questions, using speech appropriate for ELLs at different ELP levels. The teacher can also encourage the students to ask questions of each other.

Rather than asking narrow questions that require short, correct answers, teachers can ask clear open-ended questions that ask students to share their experiences and knowledge. They can start by asking questions that are personal and relevant, e.g., "How do you display your school work at home? (Hint: magnets on the refrigerator?) "Has anyone ever seen magnets at work?" Using simple structures and paraphrasing often, teachers can model vocabulary, language structures, and sentence patterns that match the academic language about the topic (e.g., "magnetic poles attracting and repelling" and "having no effect"). The teacher should encourage the students to try to use the same structures and phrases in their responses. When students give incorrect answers, the teacher can follow up with statements and questions that will improve the student's understanding and provide additional language prompts. When students give correct answers, the teacher can follow up by repeating what the students have stated, celebrating the students' use of academic language. Asking students to explain their thinking, give opinions, and share their knowledge in large-group discussions helps the ELLs understand the upcoming lessons since the English-proficient students often mix academic language with social language that the ELLs comprehend with ease.

Structuring Pre-Reading Activities to Build Vocabulary and Increase Comprehension

Teachers intuitively know that students who come to the text already knowing something about the content will find reading about the topic much easier (Gibbons, 2002). Even so, when snow days, assemblies, absences, and special events cause teachers to feel that they are "behind schedule," they may see the need to immediately engage the students in the reading passages without taking the time to implement multiple pre-reading activities. This shortcut may work with strong, independent readers; however, struggling readers and ELL students will not comprehend the texts that teachers assign when they are not familiar with the topic and when the key concepts are embedded in vocabulary that they do not understand.

Teachers need to do more than just *access* the ELL students' prior knowledge. They must also *build* upon that knowledge. Teachers can teach the vocabulary words that are absolutely necessary for understanding the passage and must provide instruction that scaffolds the information or misinformation that the students already know to the big ideas and main concepts that they will encounter in the passage. Activating and *building* prior knowledge is arguably the best strategy that teachers can use to improve their students' comprehension of their day-to-day classroom reading passages. This important first step helps learners be prepared to understand the big ideas and concepts of classroom readings that they will eventually be responsible to know on standardized tests.

In this chapter, we have discussed why ELLs need multiple prior knowledge activities to be ready to learn complex information and comprehend unfamiliar text. We have also suggested strategies and the use of instructional supports (e.g., visuals, demonstrations, and experiential activities) to ensure that ELLs experience a comprehensible introduction to the concepts and language that they will encounter in upcoming lessons and readings. In the next chapter, we discuss the importance of student interaction and how meaningful interactive activities can improve academic language development and help students share ways of thinking and problem solving.

QUESTIONS FOR REFLECTION AND ACTION

1. With your study group, share some prior knowledge strategies that you have found to be effective with your students.
2. How can sensory, graphic, and interactive supports be added to your prior knowledge strategies to enhance comprehension for ELLs with varying proficiency levels?

Recommended Readings

González, N., & Moll, L. (2002). Cruzando el puente: Building bridges to funds of knowledge. *Educational Policy,* 16 (4), 623–641.

Helman, L. (Ed). (2009). Literacy development with English learners: Research-based instruction in grades K-6. New York: Guilford Press.

Marzano, R. (2004). *Building background knowledge for academic achievement: Research on what works in schools.* Alexandria, VA: Association for Supervision & Curriculum Development (ASCD) Publications.

CHECKLIST FOR KEY PRACTICE 7

The checklist is written using measurable statements that can be used to evaluate and monitor language education programs and instruction at the district, school, and classroom levels. The district language education committee and school leadership teams can use the checklist as a diagnostic tool to identify the areas that represent the biggest challenges during the restructuring process. Various teams can use the results of the checklist as a starting point to determine the professional development that educators need to know in order to successfully implement the practices. Teacher teams can use the checklist to evaluate their own teaching practices to recognize ways in which they can immediately make instructional improvements.

SCORING DIRECTIONS:
1 = This practice IS implemented.
2 = This practice is in progress or is in place in some classrooms.
3 = This practice is NOT currently in place.

			The Common Classroom Practices for All ELL Educators
			Activating Students' Prior Knowledge: Teachers structure activities that connect ELLs' previous knowledge and cultural experiences to current lessons and build a comprehensible context for learning.
1	2	3	• Teachers plan multiple prior knowledge activities that connect students' knowledge and cultural experiences with upcoming lessons.
1	2	3	• Teachers use instructional supports (e.g., visuals, demonstrations, and experiential activities) while implementing prior knowledge activities.
1	2	3	• Teachers ask open-ended questions to encourage English-proficient and ELL students to share their knowledge and experiences.
1	2	3	• Teachers structure pre-reading activities that build vocabulary and increase comprehension before all reading assignments.

IMPLICATIONS AND COMMENTS _____

_____
_____
_____

KEY PRACTICE 8

Structuring Student Interaction

Provide opportunities for academic development and language practice by implementing activities that require students to talk with each other about what they are learning.

- Organize program configurations and classroom schedules that promote meaningful interactions among ELLs and their English-speaking peers.
- Promote learning-centered classroom talk that engages all students and requires them to share ways of thinking and problem solving.

- Implement learning tasks that ask students to use target vocabulary to talk about newly learned information.
- Structure small group instructional tasks that require students to work interdependently.

THE BIG IDEAS

- English language learners' (ELLs) language learning and academic development thrive when they have meaningful opportunities to interact with proficient English-speaking peers.

- ELLs are more likely to speak up and participate in classroom activities when they are asked to work with a partner or in small groups.

Oral language activities that require student interaction have long been a hallmark of second language learning. ELLs need meaningful opportunities to interact with more proficient English-speaking peers to practice speaking their new language. More recently, researchers have found that developing ELLs' oral English language development is also a critical component of effective English reading instruction. In 2006, a major finding of the National Literacy Panel's research report on language-minority children's literacy development states that literacy programs that include oral language development aligned with high-quality literacy instruction are the most successful (August & Shanahan, 2006). Teachers can maximize oral language opportunities for ELLs by asking them to interact with a partner or work with their peers in small groups.

Language practice, however, is only one benefit of student interaction. Vygotsky (1978) suggests that children learn by progressing from their actual cognitive developmental level toward their potential developmental level. Between these two levels is the "zone of proximal development (ZPD)." Vygotsky suggests that children will pass through the ZPD more effectively under adult guidance and collaborative interaction with more capable peers. Teachers intuitively understand this notion. For example, on the first day that an ELL enters an English-speaking classroom, one of the first steps a teacher takes is to pair the new student with a bilingual peer so that the new ELL has a mentor who can help the new student get around and negotiate the challenges of learning in a new school and a new culture. The bilingual peer becomes a friend, a problem solver, a cultural informant, and a coach.

Key Practice 8 demonstrates how teachers working in ESL, literacy, content, bilingual, and mainstream classrooms can structure student interaction in ways that enhance academic learning and language and literacy development for all students, particularly ELLs. We discuss how educators can organize program configurations and classroom schedules that foster the integration of ELLs into the school community and enable ELLs to have meaningful interactions with their English-speaking peers. We also discuss ways that teachers can implement structured activities in which all students can share ways of thinking and problem solving, use target vocabulary to talk about newly learned information, and work interdependently in engaging learning-centered tasks.

Organizing Program Configurations and Classroom Schedules That Promote Integration

Language education committees in school districts with large numbers of ELL students from a single language group may design and implement specific elementary classroom configurations (such as bilingual self-contained models) in order to offer comprehensive language education programs. These program planners must always make sure that any program configuration includes ways for ELLs to have meaningful learning opportunities with their English-speaking peers. For example, general education and language education teachers can integrate the ELLs and their grade-level English-speaking peers for music, art, and physical education instruction. In addition, they can plan and implement integrated social and academic activities. However, the ELLs should not simply attend these activities alongside their English-speaking peers. It is very important that language education and general education teachers at the same grade levels collaborate regularly to plan and implement ways that the ELLs from the bilingual or ESL classroom are often engaged in integrated learning activities with mainstream students.

Language education and general education teachers who have the responsibility to teach the same group of ELLs can also ensure that the ELLs are actively engaged in learning in their respective classrooms by coordinating classroom schedules. Primary and intermediate teacher teams can establish specific time periods for literacy blocks and content area instruction. By doing so, they can make sure that the ELLs do not miss parts of daily instruction in a particular subject area because of scheduling problems. When the ELLs move from one classroom to another, knowing the context and understanding what the students are working on will help them feel comfortable to join in and participate.

Promoting Learning-Centered Classroom Talk That Engages All Students

Children are amazing communicators—when talking with their classmates, they use gestures, facial expressions, phrasing, and social language in ways that help information become meaningful for each other. These interactions increase opportunities for ELLs to be actively engaged in classroom conversations. When teachers implement interactive learning activities, students can talk about their experiences, give each other examples, and share ways of thinking and problem solving.

Teachers who have culturally diverse students in their classrooms can create opportunities to structure learning activities in ways for the students to share their life experiences, cultural norms, and world views. For example, teachers can ask questions to their students in large-group settings using an interactive questioning technique called *think-pair-share*. This strategy provides more time for ELLs to process the question and think about the language needed to convey the answer. Therefore, the technique helps ELLs participate since they do not have to quickly raise their hands to respond. In a think-pair-share, the teacher starts by asking a thought-provoking question. The teacher gives students a brief time to *think* on their own. Then, the students are asked to share their thoughts with a partner (*pair*). According to Robertson (2006), this pairing step gives the students the opportunity to 'check out' their answer with another student or hear another possible answer. Finally, the teacher asks students to *share* their thoughts with the whole group.

Focusing Classroom Talk around Target Vocabulary and Newly Learned Information

Teachers working in any kind of classroom can implement interactive learning tasks that specifically use target vocabulary to talk about newly learned information. Cooperative learning activities like Inside/Outside Circle (Kagan 1994) are great ways to involve the whole class in an interactive activity. In an inside/outside circle structure, the teacher arranges his/ her students in two concentric circles in which the students face each other in pairs. Students in the inside circle face out; students in the outside

REFLECTIONS FROM THE FIELD

Role Playing to Encourage Student Interaction

Sue Wagner

I was teaching sheltered instruction to general education teachers in a school district. In addition to the weekly training sessions, the teachers had the option to invite me into their classrooms to see how they were implementing sheltered activities. Michelle invited me to come to her second grade classroom to see how she was increasing student interaction during vocabulary-building activities. As I entered the classroom, I heard her say, "OK, it's time for a paradigm shift." I paused—her use of such a big conceptual phrase made me nervous—did Michelle hear me say that teachers should model language a *little* above the students' competencies, not *way* above? Four children were in a circle in front of the classroom. Each student was standing in a pair of brightly painted adult empty shoes which had been nailed to pieces of plywood. The name of a character was attached to each board. The children were laughing as they got

out of one pair of shoes and switched into a different pair. "Time for a paradigm shift," the students repeated. Michelle was using a concrete, fun way to engage her students to interact with one another about a story they had read. On one side of the white board, Michelle had written "*Paradigm shift is a fancy expression that means to look at conflicts or events from another person's viewpoint. Today we are going to step into the shoes of each of the characters.*" On the other side of the board, she had written vocabulary prompts for the students to use as they slipped into the shoes (clever, courageous, truth, lies, discovered, disappointed, and frustrated). As the students moved into different shoes, they took the role of a different character, ready to express a different perspective about the events of the story. All of the students were actively engaged in the activity.

circle face in. Students use flashcards, study guides, or respond to teacher questions as they rotate to a new partner. This interactive strategy can be used to help students review vocabulary words, take a survey, check for understanding, review information for a test, retell new information, and/or express ideas and opinions. For example, in order to ask students to retell newly learned information to a classmate, the teacher can develop a short list of study questions and give a copy of the questions to every student. The activity starts when the teacher asks the inside circle students to ask their partners the first question. The outside partners respond to the question and ask the inside students another question. After a couple of minutes, the teacher asks the inside circle to move clockwise and stop two persons ahead. The teacher then asks the outside person in the newly formed pairs to share the answers in their previous pairing before asking and answering the next question.

In our work in schools, we have seen many creative ways that teachers have successfully implemented oral interactive tasks to retell and discuss newly learned information and, at the same time, practice using vocabulary words. We share an example of one creative lesson in the accompanying *Reflections From the Field*.

Structuring Small Group Instructional Tasks

Teachers can also organize small-group instructional tasks that require students to work together interdependently. Working with a partner or in groups of three to four students helps ELLs feel comfortable to take the risk to speak up and participate rather than observe from the sidelines. English-proficient students model age-appropriate language, model how to ask questions, and demonstrate appropriate social classroom behaviors. Kagan (1994) suggests that teachers plan group structures according to the language and content objective of the learning activities and recommends that teachers include social as well as academic purposes for small-group activities.

A jigsaw cooperative learning strategy (first developed in the early 1970s by Aronson) is a great way to get intermediate and secondary students (including ELLs with ELP levels 3.5 to 5) to work interdependently since the students must share different information that they have just been assigned to read. The strategy is most effective with nonfiction passages with nonsequential text. A jigsaw activity can help students develop oral language skills, practice retelling newly learned information, and learn how to present a summary of a reading passage. The social function can be to encourage students to see each other as resources and to equalize the status of all group members.

When implementing a jigsaw activity, the teacher places students in cooperative base groups of four students. Students in each base group are asked to split up for a while and go to an assigned reading group numbered 1, 2, 3, and 4. The teacher assigns four specific reading selections to each group, matching the length and difficulty of the passages to the literacy skills and language proficiencies of the students. All the "ones" from each base group move to one table or area, as do the "twos", "threes", and "fours." After they have moved, the teacher assigns the "ones" to read a particular passage. The twos, threes, and fours are responsible for different, but related passages. Each of the four passages should be short enough for students to read silently (or in pairs) in five to ten minutes. The teacher can walk around to provide individual assistance while the students read their passages. After the groups have finished reading, the teacher asks the groups to summarize their passage by writing down big ideas, key facts, and examples in order to individually present the information back in their base groups. After a predetermined length of time, the teacher sends the students back to their base groups where each of the four students presents his/her information. The jigsaw parts become a completed puzzle after the students share their summaries and complete a shared task using all of the information.

Besides working with English-proficient students, ELLs can benefit from small-group interaction with bilingual English-proficient peers who share their home language. General education and content teachers can occasionally group or pair ELLs with their primary language peers to reinforce content and vocabulary that the students are learning in English. The teacher can ask the bilingual aide to facilitate and supervise the discussion in the students' first language. In this way, the bilingual aide can model academic language, and ELL students with all levels of English language proficiency can discuss new concepts, tutor one another, work out math problems, and build academic language without any language barriers.

In this chapter, we have discussed how all teachers can enhance language learning and academic development when they implement meaningful opportunities for ELLs to interact with proficient English-speaking peers as well as have structured time to talk about classroom topics in their primary language with bilingual adults facilitating the discussions. We have shown ways in which teachers can structure classroom talk that engages learners and encourages them to share ways of thinking and problem solving. In the next three chapters, we show how the four common classroom key practices (using big ideas to plan instruction and assess learning, implementing meaningful vocabulary-building instruction, activating students' prior knowledge, and structuring student interaction) can be effectively woven into instruction in ESL, literacy, and content classrooms.

QUESTIONS FOR REFLECTION AND ACTION

1. Use a think/pair/share strategy to answer the following questions: How will you restructure a large group learning activity to improve student interaction? How can you enhance student interaction in small groups?

2. After reading the discussions about the four common classroom practices, what teaching strategies will you use during the next quarter (see caslonpublishing.com/pd-resources/twelve-key-practices)?

Recommended Readings

Calderon, M., & Slavin, R., (Eds.). (2005). *Building community through cooperative learning: A special issue of theory into practice*. New York: Routledge.

Kagan, S., & Kagan, M. (2010). Kagan cooperative learning. San Clemente, CA: Kagan Publishing. Available at http://www.kaganonline.com/catalog/cooperative_learning.php.

Kendall, J., & Khuon, O. (2005). *Making sense: Small-group comprehension lessons for English language learners*. Portland, ME: Stenhouse Publishers.

McGroarty, M., & Calderón, M. (2005). Cooperative learning for second language learners: Models, applications and challenges. In P. A. Richard-Amato and M. A. Snow (Eds.), *Academic success for English language learners. Strategies for K-12 mainstream teachers* (pp. 174–194). White Plains, NY: Pearson Education, Inc.

The checklist is written using measurable statements that can be used to evaluate and monitor language education programs and instruction at the district, school, and classroom levels. The district language education committee and school leadership teams can use the checklist as a diagnostic tool to identify the areas that represent the biggest challenges during the restructuring process. Various teams can use the results of the checklist as a starting point to determine the professional development that educators need to know in order to successfully implement the practices. Teacher teams can use the checklist to evaluate their own teaching practices to recognize ways in which they can immediately make instructional improvements.

SCORING DIRECTIONS:
1 = This practice IS implemented.
2 = This practice is in progress or is in place in some classrooms.
3 = This practice is NOT currently in place.

			The Common Classroom Practices for All ELL Educators
			Structuring Student Interaction: Opportunities for academic development and language practice are provided by implementing activities that require students to talk with each other about what they are learning.
1	2	3	• Program configurations and classroom schedules are organized in ways that promote meaningful interactions among ELLs and their English-speaking peers.
1	2	3	• Teachers promote learning-centered classroom talk that engages all students and requires them to share ways of thinking and problem solving.
1	2	3	• Teachers implement interactive learning tasks that ask students to use target vocabulary to talk about newly learned information.
1	2	3	• Teachers plan small-group instructional tasks that require students to work interdependently.

IMPLICATIONS AND COMMENTS _____

_____

_____

_____

PART III

Core Instructional Practices of Every Program for English Language Learners

KEY PRACTICE 9   Implementing English as a Second Language Instruction

Plan and implement daily content-based ESL instruction in the four language domains (listening, speaking, reading, and writing), focusing on the academic language needed to understand and express essential grade-level concepts.

KEY PRACTICE 10   Implementing Meaning-Based Literacy Instruction

Whenever possible, begin literacy instruction in the primary language; when literacy is taught in English, plan and implement meaning-based literacy instruction that builds on students' oral language and uses comprehensible text at appropriate English language proficiency levels.

KEY PRACTICE 11   Implementing Comprehensible Academic Content Instruction

Model and teach academic content using language just above ELLs' current English language proficiency levels, making new information comprehensible using appropriate instructional supports.

Part III shows how language education and mainstream teachers can work and learn together to implement comprehensible ESL, literacy, and academic content instruction in English-medium classrooms. We provide examples of how the common classroom Key Practices (practices 5–8) are planned and implemented in content-based ESL, meaning-based literacy, and sheltered academic instruction (practices 9–11). Comprehensible, differentiated instruction using shared common classroom practices with sensory, graphic, and interactive supports means that instruction in these three subject areas can be coordinated and comprehensible to ELLs at different ELP levels. We recommend that teachers read all three chapters, not just the chapter that most closely resembles their teaching responsibilities. ESL teachers, elementary general education teachers, and secondary content teachers will all find important information, helpful strategies, and useful templates. In addition, we continue to share specific examples of how primary language support can facilitate and reinforce learning in content areas.

Implementing English as a Second Language Instruction

Plan and implement daily content-based ESL instruction in the four language domains (listening, speaking, reading, and writing), focusing on the academic language needed to understand and express essential grade-level concepts.

- Coordinate academic content and language instruction with core content and language development standards.

- Connect receptive language skills and the oral language of beginning level ELLs to academic English language instruction.

- Use a content-based ESL approach for intermediate and advanced level ELLs.

- Implement common classroom practices with meaningful language learning activities for ELLs at all ELP levels by using sensory, graphic, and interactive supports.

THE BIG IDEAS

- Instruction for English language learners (ELLs) is most effective when English as a second language (ESL), bilingual, and mainstream teachers collaborate to plan units and lessons using standards-based big ideas as the conceptual focus for unit and theme development.

- Effective ESL instruction is planned and implemented so that vocabulary and language skills learned in the ESL classroom support literacy and content instruction in general education classrooms.

Some well-intentioned administrators and teachers assume that if the mainstream and literacy teachers receive substantial training in sheltered instruction methods, the need for specific, daily ESL instruction is not necessary. This assumption needs revising. Mainstream teachers who use sheltered instruction and differentiation strategies do improve instruction for the ELLs in their classrooms. They have learned to develop the academic English that ELLs need to learn in their content area classes (e.g., the language of math, the language of science, the language of social studies, the language of language arts). However, mainstream teachers cannot be held responsible for teaching all of the complex language skills that ELLs need to successfully learn the challenging concepts in their classrooms. Daily ESL instruction that connects with concepts and skills that the ELLs will encounter in their general education and content classrooms is necessary for ELLs at all grade levels. Furthermore, daily ESL instruction will increase the time and depth of learning engagement that the ELLs will experience in general education classrooms. Even at the kindergarten level, a specific time should be set aside for ESL instruction—usually for only 20 minutes to a half hour. Primary and intermediate ELLs will need daily English language instruction, usually between 35 and 45 minutes a day depending on their English language proficiency (ELP) level. At the secondary level, the ELL students have limited time to learn English before they are expected to successfully earn credits in academically and linguistically challenging classrooms. Therefore, we recommend two periods of ESL instruction for secondary ELLs.

Key Practice 9 shows how ESL teachers can implement the core ESL instructional component, which includes instruction in the four language domains (listening, speaking, reading, and writing) with an explicit focus on the academic language needed to understand and express key grade-level concepts. We describe how ESL teachers can use core content and language development standards to coordinate academic content and language instruction. They can provide comprehensible English language instruction to ELLs with beginning ELP levels that focuses on building receptive language skills and oral language development, and they can use a content-based ESL approach for intermediate and advanced ELLs. ESL teachers can also plan and implement ESL lessons with meaningful language learning activities for ELLs at all ELP levels by using the four common classroom practices and sensory, graphic, and interactive supports.

Coordinating Language and Content Instruction with Language and Content Standards

Core state standards define what all students should know and be able to do as a result of their elementary and secondary schooling. The English Language Development (ELD) standards reflect the social and academic language expectations of ELLs and focus on the academic vocabulary and language skills that ELLs need to process or produce (e.g., describe, explain, evaluate, predict) in order to learn and demonstrate what they know in language arts, social studies, science, and math lessons. Together, the standards provide the anchor for planning and implementing instruction in language education and mainstream classrooms. When teachers work in teams to use standards as starting points of the units and lessons, ESL instruction can be coordinated with academic content units.

ESL teachers cannot possibly develop ESL lessons that coordinate with all the topics in the subject areas at multiple grade levels. However, standards-based instructional planning provides a process to develop ESL units that will teach language skills and vocabulary that are used across many topics and themes. Standards do not change from one grade level to the next. What does gradually increase at higher grades is the complexity of knowledge, language skills, tasks, and products that students are expected to know and produce.

At the elementary and middle school levels, standards-based ESL instruction is most easily implemented in science, social studies, and language arts since learning in these areas does not usually require incremental gradients that require a specific sequence. High school ESL teachers often use language arts standards since ESL courses are often designated as language arts courses in order to qualify for English language arts credit.

At the elementary and middle school levels, ESL instruction can best support learning in mainstream classrooms when curriculum planning begins with collaboration among the ESL teacher and the mainstream teachers who share the responsibility for teaching the same ELLs. In schools where this collaboration is not regularly occurring, a building administrator and the ESL teacher can convene an initial planning meeting for ESL, science, social studies, and language arts teachers. The ESL teacher can explain (1) how his/her goal is to teach the language that the ELLs need to access the concepts in the content areas and (2) that the first step in developing ESL unit plans that coordinate and support content concepts is to identify the standards, big ideas, and/or themes addressed during each calendar quarter in science, social studies, and language arts. The group plans future meeting times for each grade-level team to complete this task.

Attending the grade-level meetings requires a lot of work for the ESL teacher, who may teach ESL to three or, unfortunately, perhaps more grade levels. For example, a middle school ESL teacher would have to attend the sixth, seventh, and eighth grade science, social studies, and language arts planning meetings. During the grade-level meetings, the teachers can use the core state standards, the district's curriculum guidelines, and their lesson plan books to share information. The ESL teacher takes notes about the order of units, topics, big ideas and, the vocabulary that the ELLs will be learning in the mainstream classrooms, using the *English as a Second Language and General Teachers' Curriculum Coordination Template* following this chapter.

After the grade-level teams (which include the ESL teacher) establish the order and time frame of the units in the mainstream classrooms, ESL teachers can identify topics and materials for ESL units that will provide vocabulary development and language skills needed to support the designated units and/or themes. For example, the seventh grade science teacher may spend several weeks on scientific inquiry. The ESL teacher has a picture book about archeology and knows of a trade book that has great visuals that show how archeologists discovered the Iceman (who was buried for 5,000 years in a glacier) and used scientific methods to learn more about the discovery. The ESL teacher shares this idea with the science teacher; they decide that this would make a great ESL unit in which the sixth and seventh grade ELLs can learn the verbs of scientific investigation and learn some language structures about how archeologists use scientific methods. In the best case scenario, summer writing teams develop ESL unit planning templates and figure out when the unit can be taught in order to precede the content units. The teachers can work together to develop long-range curricular planning calendars.

While developing their curriculum units focusing on the same two to three standards, collaborating ESL and mainstream teachers do not teach the same information, or use the same materials, or write daily lesson plans together. However, they do coordinate their efforts and share information regularly. The duration of content units in the mainstream classroom will vary, but most will take three weeks or more to provide several daily lessons for students to learn the big ideas and concepts, develop vocabulary, read various passages, and apply their new knowledge in meaningful ways. The ESL units generally will be shorter in duration, perhaps lasting a week or two rather than several weeks. In the units, ESL teachers can plan language instruction that helps the ELLs understand the big ideas and teaches the academic language needed to talk and write about the main concepts. These teacher-made units and lessons can be implemented using a wide range of trade books, supplementary materials, pictures, videos, websites, and other resources.

Building Receptive Language Skills and Oral Language of Beginning Level English Language Learners

When children learn to speak their *first* language, they move through stages—from babbling to one-word utterances, two-word phrases, full sentences, and eventually, extended conversations with complex grammatical and syntactic patterns. Students learning their *second* language also move through similar stages. Krashen and Terrell (1983) characterize the process of second language acquisition by categorizing oral (listening and speaking) language proficiency into four stages. The stages begin with the pre-production stage. The next three stages (early speech production, speech emergence, and intermediate fluency stage) describe a continuum of listening and speaking abilities that become more grammatically and linguistically complex over time.

The pre-production stage is characterized by a "silent period," which is a time when the learners observe, listen, and begin to understand the new language. During the silent period, second language learners are learning receptive language—in other words, they can understand more of the new language than they can speak. ELLs at early stages of second language acquisition need instruction that focuses on building receptive language skills and developing oral language. Some ELL children remain in the silent period for several months; others pass through this stage more quickly and are anxious to communicate and participate in classroom activities. Teachers help children move out of the silent period by encouraging language practice in low-anxiety, caring learning environments, especially in small group settings. Meaning is central: language learners understand, remember, and use language that is comprehensible (Krashen, 1994).

Krashen and Terrell (1992) suggest the "natural approach" as an effective ESL method for ELLs in the early stages of English language development. The principles behind the natural approach are: (1) comprehension precedes speech production; (2) speech production emerges in stages; (3) the instructional focus is on meaning rather than correct form; and (4) the student's anxiety level must be low in order for learning to take place. In ESL classrooms where the teachers implement the natural approach, fluency of ELLs' utterances is more important than grammatical accuracy. The focus is on acquiring oral language through student and teacher interaction in authentic and meaningful learning experiences. Teachers implement the natural approach by using language that makes information comprehensible through modeling, visuals, and hands-on experiences. Then, they continue to add new learning activities to that base.

James Asher (1982) suggests using commands as the first phase of ESL instruction in an approach he developed called Total Physical Response (TPR). The TPR method is an effective way to encourage ELP level 1 ELLs to begin participating and talking. When implementing a TPR lesson, the teacher gives a command, demonstrates the command, and then students respond physically to the command. Because students are actively involved and not expected to repeat the command, anxiety is low, and student focus is on comprehension rather than production. In this way, the second language learners are demonstrating that they understand the commands before they can speak English. Imperatives, such as *"Open your desk," "Bring me the book,"* or *"Pass your paper to the right,"* make language learning comprehensible and fun.

Krashen, Terrell, and Asher's contributions to language acquisition theory remain a hallmark of ESL instruction. What may have changed, however, is the dedicated focus on teaching English language development within the context of academic subject-matter learning (Echevarria et al., 2004; Gottlieb et al., 2007a). As the ELLs' oral proficiency emerges, ESL teachers can ask them to write what they say and read what they write—as long as the ELLs can understand what they are writing and reading. ESL teachers can engage the ELLs in meaningful classroom tasks and seamlessly move toward a content-based ESL approach to more closely align and coordinate the ESL lessons with the content lessons that the ELLs are studying (or will be studying) in their English-speaking mainstream classrooms.

Gordon (2007) explains that once the emergent ELLs begin to understand basic classroom language, ESL teachers can continue to use pictures, visuals, and modeling to connect commands to classroom content topics and academic concepts. In a TPR lesson, ESL teachers can introduce five to seven new vocabulary words or phrases. Gordon describes six steps for a typical TPR lesson.

1. The ELLs watch a demonstration as they hear the teacher say a command using key words (*Plant the **seeds** in the dirt. **Pour** the water into the **dirt**. Put the **container** in the **sunshine**.*).

2. Students listen again and watch as the teacher performs the action again.

3. The teacher gives a command and models the action again, this time having students perform the actions simultaneously.

4. The teacher gives a command to the group without modeling the action and then to individuals without modeling the action.

5. The teacher models variations and combinations and then asks the students to perform the same variations and combinations.

6. Finally, if some students are ready, they can give commands to classmates.

ESL teachers can help move ELLs into expressive language by modeling useful, natural language in context-rich settings. As their oral language develops, ELLs will make grammatical errors, over-generalize, and mispronounce words by using sounds familiar to them from their first language. Richard-Amato (2003) emphasizes that in order to build oral English language fluency for ELLs in the early stages of learning, teachers need to have classroom environments that support risk-taking. She suggests that teachers avoid direct grammatical correction but make corrections in context when possible. Through meaningful modeling, comprehensible instruction, and task-oriented interaction with English-speaking peers and adults, the ELLs will begin to make their own corrections and creatively construct and improve their speech production.

Using a Content-Based English as a Second Language Approach with Intermediate and Advanced Level English Language Learners

In content-based ESL instruction, ESL teachers use the big ideas of a particular content topic and the requisite terminology as the focus of English language instruction. The goal is the development of academic English language aligned with WIDA, TESOL, or other state English language development standards. Teachers often ask us to clarify the difference between content-based ESL instruction and sheltered instruction. The answer is that there is little difference in the implementation of both approaches.

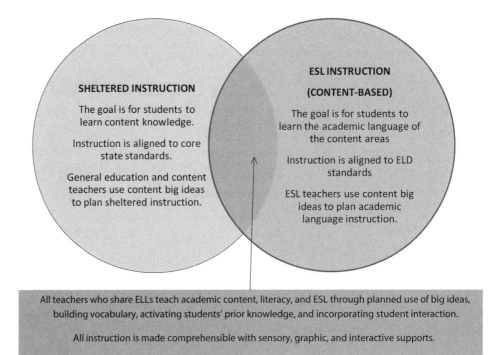

FIGURE 10.1   Comparing Sheltered Instruction and English as a Second Language Instruction

In fact, the origin of sheltered instruction is based on the principles and practices of content-based ESL instruction. The difference is that in ESL, language development is the goal. In contrast, in sheltered instruction, learning content knowledge is the goal. These distinctions are shown in Figure 10.1. In other words, ESL teachers focus on developing academic language skills using content topics as the vehicle. Content teachers teach knowledge about subject-area topics using comprehensible language as the vehicle.

ESL teachers learn content-based ESL methods during courses required for ESL certification. The Specially Designed Academic Instruction in English (SDAIE) approach (Sobul, 1995) is often used in the western part of the U.S. The SDAIE methodology was first used in California school systems to teach academic content to ELLs with intermediate or higher ELP levels. The widely used Sheltered Instruction Observation Protocol (SIOP) includes 30 steps that teachers can learn in order to teach academic content to second language learners. The SIOP model is closely aligned with the SDAIE methodology. More recently, the WIDA Consortium created a training course entitled the Content and Language Integration as a Means of Bridging Success (CLIMBS). This course trains participants in a sheltered instruction approach that is designed for teaching ELP levels 1-5 and is grounded in the WIDA ELD standards and related assessments. We recommend all of these excellent training methodologies. They suggest specific strategies and detailed steps that include the instructional supports discussed throughout this book.

Implementing Common Classroom Practices to Engage English Language Learners at all English Language Proficiency Levels

ESL teachers can find different lesson planning templates with different labels to guide their efforts to plan and implement lessons with meaningful language learning activities for ELLs at all ELP levels. These ESL lesson planning templates generally include (1) a preparation/planning stage in which teachers identify the big ideas, objectives, and requisite vocabulary; (2) an introductory stage in which teachers engage the learners in prior knowledge activities; (3) a teaching stage in which ELLs receive comprehensible instruction; (4) a literacy stage in which students read and write about the topic; and (5) an evaluation stage in which the students' learning can be expanded and assessed. Teachers use sensory, graphic, and interactive supports in their ESL lessons to scaffold ELLs' content learning and language development. This section suggests lesson planning ideas for each of these stages and demonstrates how the four common classroom key practices and instructional supports are infused in each stage of the lessons.

The discussion of the five lesson planning stages includes descriptions of examples of strategies used in a middle school ESL archeology unit. The unit is designed for sixth and seventh grade ELLs with ELP levels 2, 3, and 4. The short (six or seven classroom periods) ESL unit will precede a three-week mainstream classroom scientific inquiry unit that the seventh grade students will study later in the school year (described in Key Practice 10). Although the sixth grade ELLs will not experience the scientific inquiry unit until the next school year, the focus on the language of scientific inquiry will benefit them immediately in their science classroom. Furthermore, since both units are centered around similar big ideas, the students will be well prepared to reach the scientific inquiry objective the following year. We provide a *Content-Based English as a Second Language Planning Template* that shows the completed planning template for the middle school content-based ESL unit.

Stage 1: Planning and Preparation

District curriculum guidelines and teachers' editions of textbooks often provide standards-based big ideas, main concepts, and/or objectives of topics and themes. Furthermore, textbooks, supplementary materials, and trade books are generally aligned with core content standards. Using these resources (as well as resources from the library or the Web), ESL teachers and their mainstream colleagues can work together to write big idea statements that they will use as starting points for the sheltered unit in the mainstream classrooms and the ESL unit in the ESL classroom. ESL teachers can use the WIDA English Language Development Standards and Resource Guide to write language objectives that incorporate content topics. The Resource Guide shares multiple sample topics and genres for each content area (representative of national and state content standards) grouped by grade-level clusters. Using the WIDA model performance indicators (MPIs), teachers will find language tasks at each ELP level that can help them write language objectives within various content topics.

In our middle school scenario, the ESL teacher uses the core standards to identify and write the big ideas in the ESL unit and makes sure that the materials he/she has selected align with the big ideas. Next, he/she develops language objectives and content objectives. He/she identifies the science words and phrases that students will need to know and the kind of language skills and structures that they will need to use to discuss the work of archeologists. At this point, the ESL teacher discusses the unit plans with a science teacher. The ESL teacher and science teacher can discuss their coordinated units and talk about the academic words that each teacher plans to teach. Once the ESL teacher has developed his/her own vocabulary list, he/she is ready to plan multiple vocabulary-building strategies. In addition, the teacher must gather several trade books, pictures, and other visuals about archeology that will be displayed prominently in the classroom.

Stage 2: Introducing the Unit/Lesson to the English Language Learners

When introducing new lessons and/or a new unit, ESL teachers should plan two or more introductory activities to set the context and build upon the prior knowledge of the ELLs. These activities should require students to talk with one another. Teachers can develop an experiential activity such as a demonstration, role-play, experiment, website exploration, or a field trip. For example, the middle school ESL teacher can pack damp sand into a cake pan (perhaps with buried "*artifacts*") and, using a pencil in the sand, draw *grid* lines and show how scientists scrape, find, and map artifacts. To understand the difficulty of unearthing the Iceman from the glacier, the students could participate in an activity in which they carefully try to remove items frozen in small ice blocks. The teacher can take digital photos of students during these activities and use these photos later in the unit for a sorting/sequencing activity or as a writing prompt. Where possible, the teacher can also enlist the bilingual assistant to find a video on the internet in the students' primary language about the work of archeologists and show it to the ELLs in that language group.

In addition, the ESL teacher can conduct prior knowledge activities (e.g., a KWL, anticipation guide, word sort) that develop oral language by

Table 10.1   Anticipation Guide for Content-based English as a Second Language Archeology Unit

The Science of Archeology		
Write A (AGREE) or D (DISAGREE) for each of the following statements:		
Before Reading:		After Reading:
_____	1. Archeologists try to reconstruct past actions and events by the collection of evidence found in the earth.	_____
_____	2. Archeologists use scientific inquiry, factual information, and technology to make educated guesses.	_____
_____	3. Archeologists are even interested in the garbage found at the archeological sites.	_____
_____	4. Archeologists dig round, square, or rectangular holes depending on the terrain.	_____
_____	5. Archaeologists work all over the world, on land and in the sea.	_____
_____	6. Archeology is just about the only way that we can learn about prehistoric civilizations.	_____

asking students to talk, share ideas, and tell what they know about the topic. In addition to the student interaction that occurs naturally during prior knowledge activities, ELLs may need sensory and graphic supports to understand the big ideas (e.g., pictures and images from the selected materials). Table 10.1 shows an anticipation guide to introduce the big ideas of the archeology unit. The ELP level 3-4 ELLs may be able to comprehend the sentences on the anticipation guide, but the ESL teacher will have to clarify vocabulary words (scientific inquiry, educated guesses, reconstruct, civilization), pointing out scientists' work in pictures in order to help the ELP level 2 students. The anticipation guide includes one incorrect statement (called a foil) in order to encourage student discussion and interaction. (Archeologists dig round, square, or rectangular holes depending on the terrain.) The students can complete the anticipation guide as a whole class or in pairs. Anticipation guides generally ask students to agree or disagree rather than asking them to determine whether the statements are true or false. This seemingly simple change in wording can substantially reduce students' anxiety level when completing the task.

After the students agree or disagree with each statement, they will want to know if their opinions are right. This is a good time to state the big ideas and objectives of the lesson and/or unit and write and display them prominently in the classroom. The teacher can also introduce more of the target vocabulary words in a whole-group discussion. As they talk about the new words, the teacher writes the words on the board or on chart paper, engaging the students in definition-getting. Whenever possible, the teacher should explicitly link students' past experiences and cultural backgrounds to the vocabulary-building process.

Stage 3: Implementing Comprehensible Instruction

The next stage of implementing content-based ESL instruction is often labeled the comprehensible input phase. Krashen (1985) coined the term *comprehensible input* to describe how children learn a second language. He states that children learn a second language when instruction is comprehensible, natural, interesting, useful for meaningful communication, and approximately one step beyond the learner's current level of competence. Krashen uses the term i + 1 to describe how teachers can make lessons comprehensible by modeling, teaching, and using language a little beyond the students' current proficiency level. Richard-Amato (2003) explains that similar to the zone of proximal development, this i + 1 concept refers to the distance between actual language development (represented by i) and potential language development (represented by i + 1). In order to continually stretch ELLs' language skills into the next level, ESL teachers can model and use language one step above the ELLs' current language competence, scaffolding new information with visual, graphic, and interactive supports.

In the comprehensible input stage, ESL teachers must implement instructional strategies that promote talking and thinking (e.g., connect-twos, word sorts, two-way tasks, hands-on experiences, cooperative learning strategies, etc.). They must also make sure that they revisit and review previously learned vocabulary and provide opportunities for language practice, including writing activities. Table 10.2 shows a connect-two learning activity for the middle school content-based ESL unit.

In a connect-two learning activity, the ELLs are asked to choose two of the words and talk (and later, write) about how they are connected or related. The teacher can ask the students to share their statements, calling attention to sentences that use various words from the word bank but describe different similarities. The teacher can expand the activity by asking for volunteers to orally connect three words or ask students to create long, interesting sentences using more words from the word bank. Teachers can ask various types of questions about the relationships (e.g., knowledge, recall, interpretive, analytical, synthesis, evaluation) and give students sufficient wait time for responses. To encourage risk-taking, as students respond, teachers must accept students' approximations without overcorrection.

Stage 4: Engaging English Language Learners in Literacy Activities

ESL teachers are great at making new information comprehensible through concrete ways, using visual, hands-on, and graphic supports. However,

Table 10.2 Connect-Two Learning Activity

CONNECT-TWO: Archeology		
archeologist	radiocarbon dating	make a hypothesis
classify	satellite photos	site/dig
artifacts	make deductions	analyze
grid	educated guesses	evidence
reconstruct	excavation	draw conclusions

1. _____ and _____ are connected because _____

   _____.

2. _____ and _____ are connected because _____

   _____.

3. _____ and _____ are different because _____

   _____.

4. _____ and _____ are different because _____

   _____.

5. _____ and _____ are connected because _____ but are

   different because _____.

they need to provide multiple opportunities to actively engage their ELLs in literacy activities, planning ways for the ELLs to improve their word knowledge, comprehension, fluency, and writing. Teachers can model fluency by reading aloud specific paragraphs in the passages, asking students to listen as they follow along in the text. Then, they can ask the students to chorally read the same paragraphs. They can ask the ELLs to read selections from various materials that they have chosen that match the independent reading levels of the ELLs. Teachers can ask the ELLs to read with partners, varying the pairings depending on the task or difficulty of the passage. They can improve students' comprehension by asking them to read small chunks of text independently, teaching specific strategies within those chunks (DRTA, say something, think-pair-share). They can ask the ELLs to respond to readings through meaningful and functional writing activities using strategies such as dictation, connect-twos, sentence strips, paragraph frames, exit slips, and graphic organizers.

In the archeology unit, after reading a simple passage with the ELLs with beginning levels of English proficiency, the ESL teacher can initiate a language experience approach (LEA) activity. The LEA approach is especially effective for ELLs because the first step is to have the students talk about a learning experience using the social language that they already have. Then, the students can dictate sentences about the topic based on the discussion and the information that they have just learned. The teacher writes down what they say. The students then orally read what they have dictated. Teachers can integrate vocabulary building into an LEA literacy activity. For example, after the middle school ELLs have read and talked about the picture book about archeological digs, the teacher might write *excavation sites, grid, analyze, artifacts,* and *dating methods* on the board, asking the ELLs to use these words as they dictate a paragraph about the work of archeologists. The teacher coaches the ELL students as they dictate sentences in the LEA, which might resemble the following sample.

The Work of Archeologists
Archeologists find things called artifacts that they dig up at the excavation sites. They dig square holes so they can make a grid to show where they find things. They take the artifacts back to the lab and analyze all the things. They figure out how old the artifacts are by using dating methods.

After the students read and reread their product, the ESL teacher can implement an oral activity with the paragraph using a cloze method. He/she reads the passage slowly and deletes one word in every sentence, replacing the word with an underlined blank (_____). Then the teacher asks a student to reread the paragraph and orally insert the word that is missing. Sometimes a target vocabulary word is deleted and sometimes other words are deleted. Next, the teacher deletes a second or third word in each sentence and asks other students to volunteer to read the passage including the words that are now missing. To set context, when the teacher deletes the first word in a sentence, he/she replaces the word with the capital letter of the word followed by a blank (T_____). If the deleted word is at the end of a sentence, the teacher makes sure that a period is firmly in position (_____.). Using the LEA with the cloze method in this manner helps the ELLs retell newly learned information, practice using targeted academic vocabulary words, and develop fluency.

After reading a passage, teachers usually ask questions to check for comprehension. To encourage language development, ESL teachers must find ways to present questions that require more than one-word responses. They should use strategies that require the students to tell each other newly learned information. Table 10.3 shares a cooperative learning strategy, numbered heads together (Kagan, 1994), around the Iceman passage in the archeology unit. The teacher places the students in groups of four and gives each student a copy of the question sheet. The teacher explains that the students are to look for the answers in the reading passage, but they don't have to write down their answers. After students have had enough time to find the answers, the teacher reads one question at a time, telling the groups to consult with their teammates to make sure everyone knows the answer. Then, the teacher calls on one student to answer. By pooling their answers before they respond, the activity promotes tutoring through social interaction and allows less confident ELLs to participate in a low-risk situation.

Table 10.3   Numbered Heads Together Cooperative Strategy

DISCOVERING THE ICEMAN

Directions: Make sure that every member of your group has answers for these questions. You don't have to write the answers on your paper.

1. Find two or more sentences which give you clues that Otzi was going to die.
2. How was his body mummified and/or preserved?
3. If the archeologists found Otzi before the hikers, what steps do you think they would take to remove the body in order to preserve the most evidence?
4. Why wasn't the Iceman's body destroyed with the movement of the glacier?
5. Describe what Otzi was wearing the day he died.
6. What do you think the word *prehistoric* means?
7. Name two ways that archeologists figure out the time period in which a prehistoric mummy (like Otzi) lived.
8. Finish this sentence: Archeologists are scientists who _____

_____.

In addition to conducting literacy activities that promote vocabulary building, increase fluency, and improve comprehension, the ESL teacher also needs to advance the ELLs' writing skills. ELLs at any ELP level benefit from multiple writing strategies (e.g., exit slips, writers' workshop, dictations, graphic organizers, paragraph frames, and sentence frames). ESL teachers can create their own paragraph frames and exit slips to fit the lessons and materials used in a lesson, as shown in Table 10.4 and Table 10.5. A paragraph frame provides prompts that help students organize information (e.g., compare and contrast, complete a learning log, retell events sequentially, or write about a problem and solution, write a report). Exit slips are similar to paragraph frames but the task is short, asking the ELLs

Table 10.4   Paragraph Frame

SEQUENTIAL PARAGRAPH WRITING

In order to find out how old things are, archeologists must follow several scientific methods. First, _____

_____.

Then, _____

_____.

Next, _____

_____.

Finally, _____

_____

_____.

Table 10.5   Exit Slip

Student Name _____
Date _____ Subject _____Discovering The Iceman_____
The story was about
_____
_____
The most interesting part was
_____
_____

to write only two or three sentences. An exit slip is generally a slip of paper about the size of a student pass. At the end of the class, the teacher can assign all students to complete the slip and hand it to him/her as the students leave the ESL classroom.

Stage 5: Evaluating and Expanding English Language Learners' Learning

After the comprehensible instruction and literacy activities, ESL teachers must plan and implement assessment activities to determine how the students' learning outcomes match the content and language objectives of the unit. At this point, teachers can encourage students to expand their learning by assigning students various self-directed inquiries. For example, projects for young ELP level 1 and 2 ELLs may include pasting photos and pictures on posters under specific categories and telling and/or writing facts about the pictures they have selected. Older ELLs at this level of English proficiency can create PowerPoint slides with images and captions that demonstrate their understanding of the lesson's big ideas and language objectives. ELL students at ELP levels 3-4 can conduct their own research using supplemental materials, internet searches, and periodicals. The projects may require students to work independently, in teams, or in pairs. The tasks chosen by each student will require varying degrees of reading, writing, and research, depending on the ELL students' ELP levels and teacher expectations. Understanding that learning a new language requires some risk-taking, teachers should remember to give positive feedback as they monitor their students' progress.

Throughout a content-based ESL unit, teachers can conduct assessments using instructional strategies that they use regularly to check their students' ability to retell information, demonstrate steps, and explain concepts according to their ELP levels. In the archeology unit example, the middle school ESL teacher may divide the class by ELP levels and plan two different final assessments that focus on the same big ideas from the unit.

Table 10.6   Sentence Strips

Scientists search for clues and evidence	by digging and sifting through the dirt.
They dig carefully so they do not	break the artifacts that they discover.
They use a rectangular grid to	map the location where the artifacts are found.
They collect evidence such as	tools, materials, food particles, and bones.
Scientists classify the artifacts in categories	that describe their use or purpose.
They determine the age of the artifacts	through a process called carbon dating.
They use various methods and technology	to try to reconstruct the past accurately.
Using the evidence, they make	educated guesses called hypotheses.

One assessment could be a final test to evaluate the ELLs at ELP levels 3-4. The test might include a dictation portion, a section where the students must match definitions, and a section in which the students fill in sentence and/or paragraph frames. This assessment requires a higher level of English than would be appropriate for ELP level 2 ELLs. For that reason, the teacher plans to use an oral retelling checklist and sentence strips for the students at ELP level 2, Table 10.6. He/she cuts sets of the sentence strips in half and places the first halves of the sentences in one envelope and the second halves of the sentences in another envelope, mixing the order of the strips.

The sentence strip assessment can be implemented by pairing students of different ELP levels together. For example, the ELP level 2 ELLs could take out the strips and match the sentence endings with the beginnings of the sentences. As the students work on the task, the teacher asks the ELP level 4 partners to listen to the ELP level 2 students read their sentences. As they read each sentence strip, the more proficient ELLs ask the ELP level 2 students to point to examples of the sentences in the archeology picture book.

At the end of a unit, ESL teachers often use various listening, speaking, reading, and writing rubrics and checklists to document their students' language development over time. Teachers can incorporate language objectives into rubrics and checklists in ways that enable the ELLs to clearly understand what they are responsible for learning and how they will be evaluated. In an ESL class, summative assessment measures for ELP levels 1–2 ELLs must focus on their understanding (demonstating, sorting) and ability to state the big ideas and main concepts that the teacher has taught in meaningful ways. For example, the ELLs can show what they know through the authentic measures described previously and also through matching, sorting, or retelling basic information. Paper and pencil tests can certainly be used, especially for older ELLs with higher levels of language proficiency. These ELLs, who may be occasionally evaluated in their general education classrooms through assessments without instructional

REFLECTIONS FROM THE FIELD

Providing Instructional Supports in Classroom Assessments

Michelle Cubero, Bilingual Teacher

My fourth grade Spanish bilingual class had just completed an ESL unit in social studies about regions. I gave a "traditional" fill in the blank assessment in English. Some of my students did not do very well. Throughout the unit we defined the vocabulary with words and pictures. We created landforms and role-played the different types of climates across the regions. I couldn't figure out where I went wrong.

It wasn't until I attended Tammy's class on assessment of ELLs that I found my answer. It was the night that we discussed the role of ELD standards that a light went on for me. As we went over and discussed the layout of the WIDA standards and the Model Performance Indicators, one phrase stood out, "with sensory, graphic and interactive support." I had learned how to use these supports in WIDA's ELD standards in my instruction but using them in assessment was not emphasized during my previous training. I think that is where I went wrong. I could have included some pictures for visual support and labeling. I also could have included a word bank to aid with vocabulary and filling in the blanks. Social studies and science concepts can be difficult for ELLs to grasp, especially if they lack background knowledge in these areas. I now realize how important it is for me to scaffold information not only during instruction, but when assessing my students as well.

supports, will need test-taking practice in the ESL classroom where the instruction is most comprehensible. The assessment measures and student work samples are kept in the students' portfolios.

Many ESL teachers are not accustomed to developing their own ESL units. In many cases, their school districts have adopted particular ESL textbooks that include content area information. However, starting on page 1 and covering all of the chapters in a commercially developed ESL textbook does not ensure that the ELLs will gain the knowledge that is considered essential learning in their state. Furthermore, the sequence of the topics in these texts does not necessarily match the sequence in which these topics are taught at the school. This means that the lessons from the text do not pave the way for ELLs to have successful learning about these topics in mainstream classrooms. ESL teachers can use a better approach by selecting information from these commercial ESL texts in a sequence that matches the school's standards-based curriculum and use those materials within a sequence of stages as described previously. They can make the big ideas explicit, implement vocabulary-building strategies, conduct prior knowledge activities, and encourage the ELLs to talk about what they are learning. The results will improve the ELLs' language skills and make the commercial texts more meaningful.

In this chapter, we have shown how ESL instruction is most effective when ESL and mainstream teachers (who share the same ELL students) coordinate unit planning based on standards-based big ideas. We have provided many examples and strategies for planning and implementing comprehensible ESL instruction. In the next chapter, designed for teachers who have ELLs in their mainstream classrooms, we provide information and examples of meaning-based English literacy instruction.

QUESTIONS FOR REFLECTION AND ACTION

1. Are the core state standards readily available in your school and classroom? Does the school district have curriculum guides that drive content instruction by grade level? If so, how are these tools used to plan and implement ESL instruction at your school? If not, what is the first step for change?

2. What steps are taken at the school-wide and grade level to coordinate ESL lessons with content instruction in general education classrooms? If this is not happening, what are the obstacles? With your study group, brainstorm ideas to eliminate the obstacles.

Recommended Readings

Herrell, A., & Jordan, M. (2007). *Fifty strategies for teaching English language learners.* Boston: Prentice Hall/Pearson.

Kendall, J., & Khuon, O. (2006). *Writing sense: Integrated reading and writing lessons for English language learners.* Portland, ME: Stenhouse Publishers.

Laturnau J. (2010). Standards-based instruction for English language learners. Honolulu: Pacific Resources for Education and Learning. Available at http://www.prel.org/products/pc_/standards-based.htm.

Peregoy, S., & Boyle, O. (2008). *Reading, writing and learning in ESL: A resource book for teaching K-12 English learners.* Columbus: Allyn and Bacon.

Richard-Amato, P. (2003). *Making it happen: From interactive to participatory language teaching.* New York: Longman.

Zwier, J. (2008). *Building academic language: Essential practices for content classrooms, grades 5-12.* San Francisco, CA: John Wiley and Sons.

The checklist is written using measurable statements that can be used to evaluate and monitor language education programs and instruction at the district, school, and classroom levels. The district language education committee and school leadership teams can use the checklist as a diagnostic tool to identify the areas that represent the biggest challenges during the restructuring process. Various teams can use the results of the checklist as a starting point to determine the professional development that educators need to know in order to successfully implement the practices. Teacher teams can use the checklist to evaluate their own teaching practices to recognize ways in which they can immediately make instructional improvements.

SCORING DIRECTIONS:
1 = This practice IS implemented.
2 = This practice is in progress or is in place in some classrooms.
3 = This practice is NOT currently in place.

			The Core Instructional Practices of Every Program for ELLs
			Implementing English as a Second Language Instruction: Daily ESL instruction in the four language domains (listening, speaking, reading, and writing) is planned and implemented. Instruction is focused on the academic language that ELLs need to understand and express essential grade-level concepts.
1	2	3	• Teachers coordinate academic content and language instruction with core content and language development standards.
1	2	3	• Teachers connect receptive language skills and beginning level ELLs' oral language to academic English language instruction.
1	2	3	• Teachers use a content-based ESL approach when teaching intermediate and advanced ELLs.
1	2	3	• Teachers implement common classroom practices with meaningful language learning activities for ELLs at all English language proficiency levels by using sensory, graphic, and interactive supports.

IMPLICATIONS AND COMMENTS _____

_____

_____

_____

Grade-Level Curriculum Coordination Template

Grade-Level Curriculum Coordination   Grade _____

ESL teacher(s) _____

Gen. Ed. teacher _____   Gen. Ed. teacher _____

Gen. Ed. teacher _____   Gen. Ed. teacher _____

Bilingual teacher/assistant _____

Content Area _____   Quarter _____   School Year _____

Directions: Identify the core state standards addressed, the big ideas that will be taught, and the target vocabulary. Mark the big ideas and concepts most emphasized with an asterisk or star.

Unit/Theme	Standards addressed	Big Ideas and Main Concepts	Key Vocabulary

Content-Based English as a Second Language Planning Template

Theme/Title of Unit: __Archeology: Discovering the Iceman__

State standards addressed (Illinois Learning Standards, Science 11 and 13):
- know and apply concepts, principles, and processes of scientific inquiry;
- know and apply accepted practices of science;
- know and apply concepts that describe the interaction between science, technology, and society.

Big ideas:
- Archeologists search for evidence at excavation sites using various tools and methods to make deductions and develop hypotheses.
- Archeologists have multiple scientific technological processes that can be used to understand more about the cultures of ancient societies.

Content Objectives	Language Objectives
Using pictures, all ELLs will explain the work of archeologists and tell how they find evidence.	ELP level 2 ELLs will write dictated sentences about how the Iceman was found and how he was moved to the laboratory, matching pictures to their sentences.
Students will learn that prehistoric discoveries must be processed through careful and specific scientific methods in order to accurately reconstruct the past.	ELP level 2 ELLs will show understanding of the verbs of scientific inquiry by matching pictures of archeologists' work with appropriate sentence strips.
ELP level 2 ELLs will fill out graphic organizers that show their understanding of archeologists' tools, methods, and technology.	ELP level 3 and 4 ELLs will write sentences about the work of archeologists, identifying sequential processes with target vocabulary.
ELP level 3 and 4 ELLs will describe several ways archeologists analyze evidence using various tools, methods, and technology.	ELP level 3 and 4 ELLs will change the verbs from the present tense to the past tense while writing paragraphs about how the Iceman was found and moved to the laboratory.
	All ELL students will be able to respond to oral questions about the Iceman, how he was found, and how he was moved to the laboratory.

Vocabulary

archeologist, dating methods, site/dig, artifacts, make deductions, fossilization, scientific inquiry, grid, evidence, educated guesses, reconstruct, excavation, discover, analyze, observe, classify, deduct, determine, make a hypothesis, reconstruct, explain.

Materials

Archeology for Kids. http://www.nps.gov/archeology/public/kids/kidsTwo.htm. National Park Service, 2010.
Dockstader, N. Kanaly, Q .(2008). *Death of the Iceman* (video). National Geographic Explorer Series.
Duke, K. (2003). *Archaeologists Dig for Clues* (Let's Read-and-Find-Out Science). Demco Media.
Examining the Iceman. (2007). National Geographic. Available at http://ngm.nationalgeographic.com/2007/07/iceman/iceman-graphic-interactive.
The Iceman. (1993). *National Geographic, 183*(6), pp. 36–67.

Implementing Meaning-Based Literacy Instruction

Whenever possible, begin literacy instruction in the primary language; when literacy is taught in English, plan and implement meaning-based literacy instruction that builds on students' oral language and uses comprehensible text at appropriate English language proficiency levels.

- Begin instruction by identifying what ELLs already know about literacy.
- Use the ELLs' oral language as a pathway to reading and writing.
- Integrate meaningful and functional literacy tasks within the five essential instructional elements of reading using a balanced literacy approach.
- Implement multiple comprehension strategies before, during, and after reading.
- Improve reading and writing across the curriculum by using nonfiction text as well as fictional stories.
- Help struggling older readers improve their reading skills by using their knowledge of the English language and appropriately leveled texts.
- Document ELLs' literacy learning progress over time.
- Use bilingual support staff and ELL parents strategically so they can support the literacy development of ELLs.

THE BIG IDEAS

- Second language learners can be actively engaged in literacy instruction in the general education classroom when literacy tasks are meaningful, functional, and appropriately adapted.

- Comprehension is the most fundamental element of teaching literacy in English to English language learners (ELLs).

- Teaching literacy to ELLs is most effective when teachers use a balanced approach.

All students, particularly ELLs, need meaning-based literacy instruction. When ELLs learn to read and write in their primary language, they can fully utilize their background experiences, oral language competence, and linguistic skills while learning how to construct meaning from text. This is especially important since the experiences that students go through when they are learning to read have a lasting impact on their view of themselves as literate individuals (Miramontes et al., 2011). Therefore, we recommend that whenever possible, school districts provide beginning literacy instruction in the primary language. We recognize, however, that there are many school districts that do not have bilingually proficient teachers, appropriate primary language resources, or enough students of the same language group to offer formal literacy instruction in the children's primary language. ELLs in these districts usually learn to read and write (in English) in general education classrooms. When literacy is taught in English, teachers should plan and implement meaning-based literacy instruction that builds on students' oral language and uses comprehensible text at appropriate English language proficiency (ELP) levels.

Key Practice 10 shows general education teachers and literacy specialists how to teach meaning-based literacy instruction in English to ELLs with varying degrees of proficiency in their second language. In a meaning-based literacy approach, teachers engage learners in concrete and engaging reading and writing tasks that are meaningful, functional, and appropriately adapted. Teaching literacy in English to ELLs is similar to teaching literacy to English-proficient children; however, the essential task of building oral language proficiency and the emphasis on making literacy tasks meaningful often change the focus and sequence of instruction.

We know that general education primary teachers frequently teach literacy to ELLs during the same literacy block in which they teach English-proficient children how to read and write. Therefore, we begin our discussion of Key Practice 10 by providing information and suggestions to help elementary general education teachers adapt instruction to make literacy tasks meaningful for the ELLs who are learning to read and write for the first time in English, their second language. Then, we provide information about how teachers can combine several literacy strategies and approaches to help improve literacy for ELLs at all grade levels. We also suggest ways in which general education teachers, secondary content teachers, and English as a second language (ESL) teachers can improve reading skills of older ELLs who have intermediate levels of English language proficiency but are struggling readers. We show how teachers can document ELLs' literacy learning progress over time. Finally, we suggest specific strategies that bilingual support staff and ELLs' parents can use to support ELLs' literacy development.

Identifying Students' Prior Experiences with Literacy

The initial literacy tasks that teachers implement with emergent ELL readers depend on each child's current literacy skills. Therefore, teachers need to know what the students already know about reading and writing in English—and in their primary language. "Even teachers who are teaching only through English need to know the literacy level of their ELLs in the home language because students who come with age-appropriate literacy or emergent literacy skills in the home language are quite different learners from those who come without these skills" (Cloud et al., 2009, p. 90). Have they had literacy experiences at home? Do they know their letters? Do they know that the words tell the story, not just the pictures? Do they have a sense of word-ness and sentence-ness? Do they know that letters make sounds? When bilingual assistants are asked to participate in these assessments, teachers can easily find the answers to these questions. The informal literacy screening process suggested in the discussion of Key Practice 3 can help assess what literacy skills the newly arrived ELLs have acquired in their home language. The WIDA CAN DO Descriptors can also help teachers find out what the ELLs already know about reading and writing. The CAN DO Descriptors, written for each grade-level cluster, provide language expectations within the four domains (listening, speaking, reading, and writing) according to the five ELP levels.

Using Oral Language as a Pathway to Reading and Writing

Although ELLs at beginning stages of English language development are mostly silent in class, they are developing their ability to understand their new language. Providing low-risk environments where these learners are comfortable to speak will help them pass through this silent period. These ELLs need structured activities about classroom tasks and topics to engage them in oral language. Placing them in small groups with more proficient English speakers can provide opportunities for classroom talk. When teachers plan strategies that require student interaction, they are providing language modeling and scaffolds that help move receptive language into expressive fluency.

The primary general education teacher who is teaching formal literacy (in a two-hour literacy block) and the ESL (or bilingual) teacher who is teaching ESL (for a shorter period) must help the ELLs build oral proficiency. These teachers must communicate regularly to connect the children's oral language to reading and writing tasks in both classrooms. Both teachers can write down what the ELLs say and share information about their progress. Both teachers can observe and take notes on the social language that the ELLs are using in the classroom. While working with students in small groups, they can model and teach the ELLs how to write the classroom words, phrases, and sentences that the ELLs know. The teachers can help the ELLs orally read these phrases and sentences and can ask the ELLs to read and write them again. As the teachers build a bank of words and phrases that the ELLs understand and can say, these known words and phrases can be used as sight words, in sentence strips, in phonemic awareness, in phonics activities, and in fluency activities. In this way, the general education teacher can use the English that the children can orally produce

Initial Literacy Tasks for ELP Level 1 ELLs

Shalley Wakeman, Primary ESL Teacher

My ELP level 1 ELLs are often nervous and quiet when they first arrive. I try to get them talking and laughing so that I can connect their oral language development with literacy experiences. Right away, I give my new ELL students a spiral-bound notebook so I can help them record their first utterances in English. I begin by writing three simple phrases in the notebook: "My name is _____." "My teacher's name is _____." "I go to _____ school." When I hear them talk, we celebrate the moment and write down what they say in their notebooks. I make flashcards and word walls, and whenever possible, I illustrate the nouns. I help each student make their own word banks for the words that they know and can use. To get the new ELLs acquainted with the school staff and locations that they need to know, I take them on a tour. The children carry papers with scanned photos of the principal, secretary, nurse, and lunchroom supervisor. When they get to the office, each student meets the secretary, "My name is

_____. What is your name?" The secretary says, "My name is Mrs. _____ and writes her name next to her picture. When they return to the classroom, the children make books about the people and the places at school and read their sentences to each other. I work closely with the general education teachers to coordinate vocabulary building, ESL lessons, and literacy tasks. Since I speak Spanish, I am able to teach the children cognates, preview stories, and explain many of the words and big ideas that they are working on in their general education classroom. Once the children are comfortable and understand more of the English that is spoken, they begin to talk much more. At this point, I know I can use their sight words and phrases in phonemic and phonics tasks, starting with beginning and ending word sounds. The children use their notebooks to read, re-read, and evaluate their progress. They are proud when they notice how much English they have learned and see how their writing has improved.

to participate in many of the same literacy skills that their English-speaking peers are learning.

At the primary level, classroom talk often starts with classroom labels, greetings, and personal statements. An effective practice to engage ELP level 1 and 2 ELLs in literacy is to connect their personal experiences and stories with classroom tasks. As Hamayan (2009) states, "Let them bring their own lives into the classroom." What the ELLs can say can be written down. What they can write, they can read. Three common, effective strategies that get the ELLs talking and engaged in literacy activities are described below.

Show and Tell

This early childhood strategy is rich in context and allows primary-level children to tell each other about things they bring to school. They talk about their experiences and learn how to be audiences for one another. It is a perfect opportunity for ELLs to think about and creatively construct what they want to say (Lindfors, 1989). Teachers can take notes during the ELLs' show and tell presentation and write up one or two sentences using the ELLs' own words. After the session is over, the teacher or assistant can make individual sentence strips from the sentences. First, the teacher points to the words as he/she reads the sentence strips and then helps the

ELL read these sentences. These strips can be saved, reread, and used for phonics instruction and vocabulary development.

Getting older students to engage in classroom talk is often challenging. Although show and tell activities are not appropriate for intermediate and secondary students, teachers can engage older learners to talk about the big events and headlines that adolescents are currently talking about. When teachers see a high-interest topic on the Web or in a magazine, they can share and talk about the article with the students and elicit their opinions. As the students share information, the teacher can create various sentence strips about the topic that are comprehensible for the ELLs in the classroom. These strips can then be used as conversation starters in small-group activities.

Morning Message

At the beginning of the day, teachers can preview the day's activities for the students. They can write the day's activities on the board, following a predictable format of three to four sentences. They can say the words as they write them. The children can read the message through choral reading. For all children, this activity models how writing is organized (left to right, letter-by-letter sequence corresponding to the spoken word, spaces between words) (Ariza, 2006; Chamberlain, 2008).

```
┌─────────────────────────────────────────────────────┐
│                   Morning Message                    │
│                                                      │
│  Today we are going to _____  │
│  _____.│
│  For science (or other content), we will _____  │
│  _____.│
│  After lunch, we are going to _____ │
│  _____.│
└─────────────────────────────────────────────────────┘
```

The morning message provides a predictable format that gives a comprehensible preview about content and literacy lessons. "We are going to" and "I am going to" can be used daily to help the ELLs construct various new sentences using the oral language they are learning. At the end of the day, the teachers can revisit the message and encourage the students to talk about and write about what they have learned: "Today I learned that …." This is a powerful strategy that helps students understand the big ideas that they are learning and connects literacy with the ELLs' academic learning experiences.

This strategy can be adapted for use in intermediate and secondary reading and language arts classrooms. For example, writing the daily agenda on the board is a valuable strategy for all learners. Teachers can write the big ideas of the content and/or literary topics, write a list of the vocabulary words that will be practiced, and write the homework assign-

Table 11.1   The Language Experience Approach (LEA)

1. The teacher and students share and discuss a learning experience (e.g., a field trip, a video, a science experiment, or other classroom activity.) The children are asked to retell the events or steps. This oral discussion is important for ELLs because the more English-proficient children model age-appropriate language around classroom topics.

2. After the discussion, the teacher takes dictation from the students and writes their sentences on the board, chart paper, or overhead projector. The teacher writes down the students' words, modeling and adapting language occasionally but without explicit correction. The teacher and students develop a title for the dictated sentences. The teacher reads back the paragraph and students may make changes if they like (Enright & McClosky, 1988). Four to five sentences are enough for emergent ELL readers.

3. The teacher and students read and re-read their product together. The class may read the story in chorus, or individuals may read with or without the teacher. These repeated readings help ELLs read with fluency, become familiar with English patterns, learn to practice academic language, and retell newly learned information. The product (a paragraph or a short story) is copied so that it can be re-used.

4. Students use the dictated story in follow-up activities, including cloze activities, sentence frames, retelling activities, adding their own sentences, etc.

5. Students move from making and reading whole-class LEAs to making their own LEA paragraphs, trading and reading one another's work, and working in pairs to write stories. Regardless of how LEA activities are expanded, meaning is key; the students must understand the sentences they are saying, writing, and reading.

ment on the board. At the beginning of the class, teachers can refer to the agenda and lead a discussion about the big ideas and the vocabulary words. By encouraging the students to participate, they are providing a preview of the day's lesson and providing opportunities for oral language development.

Language Experience Approach

The language experience approach (LEA) is a widely used emergent literacy strategy that begins by talking and writing about a shared experience. Retelling what they have just learned helps ELLs develop oral language, build sentences, and learn how to organize and describe events. "But most important of all, it provides the fundamental skills ELL students need to begin retelling stories on paper" (Brandi-Miller, 2005, p. 1). LEA activities help students write, learn words, increase reading fluency, and comprehend text they have written themselves. Table 11.1 describes the basic steps in an LEA activity.

When the general education and ESL teacher both use the LEA approach in their classrooms, the ELLs become familiar and comfortable with this important literacy teaching strategy. The teachers can adjust the LEA steps to match the ELLs' ELP levels. There are many variations of LEA activities that can help children retell and write what they have learned after a meaningful learning activity. For example, the teacher can put students in groups of two to four children, integrating the ELLs within the groups. The teacher asks the students to talk about what they did and what they learned. To get the students started, the teacher can provide visuals or objects that remind the students about the steps they took during the activity. Each group gets two or three strips of chart paper. On each strip, a sentence is started, depending on the task (e.g., First we .... Then, we .... We learned that ....). After completing the task, the groups tape their strips on a wall for others to see. The teacher can ask members of each group to orally read their sentences. The teacher can save significant sentences that can be useful for skill-building. Teacher assistants can use the sentences to help individual ELLs work with words and sounds.

Integrating Meaningful and Functional Literacy Tasks

The National Reading Panel (National Institute of Child Health and Human Development, 2000) has identified five literacy components that are essential elements of formal reading instruction: phonemic awareness, phonics, vocabulary, fluency, and comprehension. Some educators have the mistaken notion that these elements should be taught in the preceding order (Cloud et al., 2009). Cloud et al. emphasize that comprehension and meaning making should be a primary concern in all literacy tasks. Teachers should use a balanced literacy approach that integrates skills development into meaningful and functional literacy tasks for all students, particularly ELLs. For example, starting with language experience activities, sharing picture books, and reading stories aloud, teachers can demonstrate that words and text tell a meaningful story (comprehension).

Recognizing the sounds in words, matching the sounds to letters, and teaching students to recognize high-frequency sight words are important emergent literacy skills for all learners, including ELLs. Teaching reading requires teachers to work with words on a regular basis, including developing phonemic awareness, helping the children understand sound/symbol relationships, helping them learn consonant/vowel sounds, and helping them understand words that rhyme, chunking words, and word families. Using the words and phrases that the ELLs can say, teachers can help the ELLs break their words into component sounds (phonemic awareness). As the children are learning the letters of the alphabet, they can identify the letters and sounds that form the beginnings and endings of meaningful words (phonics). They can build sentences and phrases using sight words (vocabulary). They can read the LEA passages that they have dictated, and re-read familiar content text and stories (fluency). When all of these tasks use known words and phrases, the ELLs can understand what they read and write (comprehension). Table 11.2 shares many examples of how teachers can engage ELLs in meaningful tasks within the five essential components of literacy instruction.

In a balanced literacy program, teachers balance explicit skill instruction with authentic reading and writing activities. They read *to* children

(text continues on page 170)

Table 11.2   English Language Learners and the Five Instructional Elements of Reading Instruction

The Five Instructional Elements of Reading	Implementing Meaning-Based Strategies for ELLs
READING COMPREHENSION: the understanding of meaning in text.	Use text designed for ELLs according to their ELP levels.
	Use picture books.
	Use pictures and headings to preview text.
	Identify and talk about the big ideas that will be encountered in passage.
	Set context and build prior knowledge through multiple prior knowledge activities.
	Set purposes for reading.
	Use bilingual assistants to model think-alouds and other reading strategies.
	Effective teaching streategies: predictions, anticipation guides, KWLs, LEA, pictures, DRTA, mapping, think-alouds, role-playing, and learning logs.
VOCABULARY DEVELOPMENT: the knowledge of words, their definitions, and context.	Match the number of new words and meanings with the ELLs' ELP level.
	Find meaningful ways to explicitly model vocabulary words in context every day.
	Work with 5–15 words that the ELLs understand or words that they will learn as a result of the activity.
	Develop word walls, cognate walls, and word banks that are functional and personally meaningful; help the ELLs use these prompts to construct sentences.
	Group ELLs with English-speaking peers to do cooperative activities that require the students to use target vocabulary and talk about classroom tasks.
	Ask bilingual assistants, tutors, and older bilingual students to work with 5–10 vocabulary flashcards to teach, discuss meanings, and build sentences.
	Use flashcards to reinforce high-frequency words, and use the flash cards to help the ELLs build sentences.
	Point out and model English words that are pronounced differently than the spelling indicates (e.g., *Wednesday, worked, though, thought*).
	When students stumble upon a new word in text, stop and determine if the word is important enough to teach. If not, simply pronounce the word and state its meaning. If the word is important, write the word on the board and explicitly teach its meaning.
	Effective teaching strategies: flashcards, word sorts, word banks, word webs, cloze tasks, sentence frames, concept maps, connect-twos, clustering synonyms, antonyms, and homonyms.

Table 11.2 (*continued*)

The Five Instructional Elements of Reading	Implementing Meaning-Based Strategies for ELLs
PHONEMIC AWARENESS: the knowledge and manipulation of sounds in spoken words.	Work with sounds within words that the ELLs know and can produce orally.
	Ask ELLs to sort pictures of known objects according to initial consonant sounds.
	Provide ELLs with three blank squares of paper placed side by side horizontally. As teacher pronounces words with three sounds, the students place checkers or game pieces in the squares, moving from left to right.
	"Clap" or count phonemes using sight words, word banks, and classroom labels.
	In whole-group instruction, pronounce word (e.g., dog) slowly and have children touch shoulders with first sound of word /d/, elbows with second sound /o/, knees with third /g/, (and toes with fourth /s/).
	Ask bilingual teachers and/or assistants to compare the sounds in English words with sounds in their primary language, asking the assistants to point out and practice new sounds that do not exist in the primary language.
	Effective teaching strategies: flashcards, word sorts, rhymes, matching pictures of known objects with sounds, working with word families with magnetic letters.
PHONICS: the systematic and predictable relationship between written and spoken letters and sounds.	Help the ELLs create their own word banks of words they know and can use.
	Provide multiple opportunities for ELLs to sound out, review, and use their new words.
	Sound out sight words, including classroom labels.
	Sound out the beginnings and endings of known oral words while writing words on paper.
	Teach word families and other common patterns in English words.
	Pronounce words slowly and carefully and ask students to retrieve matching flashcards from a group of displayed words.
	Introduce digraphs and blends using known words with pictures.
	Teach rules thoroughly before presenting exceptions.
	Effective teaching strategies: using phrases from writing products for phonics instruction and using trade books that teach common word patterns (e.g., Dr. Seuss).
READING FLUENCY, INCLUDING ORAL READING SKILLS: the ability to read with accuracy, and with the appropriate rate, expression, and phrasing.	Ask ELLs to read along with proficient readers (choral reading).
	Ask ELLs to re-read known passages.
	Use nonfiction trade books (with visuals) with concepts that the ELLs already know to practice fluency.
	Effective teaching strategies: echo reading, reading with partners, leveled books, oral reading, choral reading, independent reading, and reading journals.

REFLECTIONS FROM THE FIELD

Asking Emergent Readers about What They Understand about Reading

Doris Reynolds, ELL Assessment Coordinator

Several years ago, I worked with a first grade student, Patryk, who was an ELL from Poland. At that time, the reading program placed a great deal of emphasis on phonics. Students would daily spend a block of time at the blackboard working on phonemic awareness and phonics. By the time the first graders finished a six-week program, they were skilled in decoding. I was surprised to see how fantastic Patryk was at learning those skills. He could decode any of the first-grade text he encountered. However, he did not understand what he was reading. His comprehension was negligible. His oral language proficiency was so far behind what he had learned to pronounce (decode) that he was not receiving any message regarding the meaning of the text. This experience really underscored the notion that the ability to decode is not an indicator of being able to read for meaning.

In a graduate class I was taking, the instructor asked us to discover what our students understood about reading. When I asked my students what they thought reading was about, the most common response was related to "getting the words right." My students felt that they were successful or unsuccessful readers at the word level rather than at the meaning level. Very few of my students said that understanding the message that the author intended was part of their purpose for reading. Patryk probably thought that he was a good reader, and other children in the classroom probably thought he was too. My students' understanding of the purpose for reading was not focused on comprehension. Since that time, I still ask my students what they think reading is all about. I have had many interesting discussions with ELLs about the importance of comprehension and interacting with text.

(text continued from page 167)

and read and write *with* children every day (read-alouds, shared reading, guided reading, interactive writing, writers' workshop). Using big books and interactive read-alouds, the teachers can read and talk about the story, predicting, pointing to words as they read, and asking the ELLs comprehension questions. They can work with the ELLs in guided reading groups, literature circles, and discussions. They can write with the ELLs through modeled writing activities, writers' workshop, and the language experience approach (Pinnell & Fountas, 2007). All of these strategies make text meaningful for ELLs and move the children toward reading and writing independently (Mooney, 1990; Fountas & Pinnell, 2001). Meaning is the key; teachers must choose authentic texts that are functional and personally meaningful for ELLs and make sure that the language demands match their English proficiency levels. For example, teachers can read aloud to ELLs on a daily basis, pointing to the pictures and clarifying the events. For shared reading activities, they can read with the young ELLs by carefully choosing stories and passages. They can use trade books specifically designed for ELLs as well as many of the leveled texts in the school's collections—using criteria that correspond to the ELLs' ELP levels. Books can be selected from school collections that are categorized by difficulty and specific criteria set by teacher teams at the primary and intermediate levels. The ESL teacher can work with general education teachers to select leveled books for ELLs by matching the texts with the children's ELP and literacy instructional levels.

Implementing Comprehension Strategies before, during, and after Reading

As emergent ELL readers develop oral English proficiency, comprehend text with improving fluency, and improve their decoding and word study skills, teachers can continue to help students improve their reading skills using authentic texts and specific literacy skill instruction, keeping in mind that comprehension remains a priority at all grade levels. As the ELLs begin to read independently, teachers can utilize multiple comprehension strategies to help students interact and comprehend various content and narrative texts.

As primary, intermediate, and secondary literacy teachers prepare their lesson plans, they should always preview the passages that they will ask their students to read. By doing so, they can identify the big ideas, select vocabulary words, and look for unfamiliar and problematic concepts for the ELLs and other diverse learners. This important step of previewing every reading passage will help teachers plan several prior knowledge activities. In addition, previewing the passage will help the teachers prepare appropriate, meaningful comprehension stratiegies during and after reading the passage. The comprehension strategies that teachers routinely use to help their English-proficient students are equally effective for ELL students. According to Gibbons, comprehension strategies should "fulfill two major functions: (1) they should help readers understand the particular text that they are reading, and (2) they should help readers develop good reading strategies for reading other texts" (2002, p. 84).

Pre-reading comprehension strategies activate prior knowledge and build context. In order to ensure that ELLs and other struggling readers benefit from before-reading strategies, the tasks within the prior knowledge activities should not require much reading and writing. However, the pre-reading strategies should require student interaction so that students share knowledge, language, and ways of thinking. Some pre-reading strategies that are effective with ELLs at all grade levels are KWLs, prior knowledge surveys, predicting, brainstorming, demonstrations, experiential activities, anticipation guides, word sorts, videos, experiments, discussions, concept maps, and previewing concepts in the students' primary language.

During-reading comprehension strategies should require students to read and interact with the text and help them construct meaning from text, develop fluency, and make connections to the real world. Gibbons (2002) states that the aim of during-reading activities is to make explicit some of the unconscious reading processes and demonstrate the interactive nature of reading. Teachers can design their own and/or use commercially developed graphic organizers (e.g., T-charts, timelines, cause/effect, webs, compare/contrast charts) to help students reflect about the passage, make inferences, draw conclusions, state opinions, identify main ideas, distinguish between fact and fiction, and determine cause and effect. Other during-reading strategies that work well with ELLs are the Directed Reading and Thinking Approach (DRTA), reading "chunks" of passages independently (setting a purpose for reading each chunk), role playing, sentence strips, retelling, and learning logs.

After-reading comprehension strategies help ELL students change receptive vocabulary to expressive, assimilate newly learned information, draw conclusions, improve writing skills, and validate and build upon previous knowledge. Combining the use of word sorts with connect-twos helps readers reflect about how the words are related to the text. After-reading strategies should include asking students to retell newly learned information. Gibbons (2002) states that effective after-reading activities usually require students to keep returning to the text in order to check on specific information or language use. Teachers can use various strategies to help students make connections from the text to real world experiences. The information that students have written in their graphic organizers can now be converted into written paragraphs and reports. Activities such as student self-directed inquiries can extend concepts of the unit and can be differentiated according to students' ELP levels, abilities, and interests. Other after-reading strategies that are effective for ELLs include dictations, poster sessions, paragraph frames for different genres, developing and/or filling out rubrics, reports, culminating performances, paper/pencil tests with supports, reaction guides, and exit slips.

Improving Reading and Writing across the Curriculum

When selecting passages and texts to use when teaching ELLs to read, teachers have often relied on commercially produced ESL textbooks and/ or low-readability passages designed to exemplify discreet language skills that accompany the passages. In other words, the readings are often written in contrived language, not authentic language. ELLs who are learning to read surely benefit from the joys of stories, and it is important that teachers provide interesting authentic texts at appropriate reading levels. However, there are many nuances of the English language in authentic children's literature that can be very difficult for ELLs. Each story has different settings, unique conflicts, and challenging vocabulary. Furthermore, stories often contain cultural references that the ELLs may not be familiar with. Another problem with using only commercially made texts and fiction to teach ELLs to read is that the vocabulary and events in the stories/passages often do not support or reinforce the learning experiences, concepts, and the vocabulary that the children are learning in the classroom.

Effective literacy teachers use nonfiction texts as well as fictional texts to improve reading and writing in all content areas. In addition to appropriately leveled literary texts, teachers can select a mix of trade books about topics that the ELLs have previous knowledge about such as topics they have already learned through comprehensible, hands-on instructional activities. Trade books are usually designed around core state standards and are filled with interesting facts accompanied by illustrations, graphics, and pictures with captions. These literacy cues help readers understand and pronounce the words that they are reading. In this way, the ELLs are using their prior knowledge about the concepts as well as their linguistic skills to comprehend text. Using predictable text and texts about familiar topics helps ELL readers build fluency and sound out known words. The teacher can build on the readers' growing competency by giving them additional trade books about the same topic, gradually increasing the level of difficulty. For these reasons, nonfiction books play a significant role in teaching ELLs to read in English.

Addressing the Needs of Older Struggling English Language Learner Readers

Many teachers find that they have older ELLs (who may not have received initial literacy instruction that matched their needs) who are socially fluent in English but are poor readers. By now, these students may be designated as ELP level 3 or level 4 ELLs; or their oral proficiency may have helped them qualify as general education at-risk students who are struggling readers. Teachers who work with these students can use their oral proficiency and knowledge of the English language to help them improve their reading skills. Teachers can use fiction and nonfiction texts while working with small groups of students with similar levels of reading ability. They can coach them to intuitively use their literacy skills and teach them strategies that help them read difficult passages. The teacher will sometimes want students to read orally, using a variety of oral reading strategies. As students stumble, the teacher can pause to give prompts, allowing time for students to self-correct.

Using a balanced literacy approach for older learners is similar to the model for elementary children. Intermediate and secondary reading teachers can help struggling readers through guided reading groups. They can read and write to their students (read-alouds, journals), they can read and write with their students (LEA, prior knowledge surveys, DRTAs, graphic organizers), and they can use appropriately leveled texts for their students to read independently. If the teacher reads a passage aloud, a copy of the text should always be in front of older ELL students. The teacher will want to pause to point out words that are pronounced differently than they are spelled (e.g., *picked, through, know*). They can stop to explain and clarify when necessary and model strong literacy habits by thinking aloud and pondering about events and information. To get the students reading on their own, teachers will need to start with short, interesting texts that are personally meaningful to older struggling readers who may have previously tuned out during literacy instruction. The teachers should involve the students in previewing stories or passages rather than setting the context themselves. Teachers can ask students to look at the headings, words, and phrases (not just pictures) to predict what the passage will be about. Teachers can ask the students to point out how the headings predict information. They can get the students talking about what they already know about the subject. Prediction activities provide social support among the group members, set context that will help the ELLs comprehend the passage, and provide incentives to read. Asking students to predict what will happen is a great strategy because they will want to find out if they are right.

When asking the students to read independently, the teacher can start with high-interest fiction and nonfiction materials that are at the ELLs' current reading level. By doing so, the readers can see themselves as potentially strong readers. When working with nonfiction texts, the teacher can find a few additional readings about the same topic, moving gradually to higher levels. Here are a few other ways to coach struggling readers to learn to use their metacognitive literacy skills.

- After handing out a reading passage that has been copied onto sheets of paper, the teacher can ask the students to quickly underline or highlight the first sentence in every paragraph. The teacher gives the students a minute or two to complete this task. Then, he/she tells them to read only the underlined/highlighted sentences and turn their papers over when they are finished. When the teacher sees that most of the students have turned their papers over, he/she asks them to predict what the passage will be about and what else they think they will find out when they read the entire passage. After this discussion, the students are asked to read the entire passage to verify their predictions.

- Struggling readers often think about getting the words and sentences right rather than thinking about the text as a whole. Teachers can actively point out introductions, overviews, topic sentences, summaries, and conclusions in nonfiction texts. They can get their students talking about the plot and the characters' motives in fiction books and short stories. With the students, teachers can discuss notions of irony, foreshadowing, and the author's intent. (Older ELLs often have missed these literary practices in earlier grades.)

- After reading a passage, teachers can find specific paragraphs that express big ideas or are especially entertaining and ask the students to chorally re-read these paragraphs. Choral reading of short, interesting passages and re-reading familiar text builds fluency.

- In preparation for a test, teachers can give ELLs several sentence strips that describe the events in a story and ask them to refer to the text to arrange the strips in the correct sequence or on a timeline. This task helps the students skim through the text to find information. Then, the teacher can ask them to talk about the characters' motives and other questions that prepare students for the test. To build fluency, the teacher can ask pairs of students to orally read the strips to their partner.

Struggling readers should not be asked to read text that is at their frustration level; reading text at students' frustration level will not improve their reading skills (Shanahan, 1998; Temple et al., 2010). A huge, daily challenge for teachers of older learners is to find and use appropriate reading passages for their students, who have a wide range of reading abilities. ESL teachers, librarians, and reading specialists can help general education and content teachers find appropriate content texts, trade books, supplemental texts, and ESL materials. However, there will be times when ELLs are faced with text that is too difficult for them to read without guided support. In these situations, round-robin reading, the practice of calling on students to orally read in the classroom, one by one, can be replaced by oral reading for specific, authentic purposes in small group settings. Opitz and Rasinski (2008) share 25 ways that teachers can implement oral classroom reading without resorting to the typical round-robin approach.

It is important that teachers move older struggling readers from reading orally in a group setting to reading silently and independently. First, they can help the students be more successful readers by making sure that the students know the big ideas of the content or story that they are about to read. Also, teachers can read aloud the beginning paragraph of the passage and/or important paragraphs that lead to the big ideas of the lesson. Then, using DRTA, the teachers can divide the passage into "chunks" and ask the students to read each chunk silently. After the group reads the chunk, the teacher can pause to ask questions that will clarify and recap the events. The teachers can then set a different purpose or task for the students (e.g., predicting events, finding specific information, underlining the main idea, circling phrases that predict an event) as they continue to read each additional chunk.

Documenting English Language Learners' Literacy Learning Progress over Time

Many classroom literacy assessments used for English-proficient students are also effective for ELLs as long as teachers take into consideration the ELP level of each student. Teachers can use traditional literacy assessment procedures such as scoring guides and rubrics with a uniform set of criteria to analyze running records, miscues, retellings, writing samples, and recordings of oral readings. They can collect samples of students' work that demonstrate the ELLs' growth in various literacy skills. When these measures are maintained in student portfolios, the ELLs' work will show growth over time as the students improve their skills in literacy and in English proficiency. When the test or task that the teacher uses for the English-proficient students does not match the ELLs' English proficiency level, teachers can use instructional strategies to develop assessment measures. For example, they can use the language experience approach as an assessment by asking ELL students to dictate sentences about what they have just read. Or, they can use a connect-two activity to see if the ELLs understand the relationships of vocabulary words. Many of the recommended readings listed at the end of the chapter offer detailed discussions of assessing ELLs' literacy development.

Using Bilingual Support Staff and Parents to Support English Language Learners' Literacy Development

At all grade levels, bilingual support staff members are valuable literacy resources who can promote English literacy by working with the children in the primary language. Teachers need to be sure that bilingual support staff (assistants, tutors, parent volunteers, and older bilingual students who serve as tutors) recognize that using strategies in the primary language will improve children's literacy in their second language (Hakuta, 1986; Short & Fitzsimmons, 2007). For example, teachers can explain that pre-reading strategies activate prior knowledge and build context and that using these strategies in the primary language will help children comprehend passages written in English. They can explain that by using the primary language, the ELLs can understand, define, discuss, and clarify the meanings of new English words and classroom concepts. Once the words and concepts are known, the students will be more able to practice and use the words in English.

Teachers can ask bilingual assistants, tutors, parent volunteers, and/or older bilingual children to come to the classroom and read aloud interesting, attention-grabbing stories to ELLs in the primary language. Using the ELLs' primary language, the readers can talk about the story with the children and ask them to predict, discuss, and give their own opinions about the story. These classroom discussions will help the children attain a sense of story, improve their primary language vocabulary, learn the joys of reading, and help them create complex sentences in the language that they know. These skills will transfer into English as their proficiency improves. Meanwhile, the ELL students see that their home language is also an important language of learning.

Table 11.3   Teaching Literacy Strategies to Bilingual Support Staff (Assistants, Tutors, Parent Volunteers)

Working with small groups, bilingual support staff can effectively support English literacy development in students' primary language by:

Helping students understand big ideas

sentence frames	anticipation guides
concept maps	learning logs
working with headings and topic sentences	

Developing vocabulary

dictations	word sorts
flashcards	working with sight words
connect-twos	

Activating and building upon prior knowledge

KWLs, prior knowledge surveys	previewing study questions at end of passage
word sorts	predictions
anticipation guides	

Teaching, explaining, and clarifying newly learned concepts

retelling	connect-twos
graphic organizers	word sorts
say something	test preparation

Improving students' writing skills

modeled writing	dictations
learning logs	sentence frames, paragraph frames
converting notes on graphic organizers to sentences and paragraphs	

Encouraging student interaction through cooperative learning structures

roundtable	numbered heads together
jigsaw	think, pair, share

General education teachers, language education teachers, and reading specialists can teach and model effective literacy strategies to bilingual support staff members. In order to provide bilingual teacher assistants with ongoing professional development, they should be assigned to work with specific teachers and, whenever possible, attend workshops with the teachers in order to try out new ideas together and reflect together. Although teachers and assistants may work together on a daily basis, we suggest that the teachers plan quarterly training meetings with the school's bilingual support staff to teach and reinforce the four common classroom practices and share other teaching strategies that they all can use. Table 11.3 lists specific literacy strategies that the teachers can teach to the bilingual support staff members so that they can use the students' primary language to support the ELLs' English literacy development.

When ELLs are learning to read in English, it is important to involve their parents in the process—even when the parents do not know English. Using bilingual support staff as interpreters, teachers can explain to the parents that they can help their children become good readers and writers. The teachers and assistants can encourage the parents to tell stories and read to their children in their home language, explaining that reading stories and content books teaches the children the joys of reading, builds vocabulary, helps children be good listeners, and supports literacy learning in English. Working with the school librarian and a librarian from the public library, the ESL teacher and bilingual support staff can develop a list of suggested children's books in the primary language. The ESL teacher and bilingual assistants can work with the school leadership team to find funding to increase the number of primary language children's literature and content books in the school library. In addition, the ELL parent advisory committee can work with the school's parent organization to raise funds to purchase children's and adult books and magazine subscriptions in the primary language for the classroom libraries. The teachers and assistants can showcase the new books at parent meetings and help the ELLs' parents obtain library cards so that they can also check out books at the public library.

In this chapter, we have shown how ELLs can be actively engaged in literacy instruction in the general education classroom when English literacy tasks are meaningful, functional, and appropriately adapted. We have emphasized that comprehension is the most important element in teaching literacy in English to ELLs. In the next chapter, we focus on teaching academic content to ELLs in mainstream classrooms. Please note that the language and literacy strategies and activities that have been discussed in this literacy chapter (and the previous ESL chapter) are also effective in sheltered academic content instruction.

QUESTIONS FOR REFLECTION AND ACTION

1. Do teachers at the primary grade levels at your school plan specific activities to help the ELLs build oral language proficiency? How do they teach literacy to ELLs in meaningful ways? If initial English literacy instruction does not appear to be adapted for emergent ELL readers, discuss how the information in this chapter can be shared.

2. Do general education and ESL teachers meet regularly to coordinate vocabulary building, ESL instruction, and literacy instruction for ELLs?

3. Are bilingual assistants, tutors, and parent volunteers effectively used to support literacy in the students' primary language? If not, what can be done to encourage collaboration among these educators?

Recommended Readings

Antunez, B. (2002). English language learners and the five essential components of reading instruction. Available at http://www.colorincolorado.org/article/341.

Brisk, M., & Harrington, M. (2007). *Literacy and bilingualism: A handbook for ALL teachers.* Mahwah, NJ: Lawrence Erlbaum Associates.

Cloud, N., et al. (2009). *Literacy instruction for English language learners: A teacher's guide to research-based practices.* Portsmouth, NH: Heinemann.

Hurley, S., & Tinajero, J. (2001). *Literacy assessment of English language learners.* Boston: Allyn & Bacon.

Opitz, M., & Rasinski, T. (2003). *The fluent reader: Oral reading strategies for building word recognition, fluency, and comprehension.* New York: Scholastic, Inc.

Opitz, M., & Rasinski, T. (2008). *Good-bye round robin, updated edition: 25 effective oral reading strategies.* Portsmouth, NH: Heinemann.

Vaughn, S., & Linan-Thompson, S. (2004). *Research-based methods of reading instruction: Grades K–3.* Alexandria, VA: Association for Supervision and Curriculum Development.

Young, T., & Hadaway, N. (Eds.). (2006). *Supporting the literacy development of English learners: Increasing success in all classrooms.* Newark: International Reading Association.

CHECKLIST FOR KEY PRACTICE 10

The checklist is written using measurable statements that can be used to evaluate and monitor language education programs and instruction at the district, school, and classroom levels. The district language education committee and school leadership teams can use the checklist as a diagnostic tool to identify the areas that represent the biggest challenges during the restructuring process. Various teams can use the results of the checklist as a starting point to determine the professional development that educators need to know in order to successfully implement the practices. Teacher teams can use the checklist to evaluate their own teaching practices to recognize ways in which they can immediately make instructional improvements.

SCORING DIRECTIONS:
1 = This practice IS implemented.
2 = This practice is in progress or is in place in some classrooms.
3 = This practice is NOT currently in place.

			The Core Instructional Practices of Every Program for ELLs
			Implementing Meaning-Based Literacy Instruction: Whenever possible, initial literacy instruction is taught in the primary language; when literacy is taught in English, teachers plan and implement meaning-based literacy instruction that builds on students' oral language and uses comprehensible text at appropriate English language proficiency levels.
1	2	3	• Teachers begin instruction by finding out what ELL students already know about literacy.
1	2	3	• Teachers use ELLs' oral language as a pathway to reading and writing.
1	2	3	• Teachers integrate meaningful and functional literacy tasks within the five essential elements of reading using a balanced literacy approach.
1	2	3	• Teachers implement multiple comprehension strategies before, during, and after reading.
1	2	3	• Teachers use nonfiction text as well as fictional stories and passages to improve reading and writing across the curriculum.
1	2	3	• Teachers use appropriately leveled texts and students' knowledge of the English language to help struggling older readers improve their reading skills.
1	2	3	• Teachers document the ELLs' progress in literacy learning over time.
1	2	3	• Teachers use bilingual support staff and ELL parents strategically so they can support the literacy development of ELLs.

IMPLICATIONS AND COMMENTS _____

_____

_____

_____

Implementing Comprehensible Academic Content Instruction

Model and teach academic content using language just above ELLs' current English language proficiency levels, making new information comprehensible using appropriate instructional supports.

- Align instructional activities with district curriculum guides and core state standards.
- Include language objectives as well as content objectives in sheltered instruction lesson planning.
- Differentiate instruction according to ELLs' language proficiency levels.
- Implement specific strategies to help older struggling ELLs learn from their textbooks.

- Use authentic assessment strategies to evaluate ELLs' progress and fulfill grading requirements.
- Develop strategic ways to use the ELLs' primary language to support academic instruction in English.

THE BIG IDEAS

- Effective instruction for English language learners (ELLs) requires that general education and language education teachers use core state standards and English Language Development (ELD) standards to plan and coordinate English as a second language (ESL) and academic instruction.

- Teachers can help their students achieve instructional objectives through differentiated instruction that manipulates classroom resources, time, space, student groupings, processes, products, and assessments.

General education and content teachers in elementary, middle, and high schools know how difficult it is to teach grade-level subject matter to ELLs who spend part of their day in their classrooms. Though highly qualified to teach students who are proficient in English, these teachers may not have learned how to make content area instruction comprehensible for ELLs at different ELP levels. Therefore, ELLs, who in many cases spend the majority of their instructional time in general education classes, are often denied access to comprehensible content area instruction.

Key Practice 11 shows how teachers can adapt or "shelter" academic standards-based content instruction for ELLs by using standards-based big ideas, developing content and language objectives, implementing effective strategies, and using instructional supports that will help the ELLs learn the concepts of the lessons. We give examples of differentiated instruction and assessment according to the ELLs' ELP levels, and we suggest specific strategies that teachers can use to help older struggling ELLs learn from their textbooks. We also demonstrate how general education teachers can plan and implement authentic assessment strategies to evaluate ELLs' learning and fulfill grading requirements. We conclude with strategic ways that teachers can use ELLs' primary language to support academic instruction in English.

Aligning Instruction with District Curriculum Guides and Core State Standards

Effective academic instruction for ELLs requires that general education and content teachers use the core state standards and the ELD standards to plan and implement instruction. We suggest that general education teachers and ESL teachers develop brief planning templates of their units that include the big ideas, objectives, and target vocabulary that the students will be learning. These templates can then be shared. The general education and language education teachers can meet quarterly to discuss the lessons that the children are learning in their respective classrooms. They can discuss how they are implementing the common classroom practices and identify particular teaching strategies (e.g., word sorts, T-charts, rubrics) that they all plan to use in the coming weeks. These collaborative efforts make language and content instruction more comprehensible for the ELLs who spend their days in two (or more) classrooms.

Including Content and Language Objectives in Sheltered Instruction

General education teachers can make their content area instruction comprehensible to ELLs at different ELP levels by using sheltered instruction methods that include the four common classroom key practices (implementing the "big ideas" of themes and topics, providing vocabulary building activities, activating and building upon prior knowledge, and planning and implementing student interaction) and by providing sensory, graphic, and interactive supports throughout their lessons. Lesson plans using sheltered instruction methods can be developed in five stages, as described in the discussion of Key Practice 10. Teachers can shelter their lessons by using visuals, demonstrations, hands-on examples, and other temporary supports that provide scaffolds that make new information comprehensible. They can model and use comprehensible language just above ELLs' current proficiency level, differentiate classroom tasks and assessment activities, and select supplemental materials and reading passages according to the students' ELP levels.

As general education teachers develop their lesson plans, they are accustomed to writing content objectives in various ways, sometimes using specific terminology according to district-adopted formats. Language objectives may have previously been overlooked in the content areas. However, by looking at the content objectives they have developed, teachers can plan and implement strategies to get their students listening, talking, reading, and writing about the concepts that they are learning. Gibbons (2002) suggests that teachers ask themselves several questions to identify the language demands of a particular topic or classroom task. For example, they can ask, "What specific vocabulary does the topic require students to know? What spoken language demands will there be? What listening tasks will there be? What texts will students be reading? What aspects of grammar (e.g., tense) does the topic require?" (Gibbons, 2002, p. 122). Figuring out how they want their ELLs to talk or write about what they learn can help teachers develop language objectives that are connected with their content objectives. Writing language objectives increases the focus on academic language development; the resulting emphasis on language development benefits all of the students in the mainstream classroom.

Previously, we presented language and content objectives in an ESL template about archeology, which we created to coordinate with a future middle school scientific inquiry unit. We share the lesson planning template of the broader seventh grade science unit in Table 12.1. This planning template also includes content and language objectives. The template lists the standards and big ideas that determine the knowledge and skills that the teacher expects the mainstream classroom students to know and be able to do. The content and language objectives express the evidence that will show the desired results. This information helps the teacher select materials and plan target vocabulary. When teachers develop planning templates using this format, they are using the backward design process advocated by Wiggins and McTighe (2005).

As shown on the template, the science teacher has developed two language objectives that are connected to his/her content objectives. The first objective states that the students will *describe* their research project, stating the research question, the steps they took, and their conclusions. Using this language objective as an example, Table 12.2 shows how the science teacher can use the WIDA CAN DO Descriptors to figure out ways that the ELLs in his/her classroom with ELP levels 2, 3, and 4 can meet the objective in light of their English language proficiency. The teacher plans to have the English-proficient students present their research projects orally at a poster session. He/she plans to develop a student-friendly rubric that the students will use to plan their presentations. Guest teachers will use the rubric to evaluate the students' presentations. Using the WIDA CAN DO Descriptors, the teacher reads the language tasks (listening, speaking, reading, writing) that the ELLs can do at each ELP level. Since the unit language

Table 12.1   Sample of Seventh Grade Scientific Inquiry Unit*

Theme/Title of Unit: _Scientific Inquiry (7ᵗʰ Grade)_

Core state standards addressed (Illinois Learning Standards, Science numbers 11 and 13):

- know and apply concepts, principles and processes of scientific inquiry;
- know and apply accepted practices of science;
- know and apply concepts that describe the interaction between science, technology and society.

Big ideas:

- Scientists ask questions that are scientifically testable through investigations.
- Scientists use specific methods to conduct scientific investigations.
- Scientists think critically about experiment results and evidence that they have collected in order to draw conclusions.

Content Objectives	**Language Objectives**
Students will understand the basic aspects of scientific inquiry, e.g., generating hypotheses, collecting evidence, testing hypotheses, and reaching evidence-based conclusions.	At a poster session, the students will *describe* their research project, stating the research question, the steps they took, and their conclusions.
Students will conduct their own science research project using scientific methods.	The students will *write* paragraphs describing ways scientists conduct scientific inquiries (experiments, observations, surveys, and other nonexperimental approaches).

Vocabulary

scientific inquiry, make a hypothesis, testable, investigations, technology, data, evidence, reaching or drawing conclusions, findings, discover, analyze, observe, observations, classify, deduct, determine, establish, analyze, categorize, generalize, estimate, conclude

Materials (Not determined for this example)

*Big ideas and content objectives adapted from: National Instututes of Health (2011), Doing science: The process of scientific inquiry, teachers' guide. Available at http://science.education.nih.gov/supplements/nih6/Inquiry/guide/introduction.htm.

objective requires the student to orally *describe* their projects, the teacher uses the descriptors in the SPEAKING domain to build the language objective for the ELLs using appropriate sensory, graphic, and/or interactive supports for the ELP levels of students in his/her class. He/she sees that, according to the CAN DO chart, the ELP level 4 ELLs should be able to participate in the poster session, but he/she decides to provide support if necessary.

Writing the content and language objectives helps teachers identify the target vocabulary of the unit. The objectives, standards, district curriculum guides, teachers' manuals, and the big ideas will all generate several vocabulary words. In addition, as teachers preview the passages that they will ask their students to read, they will find additional words. In fact, there will be an overabundance of words that the students do not know. So teachers must select valuable words. They can select target vocabulary words, including high-frequency words and phrases which are important

Table 12.2 How to Use the WIDA CAN DO Descriptors* to Develop Language Objectives for English Language Learners

The Language Objective for the English-Proficient Students: At a poster session, the students will ***describe*** their research project, stating the research question, the steps they took, and their conclusions.	
The CAN DO Descriptors that apply to this task: *For the given level of ELP and with visual, graphic, or interactive support, ELLs can process or produce the language needed to:*	*The science teacher adds visual, graphic, and/or interactive supports to scaffold the objective for ELLs:*
Level 2 ELLs • State big/main ideas of classroom conversation • Describe situations from modeled sentences	With teacher guidance, the ELP level 2 ELL students will describe their projects in a small group setting, using sentence frames designed to describe each step of their research project.
Level 3 ELLs • Give brief oral content-based presentations • State big ideas with some supporting details	ELP level 3 ELLs will use sentence frames to plan and present their projects to the teacher or to a small group. They can participate in the poster session if they choose.
Level 4 ELLs • Explain and compare content-based concepts • Explain outcomes • Substantiate opinions with reasons and evidence	ELP level 4 ELL students will use the class rubric to plan and describe their research project at the poster session with teacher support.

*WIDA CAN DO Descriptors from http://www.wida.us/standards/CAN_DOs/Booklet6-8.pdf. Courtesy of the WIDA Consortium, Madison, Wisconsin.

to the concepts they are studying (e.g., make hypotheses, reach/draw conclusions). In addition, they will want to teach the words connected to future readings and lessons. In the scientific inquiry unit, the students will encounter several verbs and phrases that are similar or related to each other:

conduct	observe	analyze	classify
deduct	guess	hypothesize	analyze
categorize	generalize	estimate	conclude
develop a research question	make a hypothesis	review the data	draw or reach a conclusion

When introducing the scientific inquiry unit to the students, the science teacher plans to get the students to talk about the words and phrases in a word sort. This activity helps the students clarify their understanding of these terms. The teacher asks the students to cut out each word/phrase, using one set of words for partners or groups of no more than four students. The assignment is for students to talk about the words and phrases and place them in categories. For example, the teacher can ask the students to place the words and phrases in categories that describe what actions scientists take before an experiment, during an experiment, and after an experiment. It will be difficult for ELLs to understand the nuances and particular usage of these important science words. Therefore, the science teacher can ask the bilingual assistant to do the word sort with the ELLs in a small group setting before the word sort activity is used in English for the whole class. The bilingual assistant can use the ELL's primary language to clarify the meanings and talk about the words as the students manipulate and place them in categories. When older ELLs receive this type of primary language support, they often want to write the words in their own language on the back of the word slip. This is a perfectly acceptable second language vocabulary learning strategy, even though they will be participating in the word sort in English in the whole-group science activity.

Differentiating Instruction According to English Language Proficiency Level

The movement to standards-based instruction (which requires all students to learn the same principles and concepts) highlighted the need for differentiated instruction to ensure effective learning for diverse learners in K–12 classrooms. Differentiated instruction is a broad term that refers to a variety of processes and practices that teachers manipulate to allow for differences in students' learning styles, prior knowledge, interests, needs, and comfort zones (Benjamin, 2003). In order to differentiate instructional tasks and assessment for ELLs, teachers need to get to know their students and find out what they already know and can do. The ESL teacher can often provide this information using the interview process and survey discussed in Key Practice 3. What grade level did the student complete in his/her home country? Is he/she a strong reader? What are his/her interests?

ELP level 1 and level 2 ELLs do not understand instruction in English without visual support (Gordon, 2011). Elementary general education and secondary content teachers can initiate differentiated instruction for these ELLs by using sensory, graphic, and interactive supports. They can start with visuals to introduce new units, themes, and/or concepts. Teachers can find a wealth of videos, pictures, and other images on the Web about almost any curricular theme or content topic. In fact, multiple videos about school topics can be found online often narrated in languages other than English.

General education teachers often differentiate instruction for ELLs by giving them alternate tasks. For example, when the English-speaking students are asked to write paragraphs summarizing information, the ELLs are asked to fill out a structured T-chart. Although this practice is a good one, differentiating instruction requires more than applying a variety of teaching strategies and tasks. Rothenburg and Fisher (2007) state that when teachers know their students' levels of readiness and are aware of their interests and specific learning styles, they can select varied sources, use different processes, and adjust assessment practices to match instruction.

An important way in which teachers differentiate instruction for ELLs is to provide reading materials that match their ELP levels. Fortunately, there are numerous trade books on most curricular topics (at readability levels lower than academic textbooks) available in schools, public libraries, and online. Vocabulary on the topic is often accompanied by visuals and diagrams that make the words and concepts comprehensible. Elementary teachers are accustomed to checking out multiple trade books with lots of pictures, diagrams, and charts. Secondary teachers, who may have previously relied only on textbooks, will find that trade books generally address the same standards that the textbooks do. Furthermore, trade books are often much more engaging than textbooks. When trade books are displayed prominently in the classrooms, students often pick them up, browse through the pages, and read captions, text boxes, and other information.

Tomlinson and McTighe (2006) suggest several elements that teachers can manipulate daily to help their students achieve instructional objectives: time, space, resources, student groupings, instructional strategies, presentation strategies, and student pairings. For example, elementary and secondary teachers can use classroom space to display current vocabulary words, use chart paper to display big ideas of curriculum topics, and use walls to provide word walls, sentence frames, and other writing prompts. Fairbairn and Jones-Vo (2010) emphasize the critical need for teachers to make changes to the processes and products of instruction according to the students' language proficiency levels. Table 12.3 suggests ways that teachers can specifically differentiate instruction and assessment for ELLs.

One of the objectives of the seventh grade science inquiry unit requires the students to understand the basic aspects of scientific inquiry. They will be asked to generate hypotheses, test their hypotheses, and reach evidence-based conclusions. These are demanding linguistic tasks. Using the above chart, the science teacher can get ideas of how to differentiate learning for the ELLs as well as for other English-proficient students who may need differentiated instruction. For example, the teacher can use videos and trade books that clarify the steps of scientific investigation. He/she can prepare a study guide and graphic organizer that guide the students through each step of the project. The teacher can assign a partner to help the ELLs prepare their oral presentations. Instead of a large group presentation, the oral presentations can be presented in small groups in which the group members use rubrics to evaluate their peers.

Table 12.3   Differentiating Instruction and Assessment for English Language Learners*

Elements	Examples, Strategies, Ideas, and Instructional Supports
Sources and Resources	Visuals, videos, video streaming, diagrams, Google images
	Trade books at various reading levels
	Thesauruses, dictionaries designed for ELLs, bilingual dictionaries
	Leveled readers
	Content materials designed for ELLs
	Bookmarked websites in languages other that English
	Realia (real-life objects like maps, globes, yard/meter sticks)
	Illustrations of processes and cycles
	Bilingual assistants/tutors
	Parents and other community human resources
Time	Additional time for tasks
	Increased wait time
	Increased time activating and building upon prior knowledge
	Coordinated time schedules with general education, bilingual/ESL teachers
Space	Equitable school and classroom environments for culturally diverse students
	Rearrangement of seats according to task
	Quiet zones, student work centers
	Word walls, cognate walls, writing prompts, prominently displayed
	Big ideas, sentence frames, paragraph frames, prominently displayed
	Daily homework assignments written on board
Processes	Assigning different tasks and readings according to ELP level
	Frequent use of visuals, visual cues (e.g., gestures, pointing), voice cues (e.g., intonation, volume, pause)
	Decreased speaking rate, dramatization, repeating when necessary
	Use of the primary language to preview, explain, and clarify concepts
	Modeled, shared, and guided writing activities
	Modeled use of graphic organizers
	Increased focus on the big ideas of themes and topics
	Implementing common practices in the classrooms that ELLs attend
	Daily morning message that describes the day's learning tasks
	Connecting student's culture and experiences to tasks
	Sentence frames, paragraph frames, and other language prompts to help ELLs write correct text structures, genres, and academic writing styles (e.g., reports, biographies)
	Cooperative learning structures and strategies
	Shared reading (big books), guided reading
	Asking students to independently read passages one chunk at a time, providing instructional supports and strategies within each chunk
	Increased focus on vocabulary-building activities

Table 12.3 *(continued)*

Elements	Examples, Strategies, Ideas, and Instructional Supports
Student groupings	Planning and implementing student interaction, cooperative learning
	Grouping for purposeful instructional objectives (language practice, social interaction, learning styles, interests, readiness)
	Partners, triads, and small groups
	Grouping by primary language for concept development
Products and Assessments	Matching, sorting, pointing to, categorizing, constructing charts to evaluate ELP level 1 and level 2 ELLs
	Converting instructional strategies to use as assessments to evaluate ELP levels 3–5 ELLs (e.g., paragraph frames, closed word sorts, graphic organizers, connect-twos, learning logs)
	Adding criteria and evidence to instructional strategies to evaluate ELLs (e.g., using checklists or rubrics that match the lesson's objectives)
	Concentrating on student meaning rather than correctness of expression or grammatical form
	Using alternatives to paper/pencil tests (graphic organizers, diagrams, poster sessions)
	Test accommodations

*Sources: Gottlieb et al., (2007); Rothenburg & Fisher (2007); Tomlinson & McTighe (2006); Fairbairn & Jones-Vo (2010).

Helping Older Struggling English Language Learners Use Their Textbooks

Intermediate and secondary content teachers have ELLs of various abilities and ELP levels, including older ELLs who are socially fluent in English. These students often have low literacy levels and have missed major concepts during their previous schooling. Their social fluency masks these gaps as they make friends and become assimilated into the mainstream. However, when they are required to use classroom texts to find and learn new information, they struggle. Here we share three effective ways that teachers can help these students learn from their textbooks: teaching the text backwards, teaching text structure, and using graphic organizers.

Teaching the Text Backwards

Not surprisingly, we teachers find ourselves teaching in ways that we were taught ourselves, especially at the secondary level. We often use the traditional "direct" instructional approach. We begin by teaching new vocabulary and ask students to write sentences with the new words. After that, we ask students to read the chapter and ask them to answer the study questions. Then, as a group, we check the answers to the study questions and have a discussion about the topic. Finally, we ask the students to apply the new knowledge into various contexts. Jameson (2003) suggests that general education and content teachers use a reverse approach which she calls "teaching the text backwards."

When teaching the text backwards, the teacher and students look at the concluding paragraph in the chapter and look over at the study questions. This task helps the teachers set the context and establish the application and relevance of the information in the chapter. The teacher designs activities for students to use oral language and introduces the vocabulary that is essential to understanding the passage. Then, the teacher and students use chapter headings to predict the content of the passage and identify the key concepts and big ideas. After these prior knowledge activities, the teacher asks the students to read the text in "chunks," guiding their reading using appropriate sheltered strategies. Finally, after the students learn the new information, see and hear the new vocabulary words in context, and talk about the new concepts, the teacher finds ways for students to use the newly learned information and academic language through meaningful writing activities.

Teaching Text Structure

Middle and high school curricula become increasingly demanding when independent reading becomes the primary way to learn. Older ELL students may not have learned that science textbooks, newspaper articles, and biographies are organized in specific ways. They may not know the difference between expository text and narrative text. They may not know the characteristics of various genres or how to read charts or how to use a map. ELLs are not alone when it comes to having difficulty finding information in their textbooks—many other struggling learners lack knowledge of text structures. Here are some suggestions to help these students:

- Preview the selection with students and identify the text structure: expository or narrative (fact or fiction, timeline or not).
- Point out and review the many common components of expository and narrative texts (table of contents, index, headings, glossary, prologue, epilogue, etc.).
- Familiarize the students with the many ways that narrative texts are organized (biographies, novels, fairy tales, short stories, first person, etc.).
- Model a teacher-directed think-aloud about how to use a table of contents and index before, during, and after reading.
- Ask students to look up words and concepts in an index to find that information and use a specially designed graphic organizer to list the page number and write notes about the information.
- Ask the class to read only the title and headings of the passage. Then, ask what information they think they will find in the passage. Be sure

to ask them why—the English-proficient students will provide a comprehensible preview of the passage for the ELLs.

- Occasionally, write down the title or heading on the white board. Ask the whole class what important words they think they will find in the passage and why they think these words will be present. Write the words that students suggest on the board. The teacher can also suggest words that might be in the passage, explaining why he/she thinks these words are important. This activity helps the ELL students see and talk about words in isolation before they encounter the words in the passage. The students will feel successful when they see the words that they predicted in the passage.

- After predicting the content of a chapter, place the students in small groups. Ask the groups to go to the end of the chapter and read the study questions. Do the questions suggest that their predictions are correct? Why or why not? Have them report back to the big group. This activity sets the context of the chapter and establishes a purpose for reading.

- Make sure that ELL students understand the meanings of academic language used to direct students to use their textbooks (*find, refer to, locate, skim, summarize, look up, main ideas, topic sentence*). Review and model these particular skills with the whole class.

- Make sure that ELL students understand the meanings of academic language arts skills (e.g., predicting, organizing facts, character analysis, persuasive writing, compare and contrast, making inferences, drawing conclusions).

Implementing Multiple Graphic Organizers

Graphic organizers are visual or pictorial representations of key concepts of a lesson that are visually displayed in ways that help explain the relationships among the big ideas and concepts (Gordon, 2007). Visual charts, graphs, and/or diagrams help students organize facts, ideas, and examples. Graphic organizers are especially useful for ELLs since facts and concepts are written where they are clearly seen rather than embedded in text that is written at higher reading levels than the students' actual reading levels. Filling out the cells within graphs and charts can help ELLs learn and remember vocabulary words because they can see how these academic words relate to the concepts in the other categories and cells. Teachers can select or develop a graphic organizer by determining what big ideas they want the students to understand and by matching the organizer with the way the information in the text is organized. Some passages are clearly made for a cause and effect graphic just as information from another text can be represented best through a timeline. There are multiple websites which contain a myriad of useful applications of graphic organizers. Here are a few more tips about using graphic organizers.

- Be sure that ELL students understand and can use the words that they will need to fill out and report the information that they are recording (e.g., *find, fill in, identify, list, sort, jot down, estimate, outline, organize, rate, give opinions, analyze*).

- Model how to write information on the graphic organizer and also how to refer back to the textbook to review or add information. For example, help them add to their timelines as new events happen.

- Use specific graphic organizers (e.g., compare and contrast, flow charts, timelines) on a regular basis. The ELLs will become more successful as they become familiar with how they are supposed to complete the tasks.

- Share information about how you use a specific graphic organizer with the other teachers who teach the same group of ELLs.

- Create graphic organizers that use headings within the chapter as categories, asking for specific information (big idea, examples, dates, events, etc.).

- After students have several experiences using various graphic organizers, ask them to create their own organizer that represents information in a particular passage.

Asking students to find information and insert information into the cells, diagrams, timelines, and charts is only the first step in using graphic organizers. It is important that oral activities follow so that students have opportunities to retell the information that they have written. In a classic study about cooperative learning, Wood (1987) states that "retelling newly learned information is one of the most powerful study techniques known to psychologists" (p. 12). The teacher can place the ELLs in small, integrated groups and ask the students to share, compare, and edit their information from the graphic organizer with other group members or with a partner. The teacher can set a purpose for the discussion by telling them that after the activity, the students will be writing paragraphs using their own graphic organizers as prompts. The isolated information within graphic cells provides a visual assist as students retell information from the charts. Then, after they have debriefed information in small groups, the students use their graphic organizers to write paragraphs that summarize the information that they have learned. In evaluating the ELL students' written work, the teacher takes their ELP levels into account.

Using Authentic Assessment Strategies to Evaluate Learning

ELLs need to be accountable for the knowledge that they have learned. Teachers can differentiate assessment in order to effectively evaluate and measure their ELLs' progress. Rather than giving ELLs traditional paper-pencil tests, teachers can use various instructional strategies that are appropriate for ELLs at different ELP levels. For example, teachers can figure out ways to ask ELLs with ELP levels 1 and 2 to show what they know by demonstrating, pointing, sorting, drawing, matching, etc. They can ask students to match or write labels on pictures to demonstrate knowledge of vocabulary words. Using a predetermined set of criteria, they can ask students to illustrate a story, read a group LEA activity out loud, and retell information that they have read. Teachers can use paragraph frames, closed word sorts, graphic organizers, and connect-twos for students in ELP levels 3 through 5. All students will be evaluated by the facts and information that the teacher has identified as essential learning. Retelling information by building sentences from words and phrases written within cells of a graphic organizer can also demonstrate that the students comprehend a passage.

Secondary content teachers who have multiple sets of students in various courses generally rely on paper/pencil tests. Therefore, secondary level ELLs need to learn to take written tests since they will be continually exposed to this useful and commonly used assessment. Working together, secondary content and ESL teacher teams can plan ways to teach the specific language of test-taking in the various content areas. They can provide opportunities for ELLs to practice taking tests in low-anxiety settings. Some secondary content teachers may resist differentiating classroom assessments. In this case, ESL teachers can suggest testing accommodations. For example, they can suggest that teachers take the surprise out of tests by providing comprehensible study guides. They can suggest that teachers allow ELLs to retake a portion of a test when it is clear that they did not understand the directions. Also, they can allow ELLs more time to complete written tests by finding a counselor or assistant who is willing to proctor the test completion. The proctor can read the test to older ELLs with low literacy levels and allow the students to dictate their answers to test items. If newly arrived ELLs have been in school regularly in their home countries, teachers can allow them to use their bilingual dictionaries.

Gottlieb suggests differentiating assessment data to tackle the question, How do I grade ELLs? She suggests a system for grading ELLs that capitalizes on students' strengths at the various ELP levels. In her system, an ELL can earn a total of 100 points. These points are earned in four subcategories of student data: performance on assessment of learning standards, self-assessment, teamwork/personal responsibility, and motivation/effort. A maximum number of points in each subcategory depends on the student's ELP level. The idea is that the various components of students' grades are the same for all students in the class; the difference is in how the components are weighed according to each student's ELP level. For

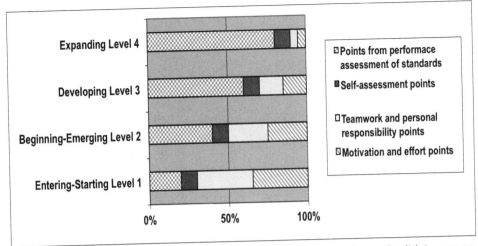

FIGURE 12.1   System for Grading English Language Learners According to English Language Proficiency Level. Gottlieb, M. (2006) Assessing English language learners: Bridges from language proficiency to academic achievement. Thousand Oaks, CA: Corwin Press. Used with permission of the publisher.

students beginning to learn English, more of their grade is determined by activities that focus on their oral language production, how they take responsibility to learn, and how they work with others. As their English develops, the focus shifts more and more to points earned on performance-based assessments. Figure 12.1 illustrates how students' grades can be calculated using Gottlieb's system. The system can be used for grading projects as well as assigning end-of-term grades for report cards (Gottlieb, 2006).

Planning Strategic Use of the Primary Language to Support Instruction in English

In Key Practice 4, we share ways that bilingual assistants and tutors (and in some cases bilingual English-proficient peers) can effectively use the primary language to support ELLs' learning in their English-speaking classrooms. These strategies, ideas, processes, and other tips can be used as a menu of options to help elementary and secondary teachers figure out more specific ways that they can ask primary language support staff to support content learning. As general education and secondary content teachers build their units and plan their lessons, it is important that they share planning templates containing the big ideas and the objectives of the unit with the ESL teacher and bilingual assistants. The completed template serves as an executive summary of what the students are learning. The teacher and the assistant can use the template to identify the concepts and vocabulary that can be best introduced or learned through the students' primary language.

Administrators can facilitate the effective use of primary language support by making sure that mainstream teachers who have ELLs in their

REFLECTIONS FROM THE FIELD

Planning Primary Language Support
Joe Smith, Science Teacher

Mr. Smith, the seventh grade science teacher shares a bilingual assistant with four seventh and eighth grade teachers who also have ELLs in their classrooms. The teachers have established a schedule for the bilingual assistant, Miss Garcia. Miss Garcia only works with the ELL students in Mr. Smith's science class two days a week. Therefore, Mr. Smith uses the unit planning template to figure out the most important ways that Miss Garcia can help the ELLs complete the tasks and meet the objectives of the unit. The science teachers collaborate monthly with the ESL teacher, so he knows that the ELLs in his seventh grade science class completed the ESL archeology unit last semester. He meets briefly with the ESL teacher to talk about the objectives for the scientific inquiry unit. They discuss how Miss Garcia can be used most effectively. They decide that she should preview the unit by having students share what they already know about scien-tific investigations. Miss Garcia should point out that some scientists conduct experiments to investigate a question and other scientists, like archeologists, use existing data to make observations and reach conclusions. After the archeology unit, most of the ELLs are familiar with some of the vocabulary; however, there are new ELLs who were not present during the archeology unit. They decide that Miss Garcia should use a word sort to refresh and clarify the scientific terms in the primary language. Mr. Smith points out that there are multiple websites that provide ideas for student science projects so he will ask Miss Garcia to do some searches with the ELLs (in Spanish as well as in English) to explore project topics. The ESL teacher suggests that Miss Garcia can also search the Web for videos in Spanish that focus on the processes of scientific inquiry.

classrooms have access to bilingual support personnel or have bilingual assistants assigned to their classrooms. Bilingual assistants should not follow individual students' schedules but should be assigned to work with specific teachers. General education and secondary content teachers who have substantial training in sheltered instruction can work with the ESL teacher to teach the assistants how the students' primary language can be used without direct translation to implement specific strategies. For example, the teacher and assistant can search for information in the primary language on multiple sites on the internet that can reinforce and explain concepts that the students are learning in English. In Reflections from the Field, *Planning Primary Language Support,* we provide an imaginary scenario about how the seventh grade science teacher effectively plans primary language support in his scientific inquiry unit.

At this point in the book, we have discussed eleven of the twelve key practices. We have shown how language education and mainstream teachers can use the four common classroom practices and sensory, graphic, and interactive supports to effectively implement ESL, literacy, and academic instruction. We have discussed the importance of developing appropriate common assessments and we have shared ways in which the primary language of ELLs can be used as a valuable learning resource. In the next chapter, we discuss the twelfth key practice: how the language education committee can use all of this information to develop and/or restructure the district's language education program configurations in ways that meet the needs of the district's ELL student populations.

QUESTIONS FOR REFLECTION AND ACTION

1. Look at the district curriculum guide, teacher's guide, or your lesson plans to locate the content objectives in an upcoming unit or theme. Using one of the objectives, develop a language objective that will enable your students to talk or write about what they have learned. Then, using the WIDA CAN DO Descriptors, figure out how the ELLs in your classroom can meet this objective. First, use a language function (describe, tell, make a list); then, provide an instructional support (visuals, teacher's guidance, graphic organizer) as you develop the language objective for various levels.

2. Review and discuss the differentiated instruction suggestions (see Table 12.3). Which of these suggestions have you implemented? With your study group, discuss ways to improve your current lesson plans by manipulating space, resources, processes, grouping, and products for the ELLs and other diverse learners in your classroom.

Recommended Readings

Coggins, D. et al. (2007). *English language learners in the mathematics classroom.* Thousand Oaks, CA: Sage Publications.

Cruz, B., & Thornton, S. (2008). *Teaching social studies to English language learners.* New York: Routledge.

Echevarria, J. et al. (2007). *Making content comprehensible for English learners: The SIOP model.* Boston: Allyn-Bacon. (3rd Edition)

Fairbairn, S., & Jones-Vo, S. (2010). *Differentiating instruction and assessment for English language learners: A guide for K-12 teachers.* Philadelphia: Caslon Publishing.

Freeman, Y., & Freeman, D. (2008). *Academic language for English language learners and struggling readers: How to help students succeed across content areas.* Portsmouth, NH: Heinemann.

Gibbons, P. (2002). *Scaffolding language, scaffolding learning: Teaching second language learners in the mainstream classroom*, Portsmouth, NJ: Heinemann.

Gottlieb, M. et al. (2007). Understanding the WIDA English language proficiency standards: A resource guide. Madison: University of Wisconsin. Available at http://www.wida.us/standards/Resource_Guide_web.pdf.

Hill, J., & Flynn, K. (2006). *Classroom instruction that works with English language learners.* Alexandria, VA: Association for Supervision and Curriculum Development.

Jameson, J. (2003). *Enriching content classes for secondary ESOL students.* Washington, D.C.: Delta Systems Co., Inc.

Marzano, R., Pickering, D., Pollack, J. (2004). *Classroom instruction that works: Research-based strategies for increasing student achievement.* Upper Saddle River, NJ: Prentice Hall/Pearson.

Rosebery, A., & Warren, B. (Eds.). (2008). *Teaching science to English language learners: Building on students' strengths.* National Science Teachers Association.

Rothenberg, C., & Fisher, D. (2007). *Teaching English language learners: A differentiated approach.* Upper Saddle River, NJ: Pearson.

WIDA Consortium. (2009). WIDA's CAN DO descriptors. Madison: University of Wisconsin. Available at http://www.wida.us/standards/CAN_DOs/index.aspx.

CHECKLIST FOR KEY PRACTICE 11

The checklist is written using measurable statements that can be used to evaluate and monitor language education programs and instruction at the district, school, and classroom levels. The district language education committee and school leadership teams can use the checklist as a diagnostic tool to identify the areas that represent the biggest challenges during the restructuring process. Various teams can use the results of the checklist as a starting point to determine the professional development that educators need to know in order to successfully implement the practices. Teacher teams can use the checklist to evaluate their own teaching practices to recognize ways in which they can immediately make instructional improvements.

SCORING DIRECTIONS:
1 = This practice IS implemented.
2 = This practice is in progress or is in place in some classrooms.
3 = This practice is NOT currently in place.

			The Core Instructional Practices of Every Program for ELLs
			Implementing Comprehensible Academic Content Instruction: Teachers model and teach academic content using language a little above the ELLs' current English proficiency levels, making new information comprehensible by using appropriate instructional supports.
1	2	3	• Instructional activities are aligned to district curriculum guides and core state standards.
1	2	3	• Teachers include language objectives as well as content objectives in sheltered instruction lesson planning.
1	2	3	• Teachers differentiate instruction according to ELLs' language proficiency levels.
1	2	3	• Teachers implement specific strategies to help older struggling ELLs learn from their textbooks.
1	2	3	• Teachers use authentic assessment strategies to evaluate ELLs' progress and fulfill grading requirements.
1	2	3	• Teachers develop strategic ways to use the ELLs' primary language to support academic instruction in English.

IMPLICATIONS AND COMMENTS _____

_____

_____

_____

PART IV

Organizing the Key Practices into Effective Program Configurations

KEY PRACTICE 12 Structuring the Language Education Program

Organize the instructional program for ELLs to effectively meet the literacy, academic, and language needs of the district's ELL population.

Well-planned language education program structures are instrumental in implementing effective instruction for English Language Learners (ELLs). In this final chapter we show how all of the key practices can be effectively woven into comprehensive language education program configurations. We describe how a district-wide language education committee can work and learn together to design or restructure language education programs to ensure maximum opportunities for ELLs to reach high levels of English language proficiency, achieve grade-level literacy skills, and acquire academic knowledge. We provide descriptions of how various program configurations can be implemented in elementary and secondary schools with varying number of ELL students. This lengthy chapter provides information and examples that the language education committee needs to take on the challenge of restructuring and developing comprehensive language education programs.

Structuring the Language Education Program

Organize the instructional program for ELLs to effectively meet the literacy, academic, and language needs of the district's ELL population.

- Establish a district language education committee to develop or restructure the language education program.

- Determine the extent of the use of the ELLs' primary language according to the specific needs of the district's ELL student populations.

- Identify how the three core instructional practices (ESL, literacy, and academic content instruction) will be implemented in the new or restructured program configuration.

- Prepare program recommendations through a process that defines the purpose of the language education program, grounds the program in standards, includes short- and long-term professional development plans, and shares information with parents and other stakeholders.

- Monitor the new or restructured program by annually assessing professional development needs and reviewing student data to evaluate the ELLs' progress.

THE BIG IDEAS

- A well-planned language education program is instrumental in implementing effective instruction for English language learners (ELLs).

- By working and learning together, language education committee members can design or restructure language education programs to ensure maximum opportunities for ELLs to reach high levels of English language proficiency, achieve grade-level literacy skills, and learn academic content.

- Structural program changes are most effective when the language education committee encourages principals and school leadership teams to participate in the restructuring process.

Effectively meeting the literacy, academic, and language needs of the district's ELL population requires planning, implementation, and evaluation. We begin our discussion of Key Practice 12 by emphasizing the importance of establishing a district language education committee that is charged with developing or restructuring the language education program. Then we describe the steps that the language education committee can follow to plan effective program configurations that address the preceding eleven key practices. The first step includes several learning processes: studying and reviewing the research in the field, identifying the needs of the district's ELL population, and reviewing the current programs. Then, the committee must determine the extent of the use of the ELLs' primary language according to the ELLs' needs and identify how the three core instructional practices (ESL, literacy, and academic content instruction) will be implemented in the new or restructured program configuration. The next step is to prepare program recommendations through a process that defines the purpose of the language education program, grounds the program in standards, includes short- and long-term professional development plans, and shares information with parents and other stakeholders. The last step in the process is implementing and monitoring the new or restructured program by annually assessing professional development needs and reviewing student data to evaluate the ELLs' progress.

There is no one-size-fits-all program type that all districts or schools can implement to address the needs of their ELLs. However, as we have shown throughout this book, there are key practices that district, school, and teacher leaders can follow as they develop program configurations that are appropriate for their schools and community. In this chapter, we provide several promising program configuration models to help the committee (assisted by principals and school leadership teams) explore programming options. Within these discussions, we provide several recommendations for elementary and secondary programs. We also discuss the role of the language education committee during the implementation of the newly developed or restructured programs.

Establishing a District Language Education Committee

The goal of the language education committee is to design or restructure language education programs that will ensure maximum opportunities for ELLs to achieve grade-level literacy skills, grade-level academic knowledge, and reach high levels of English language proficiency. We recommend a three-phase process, which roughly parallels the Castañeda v. Pickard federal court case ruling of 1981 that establishes a three-part test for evaluating districts' language education programs.

During the first year (phase one), the committee meets monthly to read and discuss this book, learn what the laws and research have to say about educating ELLs, and review and evaluate the current program. Then, the committee members can develop the goals and purposes of the language education programs, make changes and/or reconfigure instructional approaches, and prepare recommendations to present to the school board.

The following year (the implementation phase), the committee monitors the new program, reflects about how things are working, and refines

Table 13.1   Outline of Language Education Committee Phases and Tasks

Phase	Members and Meetings	Tasks	Castañeda v. Pickard Standards (1981 Court Ruling)
Phase 1: Strategic Planning	Representatives of various stakeholder groups meet monthly.	Review research about educating ELLs, evaluate current program, conduct data analysis, develop action plans, make recommendations.	Services for ELLs must be grounded in educational theories recognized as valid by experts in the field.
Phase 2: Implementation	Same committee members (as in Phase 1) meet every other month.	Monitor the program implemented across the district, analyze data, solve problems, refine professional development, provide human resources, and instructional resources.	The program must be implemented with an adequate amount of resources (staff, materials, time, and professional development).
Phase 3: Ongoing Analysis and Evaluation	One third of the committee rotates out and is replaced with new representatives for that stakeholder group; committee meets 2-4 times per school year.	Review data and refine language education programs; at any time, revisit phases one and two due to data analysis or significant changes in ELL populations.	The program must be evaluated and if the desired results are not being attained, then the program should be adjusted or restructured to ensure that the ELLs' language barriers are overcome.

professional development needs. Typically in this phase, the committee meets every other month. During the final phase, year three and beyond, the committee meets two to four times a year to review and analyze the district's demographics and assessment data to determine program effectiveness and tweak the program's structure. It should be noted that this third phase continues indefinitely because the program should be engaged in a continuous cycle of review and improvement—like all district programs. In fact, if there are significant changes in the student demographics, legal requirements, or district curriculum, the language education committee can decide to revisit phases 1 and 2. Table 13.1 outlines the three phases.

After the committee has met several times during the first year to discuss the key practices, learn what the laws and research recommend about educating ELLs, and evaluate the current program, they are ready to take on the challenge of developing or restructuring the districts' language education program configurations at the elementary, middle, and secondary levels. In the following pages, we suggest several processes to guide the team's tasks.

Preparing Student Demographics

One of the first steps in creating or restructuring a program is to identify and sort all of the ELLs in the district. As stated previously, recently arrived ELLs are relatively easy to count; identification of language-minority students born in the U.S. is problematic. The assessment strategies, templates, and suggestions provided in Key Practice 3 can help ESL and bilingual teachers conduct a thorough count. Once the ELLs are assessed, identified, and counted, they should be categorized according to their English language proficiency (ELP) levels using the state-adopted ELP definitions and procedures. (Reminder: in this book, we use the criteria set forth in the WIDA ELP performance definitions.) Next, the ELLs at each ELP level should be counted and sorted by language groups and by grade levels within each school in the district. The *Sample of English Language Learners Student Demographics Template,* following this chapter, represents a sample template that can be completed for each school.

Using additional copies of the student demongraphics template, the committee should record student demographics for the past several years to determine any trends of growth, stability, or decline of the ELL student population numbers. Comparing and contrasting the district's academic achievement data with the ELP data is a worthwhile task at this point as well. Often the ELP data will serve as a lens for understanding the academic achievement data. For example, an ELL who has not yet attained a ELP level of 5 or higher (grade-level English proficiency) will have difficulty understanding the test and, therefore, difficulty meeting grade-level expectations on a state academic achievement test that is given in English. This data analysis process will set the stage for programmatic decisions and short- and long-term program development planning and evaluation for the school district.

Reviewing Current Programs and Practices

After becoming familiar with the district's ELL student populations, the language education committee will be ready to begin a review of the current program. The purpose of this step is to collect information that will allow the committee to complete the Twelve Key Practices Checklist. First, the members of the committee can interview a sampling of the current language education (ESL and/or bilingual) teachers and several mainstream classroom teachers that have ELLs in their classrooms at the elementary, middle, and high school levels. The basic interview questions are the following:

1. How are the ELL students currently learning to read and write (primary level) or improving their literacy skills (intermediate level and beyond)?

2. How are they learning grade-level academic concepts?

3. How are they acquiring academic language proficiency in English?

As the interviewers talk with the teachers, they can use the template *Current Practices: Language Education Program Template*, to record the information they gather. The committee members' knowledge of the twelve key practices will make them keen observers. For example, if literacy instruction is taught in English in mainstream classrooms, the interviewers will want to know how instruction is adapted to provide meaningful reading and writing activities for ELLs. They will want to know how content area instruction is adapted for ELLs and if subject area instruction is based on the core state standards. They will want to know if the ELLs are actively engaged in comprehensible learning activities throughout their school day.

When the committee gets together to discuss the information they receive from the interviews, they will have gained authentic information about the structure of the current program services. The committee will undoubtedly find that the answers to these questions vary greatly in different buildings and at primary, intermediate, and secondary levels. Based on this information, the committee may decide to develop a survey to collect information from all certified staff members in the district who work with ELLs.

Surveying Teachers with English Language Learners in Their Classrooms

The language education committee can develop a written survey for all teachers who have ELLs in their classrooms. In districts with fewer than 50 ELLs, the survey can be constructed in an open-ended format with the same three questions discussed previously as the conceptual focus of the survey. Each question can be followed by these prompts: "What is working?" "What is not working?" These open-ended questions can provide valuable insights into the challenges of educating ELLs across the district. Or, in larger districts, in order to facilitate the process, they can use the Twelve Key Practices Checklist to create a survey. Rather than using the entire checklist, the committee can develop one or two locally appropriate questions from each key practice area. To encourage teachers to participate in the survey, we recommend that the survey questions fit on one sheet of paper. Using a website to create a survey and tabulate responses will facilitate the entire process (e.g., SurveyMonkey™).

Armed with the interview information and the survey results, the committee will be ready to discuss and summarize their findings about their current program. The Twelve Key Practices Checklist will serve as a quantitative tool for summarizing this data. The checklist can be discussed and completed at a language education committee meeting. The results will provide a needs assessment for the program restructuring process and indicate professional development needs. Effective language education planning should include wide participation of educators at the district, school-wide, and classroom levels. Therefore, the results of the interviews, surveys, and checklist can be shared at a meeting with principals and the district's language education professional learning community (PLC) teams. The rich discussion about the district's strengths and challenges will influence and enhance the language education committee's work.

Becoming Familiar with Typical Program Approaches for English Language Learners

The language education committee can review the research about educating ELLs to find program approaches that most closely match the needs of the district's ELL student population. In other words, the task is to develop research-based approaches that are locally appropriate. As stated previously, there are various labels that traditionally have been used to describe language education programs that serve ELLs. The most common bilingual education approach is called a transitional bilingual education (TBE) program. TBE programs usually provide primary language instruction for one to three years and then transition the students into English-speaking classrooms. Comprehensive, late-exit TBE programs provide primary language instruction for up to six or seven years, and the certified bilingual teachers work closely with mainstream teachers who are also trained in sheltered instruction methods. Dual-language programs are long-term bilingual programs that continue to provide primary language *instruction* in addition to English instruction throughout the student's entire education.

Language education programs that use English as the language of instruction have traditionally been called English as a second language (ESL) or English for speakers of other language (ESOL) programs. In comprehensive ESL programs, certified ESL teachers work closely with mainstream teachers who are trained in sheltered instruction methods. In some districts, ESL programs use *only* English as the language of instruction. However, in many comprehensive ESL programs, administrators and teachers have recognized the value of providing primary language *support* (especially for ELLs with beginning ELP levels) through the use of bilingual adults as teacher assistants and/or tutors.

Determining the Role of the Primary Language in District Program Configurations

As the language education committee begins the task of exploring program options, they need to determine the extent of the use of the ELLs' primary language in the new or restructured elementary and secondary program configurations according to the specific needs of the district's ELL student populations. To increase the number of educators involved in making recommendations about the use of the primary language, the committee can engage other members of the PLC teams in this important task. The *Factors to Consider about Implementing Primary Language Instruction and/or Primary Language Support Template*, provides questions that can help committee members determine which use of the primary language is most appropriate for their specific ELL student populations: primary language support or primary language instruction.

Structuring Program Configurations around the Core Instructional Practices

To determine how instruction in ESL, literacy, and academic content will be implemented, the language education committee must figure out what language of instruction will be used in each area. This is especially important in the early grades, in which children learn to read and write. Emergent readers who have successful literacy experiences will see themselves as successful learners, creating a jumpstart for academic success (Miramontes et al., 2011). Therefore, we recommend that ELP levels 1, 2, and 3 ELLs in the primary grades receive literacy instruction in their native language. If this is not possible, they will need meaning-based literacy instruction in English. In addition, primary language support can support their literacy development in English. We present our recommendations about language use and instructional methods in elementary classrooms in Table 13.2. In this table, we show how planners can reduce the language demands in order to make instruction comprehensible in the three core instructional practices: implementing ESL instruction, implementing meaning-based literacy instruction, and implementing comprehensible academic content instruction. These program components are the heart of language education programming. When these three areas are appropriately implemented, the big picture practices (providing equitable school and classroom environments, addressing challenges through collaboration, designing and using a balanced assessment system, and embracing an additive bilingualism perspective) can be appropriately addressed.

Constructing Program Configurations to Match English Language Learner Needs

The reality is that the program types, program models, and program labels vary significantly from district to district throughout the United States and Canada. For this reason, we suggest that the language education committee create its own program configurations. First, they must consider the literacy and academic backgrounds of their specific ELL language group(s). Then committee members can decide if they will provide primary language instruction in bilingual classrooms or if they will provide primary language support in English-speaking classrooms. The resources at the end of this chapter can help with these tasks.

Table 13.2 Recommended Language Use for the Three Core Key Instructional Practices According to English Language Proficiency Levels of English Language Learners in Kindergarten–Fifth Grade

The Three Core Instructional Practices	Recommended Language of Instruction and Assessment	
Key Practice 9. English as a Second Language Instruction: Plan and implement daily ESL instruction in the four language domains (listening, speaking, reading, and writing), focusing on the academic language needed to understand and express essential grade level concepts.	ELP Levels 1–2	ESL Instruction (natural approach) and ESL Instruction (content-based)
	ELP Levels 3–4	ESL Instruction (content-based)
	ELP Level 5	ESL Instruction (content-based) and/or grade-level English instruction*
Key Practice 10. Meaning-Based Literacy Instruction: Whenever possible, begin literacy instruction in the primary language; when literacy is taught in English, plan and implement meaning-based literacy instruction that builds on students' oral language and uses comprehensible text at appropriate English language proficiency levels.	ELP Levels 1–3	Primary language whenever possible; meaning-based instruction using primary language support
	ELP Levels 4–5	Meaning-based instruction and/or grade-level English instruction
Key Practice 11. Comprehensible Academic Content Instruction: Model and teach academic content using language a little beyond the ELLs' current English proficiency levels, making new information comprehensible by using appropriate instructional supports.	ELP Levels 1–2	Primary language whenever possible; sheltered content instruction with primary language support
	ELP Levels 3–4	Primary language and/or sheltered content instruction
	ELP Level 5	Sheltered content instruction and/or grade-level English instruction

* Grade-level English instruction refers to providing classroom instruction and assessment at a level of English typical for that grade level, without language supports (sensory, graphic, or interactive supports), that is, without the use of sheltered instruction.

As the planners design program configurations, they must stop to consider how they will implement the other key practices within the structural configurations that they are considering. This step includes figuring out the time periods for the three core practices and figuring out how to provide the additional time needed to implement all of the key practices in the proposed program structures. For example, they will have to figure out how to provide time for teachers to plan and coordinate the four common classroom practices (providing vocabulary-building activities, planning and implementing the "big ideas" of themes and topics, activating and building upon prior knowledge, and planning and implementing student interaction). Table 13.3 suggests specific questions to help them with this task.

As the committee members prepare to construct program configurations, they will reflect about what they have learned and discuss the challenges identified on the Twelve Key Practices Checklist. Some of the committee members may want to visit programs in other school districts with

Table 13.3   Incorporating Sufficient Time to Successfully Implement Key Practices

Key Practice	TIME CHALLENGES
1	Will the program configuration allow ELLs to be actively engaged in learning throughout their school day?
	Will the mainstream teachers who have ELLs in their classrooms have substantial training (more than 5 days) in sheltered instruction?
2, 3, 9, 10, 11	Will language education teachers and mainstream teachers who share ELL students have structured time to share assessment responsibilities, coordinate instruction, learn from each other, solve problems, and have purposeful and reflective conversations?
9, 10, 11	Will the language education and mainstream teachers have time to coordinate instruction and assessment?
9	Does the program configuration allow the ESL teacher to teach English language development every day for 30–50 minutes, depending on age and ELP level?
4, 10	Does the program configuration allow enough time (two-hour block) for ELLs to develop reading and writing skills through comprehensible literacy instruction (taught either in primary language or in English using a meaning-based approach)?
10, 11	If the ELLs will be receiving literacy and content instruction in English in general education classrooms, is additional time planned for the ESL teacher or bilingual teacher to work with ELP levels 1 and 2 ELLs to support literacy and academic instruction?
2, 5, 6, 7, 8	Will language education and mainstream teachers have time to collaborate as they develop and implement the four common classroom practices?

similar student demographics. Undoubtedly, the learning experienced through the committee processes will make them wise observers as they visit other programs. The committee should also be sure that they are familiar with their state's rules and regulations regarding ELLs and review the state's English language development standards and assessment practices. The language education committee can meet with principals and school leadership teams to discuss options, share opinions and provide a forum to try to figure out some tentative program configurations that align with the twelve key practices. The *Long-Term Language Education Program Planning Template* and the *Program Configuration Templates* can guide their discussions.

Formulating Short- and Long-Term Language Education Action Plans

In many districts, the language education committee will want to make some immediate changes. For example, they will want to make changes necessary for the district to be in legal compliance with state and federal mandates. They may want to provide more time for the ESL and bilingual teachers to work with the ELLs with limited prior schooling. In order to make short-term general improvements to their existing program structures, the committee can find the program description in this chapter that most closely resembles their current program and find ways to maximize the strengths and minimize the challenges listed after the program's description. The *Short-Term Action Plan Template* can be used for short-term action planning.

Long-term programming action plans for specific buildings, language groups, and/or grade levels will require a more comprehensive approach. Since most school districts have ELLs with different literacy levels, diverse backgrounds, and varying levels of English at all grade levels, it is quite likely that the language education committee will implement more than one program approach. For example, a large school district may have a large number of ELLs in one language group, a large number of older ELL students who arrive in secondary schools with limited schooling and low literacy in their first language, and a few ELLs in grades K through 12 from many diverse language groups. These districts will need to look at each of these groups at the primary, intermediate, and secondary levels. As stated previously, program planners can start by planning how the three core instructional practices (ESL, literacy, and academic content instruction) will be implemented in the new or restructured program configuration, according to the needs of the specific groups. The *Long-Term Language Education Program Planning Template* can be used for long-term planning for the language education programs.

Constructing Program Configurations

In the following several pages, we provide descriptions of various promising elementary and secondary program options. The descriptions include how ESL, bilingual, and mainstream classroom teachers divide responsibilities for teaching literacy, academic, and ESL instruction according to the ELLs' ELP levels and the number of ELLs served in schools. We list the strengths and challenges of these program options and provide some general recommendations. We believe that the language education committee can implement the twelve key practices in these promising configurations. However, in addition to the program descriptions that we provide, we suggest that the committee read about various language education program approaches described in texts listed in the Recommended Readings section at the end of this chapter.

Elementary Language Education Program Options. Regardless of the program label or program approach (e.g., ESL or bilingual program), the language and academic needs of ELLs in grades K through 5 are primarily addressed in four different structural configurations: (1) self-contained classrooms, (2) resource classrooms, (3) pull-out programs, and (4) push-in programs. The language education teachers are either certified bilingual teachers or certified ESL teachers.

In a self-contained classroom, approximately 15 or more ELLs stay in the classroom for most of the day with a certified bilingual or ESL teacher who teaches all content area subjects as well as ESL instruction. In a resource classroom, a certified bilingual or ESL teacher teaches fewer than 15 ELLs from two to three grade levels (e.g., grades 3-4, grades 3-4-5) for half of their school day. In a pull-out program, an ESL or bilingual teacher pulls out ELLs individually or in small groups for a shorter duration, often in an office or a small space. The pull-out teacher teaches ESL and, in some schools, helps the ELLs understand content instruction taught in mainstream classrooms. A resource classroom is different from a pull-out classroom because formal literacy instruction is taught by a certified bilingual or ESL teacher. Also, the resource classroom serves as the ELLs' homeroom, and the bilingual or ESL teacher determines when the ELLs have the English proficiency and literacy skills to succeed in particular subjects in the general education classroom. In a typical pull-out classroom, the teacher's schedule determines when the ELLs are pulled out for ESL instruction, and the pull-out sessions are usually conducted for less than one hour. In a push-in program, a bilingual or ESL teacher works directly in the general education classroom. Of course, in all of these elementary-level configurations, we recommend that the general education teachers have substantial training in sheltered instruction.

Elementary Bilingual Education Programs. In many elementary bilingual programs, ELLs in grades 1 to 3 are served in full-day self-contained classrooms where they can be active, engaged learners in all subject areas. The full-day primary self-contained classroom allows the certified bilingual teacher to teach literacy in the primary language in a two-hour literacy block, teach ESL, and teach standards-driven academic content. The bilingual teacher plans instruction in both the primary language and English, often planning units that integrate language development and content instruction. The bilingual teacher is responsible for teaching to the state content standards and language development standards. The students are integrated with their English-speaking grade-level peers for social activities and instruction in art, music, physical education, and computer education.

By the third or fourth grade, many of the ELLs have reached ELP levels 4 and 5. Therefore, there are usually fewer ELLs with levels 1, 2, and 3 in the intermediate grades. For this reason, a bilingual resource classroom often serves ELLs from two to three grade levels, i.e., grades 3–4, grades 4–5, or even grades 4–6 (Table 13.4).

In bilingual self-contained and resource classrooms, literacy is taught in the primary language for ELP levels 1, 2, and 3 ELLs. The transition from primary language literacy to English literacy instruction occurs gradually in the bilingual classroom, initiated by the bilingual teacher. At the intermediate grade levels, the ELLs with ELP levels 4 and 5 spend increasing amounts of time in general education classrooms as they are able to succeed in particular subjects (initially math and science). Newly arrived

Table 13.4   Strengths and Challenges of Elementary Bilingual Self-Contained Classrooms and Resource Classrooms

STRENGTHS	CHALLENGES
• Initial literacy is more fully achieved when children can construct meaning in their L1.	• Bilingual and general education teachers must make sure that ELLs have multiple opportunities to interact with English-speaking peers and teachers.
• Content instruction can be parallel to district curriculum and core state standards.	• The bilingual classrooms should have equal status as general education classrooms and not be seen as remedial.
• ESL instruction can be aligned and integrated with content area instruction.	
• Appropriate primary language materials and resources in literacy and in content areas are readily available for high-incidence language groups.	• The main criterion for transitioning ELLs out of L1 should be their English language proficiency level, not the students' grade level or years in program.
• The children's cultures and prior knowledge are integrated into classroom tasks.	• Bilingual teachers must strategically plan the use of L1 and L2.*
• Gradual transitioning practices can be planned and implemented.	• Bilingual teachers should participate in grade-level team planning and curriculum development.
• Parents can be more involved in the children's learning because they can communicate with their children's teachers.	• Bilingual classrooms must contain abundant literacy and content books, charts, and other materials in two languages.
• Students who arrive late in the year are easily absorbed.	
• Classroom environments are language rich in two languages.	

* L1: primary or first language; L2: second language (English).

third, fourth, and fifth grade ELL students with limited literacy will spend most of their day in the bilingual resource classroom. The primary language instruction will improve their literacy skills, provide immediate access to grade-level content, and support English language development. Bilingual teachers and general education teachers who share teaching and assessment responsibilities for ELLs need to collaborate regularly to maximize instruction in both classrooms. Through their collaborative efforts, they can plan integrated social and academic activities so that all children have opportunities for cross-cultural friendships as well as ensure that ELLs are not isolated from their English-speaking peers. When general education teachers have substantial training in sheltered instruction methodology, all twelve key practices can be successfully implemented in comprehensive bilingual programs. Detailed descriptions of two promising elementary bilingual programs are found in Table 13.5.

Elementary English as a Second Language Programs. In elementary schools where bilingual programs are not an option, certified ESL teachers can make literacy and content meaningful and comprehensible in ESL self-contained or ESL resource classrooms. A full-day primary self-contained classroom allows a certified ESL teacher to teach meaning-based English

Table 13.5 Bilingual Education Program for Grades K through 5*

Promising Program for Schools with 20–50 ELLs from One Language Group and Small Numbers from Other Language Groups

1–2 Bilingual Teacher(s)	Integrated Time	General Education Classroom Teachers
Bilingual teacher serves as an ESL teacher when working with students from other language groups.	ELLs are grouped with their fluent English speaking peers.	Courses are taught by general education teachers with substantial ESL training.
• Daily ESL instruction	• Physical Education	• English Literacy for ELP level 5
• Primary language literacy for students from predominant language group with ELP levels 1–3	• Fine Arts	• Math
• Meaning-based English literacy for ELP levels 1–4 for students from low incidence language groups	• Music	• Science
• Support for content area instruction through primary language support	• Recess	• Social Studies
	• Technology	*Bilingual assistant can be scheduled to provide primary language support in content areas.*

Promising Program for Schools with more than 50 ELLs from One Language Group and Small Numbers from Other Language Groups

2 or more Bilingual/ESL Teachers**	Integrated Time	General Education Classroom Teacher
One of the certified bilingual teachers serves as an ESL teacher when working with students from other language groups	ELLs are grouped with their fluent English speaking peers	Courses are taught by general education teachers with substantial ESL training
• Daily ESL instruction	• Physical Education	• English Literacy for ELP level 5
• Primary language literacy for predominant language group with ELP levels 1–3	• Fine Arts	• Math for ELP levels 4 and 5
• Meaning-based literacy for ELLs with levels 1–4 and students from low-incidence languages	• Music	• Science for ELP levels 4 and 5
• Math, science, social studies provided in primary language for predominant language group, levels 1–3, and some 4s	• Recess	• Social Studies for ELP level 5 and some 4s
• Sheltered content instruction for other language groups	• Technology	*Students gradually transition into the general education classroom according to established transition criteria.*
		Bilingual assistant can be scheduled to provide primary language support.

* General education subject area instructional schedules must be coordinated across grades in order for the program model to operate successfully.

** The number of ESL teachers needed will depend on the number of ELLs served.

Table 13.6 Strengths and Challenges of Elementary English as a Second Language Self-Contained and Resource Classrooms

STRENGTHS	CHALLENGES
• Where there are ELLs from many different language backgrounds at similar grade levels, ESL self-contained and resource classrooms are more effective than pull-out programs. • Daily ESL instruction can be integrated with literacy and content instruction. • Formal literacy instruction in English can be comprehensible to ELLs and taught with appropriate methodology. • The big ideas of content instruction can be parallel to district curriculum and core state standards. • Transition into general education classes can be gradual and planned. • Appropriate content-based ESL materials and resources in literacy and in content areas are readily available. • The ELLs' diversity is recognized and their cultural experiences are integrated into lessons. • ESL classroom environments recognize the diversity of the learners and their ELP levels; walls and tables are filled with appropriate language prompts and trade books.	• ESL and general education teachers must plan and implement multiple opportunities for ELLs to interact with English-speaking peers. • When implemented without primary language support, even with sheltered instruction, ELP level 1–2 ELLs will have trouble understanding many concepts. • ESL teachers should participate as equal partners in grade-level team planning and curriculum development. • ESL and general education teachers must value and support the ELL children's primary language in order for the children to maintain and improve their L1 skills. • The ELLs' parents will have difficulty communicating with their children's teacher. • It will be difficult for the additive bilingualism key practice to be fully implemented in this classroom model.

literacy instruction in a two-hour literacy block, teach ESL, and teach standards-driven academic content through sheltered instruction. Resource classrooms at the intermediate level can be blends of two or even three grade levels, as described previously. When districts with small ELL student populations provide half-day ESL resource classrooms for K-5 ELLs and provide substantial training in sheltered instruction for general education teachers, the children can be active, engaged learners for most of their school day. This is a great improvement over pull-out programs in which ESL teachers pull out students for too little time to effectively support academic content and literacy instruction in addition to teaching ESL (Table 13.6).

In an ESL classroom approach, the ESL teacher is responsible for teaching to the core state standards and the ELP standards. The teacher can plan comprehensible instruction, targeting academic vocabulary and planning thematic units that integrate language and content instruction across all subject areas. While many of the twelve key practices can be successfully integrated in ESL classrooms, the key practices of teaching meaning-based literacy and using the primary language as a valuable re-

Table 13.7 English as a Second Language Program for Grades K through 5

Promising Program for Schools with 1–50 ELLs from Various Primary Language Groups

1–2 ESL Classroom Teacher(s)

- Daily ESL instruction
- Meaning-based literacy instruction in English for ELP levels 1–3 in schools with 20 or more ELLs
- Sheltered instruction in math, science, social studies for ELP levels 1–3 in schools with 20 or more ELLs
- Support for content instruction for levels 4 and 5 or when all ELLs receive content instruction in general education classroom

Bilingual assistant can be scheduled in ESL classroom to provide primary language support. *

Integrated Time

ELLs are grouped with their fluent English-speaking peers.

- Physical Education
- Fine Arts
- Music
- Recess
- Technology

General Education Classroom Teacher

Courses are taught by general education teachers with substantial ESL training.

- Meaning-based literacy in English for ELP levels 1–4 (in schools with fewer than 20 ELLs)
- English Literacy for ELP levels 4 and 5
- Math
- Science
- Social Studies

Bilingual assistant can be scheduled to provide primary language support during literacy and/or content instruction.

Promising Program for Schools with More than 50 ELLs from Various Primary Language Groups

2 or more ESL Teachers**

Self-contained ESL classrooms are formed when there are enough students

- Daily ESL instruction
- Meaning-based literacy taught in English for ELP levels 1–4
- Sheltered Math for ELP levels 1–3
- Sheltered Science for ELP levels 1–3
- Sheltered Social Studies for ELP levels 1–4

Bilingual assistant can be scheduled to provide primary language support.

Integrated Time

ELLs are grouped with their fluent English speaking peers

- Physical Education
- Fine Arts
- Music
- Recess
- Technology

General Education Classroom Teachers

Courses are taught by general education teachers with substantial ESL training

- English Literacy for ELP level 5
- Math for ELP levels 4–5
- Science for ELP levels 4–5
- Social Studies for ELP levels 5

Students transition into the general education according to district transition criteria.

* When primary language support is provided by assistants rather than bilingual teachers, the students are considered to be in an ESL program.
** The number of teachers depends on actual ELL student enrollment.

source will be a challenge for ELP level 1 and 2 ELLs. In school districts with very few ELLs scattered throughout grades K to 5, program planners usually determine that general education teachers will teach initial literacy to ELLs rather than ESL teachers. When this is the case, it is extremely important that the general education teachers receive training in sheltered instruction methodology and meaning-based literacy instruction. It is important to remember that ELLs who have not been to school regularly and appear to be far behind their grade-level peers will not thrive in English-only classrooms. Detailed descriptions of two promising elementary ESL programs are located in Table 13.7.

Secondary Language Education Program Options. The language education committee and secondary school leadership teams have a difficult challenge to try to develop programs for secondary ELLs with a wide range of diverse needs. Secondary program planners can start by figuring out how to offer ESL courses and required content courses for the ELLs. We suggest that secondary ELLs receive two periods of daily ESL instruction. These two classes should not focus on one topic taught in a double period. The focus of instruction should vary in both classes. Using the core state standards and English language development standards to plan English instruction, both ESL courses can help ELL students learn the academic language they will need when they enroll in departmental content courses. For ELLs with intermediate ELP levels 3–4, instruction in one period can be aligned with language arts standards and articulated with English language arts courses, using materials and literature appropriate for the ELLs' ELP levels. The corresponding course can focus on academic language needed to succeed in a required or popular elective academic course. Although these classes are focused on language development, the curriculum can be aligned with the big ideas of various departmental course offerings (e.g., Consumer Education, World Geography, and Earth Science). Both types of ESL courses should award English language arts credits to ELLs who have completed required assignments.

Secondary program planners also must provide courses required for graduation taught through comprehensible approaches. These courses can be taught in three different ways: (1) a required course can be taught in the primary language; (2) a required course can be taught by an ESL teacher who is also certified in the content area; and (3) a required course can be taught in a designated section by a content teacher who has received substantial ESL training. When district administrators and teachers provide at least two of these options, secondary ELLs can be actively engaged learning the content that the state has deemed required knowledge.

Nonsequential courses can be alternated or rotated over a two- or three-year period. When required courses are rotated, ELLs may not take a particular course during the grade level that it is customarily taught. For example, in many states, juniors take U.S. History; however, ELLs may be taking it as sophomores or seniors. Full credit should be awarded to ELLs who have completed required course assignments.

It is also important that ELLs have access to the many interesting elective courses that high schools offer. Therefore, program planners must plan ways that ELLs can have comprehensible sheltered instruction in the basic course of popular electives within each department. For example, drafting is often a prerequisite course for other industrial arts courses, such as auto mechanics or graphic design. ELLs should be clustered in a designated section of drafting taught through sheltered instruction so that the students will learn the language of architectural drawing and understand the information they will need in order to have access to the other departmental courses. Some schools provide primary language support in the basic courses using English-proficient bilingual students who are enrolled in advanced levels of the course. These student tutors use their "free period" to earn a half credit by serving as tutors in prerequisite courses to explain and clarify concepts for the ELLs.

Secondary program planners need to prepare a scope and sequence framework of courses that provides course offerings for ELLs for multiple years (three to five years). The scope and sequence chart can include several middle and high school courses, including electives, which are alternated with other courses from year to year. A well-planned multi-year secondary program sequence ensures that ELLs with beginning English proficiency levels will have opportunities to take courses in which they can be successful learners and earn credit toward graduation requirements. In the following pages, we suggest four potentially promising secondary language education programs: two bilingual programs and two ESL programs, differentiated by the number of ELLs in the school. In all of the promising programs, the course titles in the tables are labeled to resemble typical required courses and typical electives. Program planners must change the course titles to align the bilingual and/or ESL program courses with their local course offerings and requirements.

Secondary Bilingual Education Programs. A secondary school with 20 or more ELLs from a single language group (in addition to students from low-incidence language groups) can initiate a bilingual education program that includes ESL courses, content courses taught in the primary language of the predominant language group, and content courses taught in English by teachers with substantial training in sheltered instruction. ELLs at all grade levels and all language groups are placed together for ESL classes, according to their ELP levels. The bilingual teachers can teach required courses (e.g., Earth Science, Biology, Health, U.S. History, Government, and Economics) within their certification. The bilingual teachers, who teach content mostly in the primary language, are responsible for providing instruction that is parallel to district curriculum guidelines and core state standards. In many districts, there will be situations in which the

Table 13.8 Strengths and Challenges of Secondary Bilingual Language Education Programs

STRENGTHS	CHALLENGES
• ELLs at all grade levels and from all language groups can have two periods of ESL designed for their ELP levels.	• Scheduling ELLs into ESL and bilingual courses and singleton sections of many different courses in different class periods is problematic.
• Literacy improvement can be addressed in courses taught in the primary language and in the ESL courses.	• Mainstream content teachers may need help finding appropriately adapted materials, trade books, and other resources.
• New ELLs in predominant language group with ELP level 1 and level 2 will have immediate access to required content courses through primary language instruction.	• Content teachers in several different departments must have training in sheltered instruction methods.
• ELLs receive required instruction in classrooms where they have opportunities to be actively engaged.	• Language-rich environments are not always available in secondary content classrooms, especially when teachers do not have their own assigned classrooms.
• ELL students can plan coursework leading to graduation.	• On-going professional development on key practices topics will help sustain quality instruction in all areas.
• Textbooks and supplementary materials are available in many high-incidence languages.	
• Newly transferred ELLs who have social English fluency but are behind academically will benefit from sheltered instruction in designated sections.	
• Limited English parents can communicate regularly with their children's teachers.	
• The prior experiences, knowledge, and cultures of ELLs are utilized and valued.	

bilingual teachers do not have certification in specific content areas and therefore are not qualified to teach certain courses. In these situations, it may be possible for the bilingual teacher and a content teacher to team teach the course. It may also be possible to assign a bilingual assistant to work with a secondary content teacher in a designated class section (Table 13.8).

Courses taught by content teachers with training in sheltered instruction can serve the low-incidence language groups as well as the intermediate-level ELLs identified as having social English fluency but low literacy and academic skills. ELL students can be integrated for physical education and, as their English proficiency allows, many elective courses with English-proficient students.

In secondary bilingual language education programs, primary language literacy and language arts instruction are often implemented through world language programs, formerly known as foreign language programs. Historically, the students taking foreign language classes have been English-speaking students learning a second language for the first time. Currently, since the language needs of native speakers are totally different from the English-speaking students learning a new language, many world language departments have revised their curriculum by offering additional language courses for ELLs, such as "Spanish for Native Speakers." Today, world language programs value and promote bilingualism by serving English-speaking students studying a new language, recently arrived ELLs, continuing students who were enrolled in two-way immersion (dual-language) programs at the elementary level, and language-minority students who want to improve their heritage language.

Detailed descriptions of two promising secondary bilingual programs are provided in Table 13.9. The first secondary bilingual education program described serves 20 to 50 ELLs from one language group (and a small number of ELLs from other language groups). Secondary schools with fewer than 20 ELLs from one single language group can provide primary language instruction by adding a half-time bilingual teacher to the secondary ESL program (Table 13.10). The second secondary bilingual education program is designed for schools with more than 50 ELLs from one language group (and several ELLs from other language groups) (Table 13.11).

In order to comply with federal law that mandates that teachers be highly qualified in their content area, schools with 20 to 50 ELLs will require two or more ESL and bilingual teachers. The tables suggest specific courses; however, districts must select courses and adapt teacher loads according to the certifications held by their bilingual and ESL teachers. These configurations provide literacy instruction in ESL classroom settings, offer content instruction in the primary language taught by certified bilingual teachers, and offer sheltered content courses taught by content teachers with substantial ESL training.

We recognize that secondary schools with small ELL populations often have limited choices for course offerings. Therefore, as shown in the promising program configurations, we recommend looping the curriculum in middle school content courses when there are small numbers of ELLs. Rather than offering sixth grade science, seventh grade science, and eighth grade science, a designated, looped section of standards-based science can serve ELLs in all three grades. Newly arrived ELLs can be easily absorbed into a standards-based looped curriculum that is implemented during a three-year cycle.

In secondary schools with large numbers of ELL students (more than 50), ESL teachers and bilingual teachers can be hired with content certifications that match the coursework needs of the ELLs. Simply stated, the more ELLs a school has, the more sophisticated the program can be. For example, courses such as Spanish for Native Speakers can be taught by a bilingual teacher or a world language department teacher, depending on the teachers' certifications. Teachers in large secondary bilingual programs can successfully plan and implement the twelve key practices. The fortunate ELLs that arrive in schools with well-planned comprehensive bilingual

(*text continues on page 223*)

Learners from Other Language Groups

Middle Schools (Grades 6, 7, 8)

1 or 1.5 ESL Teacher(s)	1.5 or 2 Bilingual Teacher(s)	Content Teachers
ESL courses are taught using content-based ESL methodology.	Bilingual courses are mostly taught in the primary language with planned use of sheltered English.	Courses are taught content teachers with substantial ESL training.
ESL I (ELLs in all grade levels with ELP levels 1–2)	Standards-based math for ELLs with limited formal schooling	Sixth grade math*
ESL II (ELLs in all grade levels with ELP level 3)	Sixth and/or seventh grade math (as determined by student counts) or	Seventh grade math*
ESL III (ELLs in all grade levels with ELP levels 4–5)	Seventh and/or eighth grade math (looped)	Eighth grade math*
ESL Literacy (ELLs in all grade levels with ELP levels 1–3)	Science (looped, multi-grade)	ELL reading (designated section for ELLs with ELP levels 4–5)
ESL U.S. History rotated annually with other locally appropriate content-based ESL courses	Social Studies (looped, multigrade)	Sheltered Science (as determined by student counts)
		Sheltered Social studies (as determined by student counts)
		Bilingual assistant can be scheduled to assist content teachers.

High Schools (Grades 9–12)

1 or 1.5 ESL Teacher(s)	1.5–2 Bilingual Teacher(s)	Content Teachers
ESL courses are taught using content-based ESL methodology.	Bilingual courses are mostly taught in the primary language with planned use of L1 and L2.	Courses are taught in designated sections by teachers with substantial ESL training.
ESL I (ELLs in all grade levels with ELP levels 1–2)	Pre-Algebra	Algebra
ESL II (ELLs in all grade levels with ELP level 3)	Algebra	Sheltered Required Science Course (rotated annually with other science course)
ESL III (ELLs in all grade levels with ELP levels 4–5)	Health	Sheltered Required Social Studies course (rotated annually with other social studies course)
ESL Literacy (ELLs in all grade levels with ELP levels 1–3)	Earth Science (rotated annually with Biology)	Driver's Education (when possible)
Content-based ESL course	U.S. History (every other year)	ELL Reading (for ELLs with ELP levels 4–5)
	Government (rotated annually with Economics)	Spanish for Native Speakers (if not taught by bilingual teacher)
	Spanish for Native Speakers (in schools with 20+ Spanish-speaking language-minority students)	*Bilingual assistant can be scheduled to assist content teachers.*

* for ELLs with ELP levels 4–5 and ELLs in low-incidence languages

Table 13.10 Secondary English as a Second Language Program

Promising Program for Schools with 1–20 English Language Learners from Multiple Language Groups

MIDDLE SCHOOL

1 ESL Teacher	Content Teachers
ESL courses are taught using content-based ESL methodology (looped, multi-grade)*	Courses are taught by content teachers with substantial ESL training.**
ESL I (ELLs in all grade levels with ELP levels 1–2)	Designated Sections:
ESL II /III (ELLs in all grade levels with ELP levels 3–4)	Sixth grade math
Transition ESL (ELLs at all grade levels with ELP level 5)	Seventh and/or eighth grade math (looped)
ESL Social Studies or	Exploratories (fine arts, vocational education, etc.)
ESL Science* (rotated annually with other course)	Science (looped, multigrade)
	Social Studies (looped, multigrade)
	Designated linguistically demanding content courses as needed
	ELL Reading (designated section)

ELL students are placed in designated sections that often include general education students. A trained bilingual assistant can be assigned to work with teachers in designated classes to provide primary language support.

HIGH SCHOOL

1 ESL Teacher	Content Teachers	
ESL courses are taught using content-based ESL methodology*	Courses are taught by general education teachers with substantial ESL training.**	
ESL I (ELLs at all grade levels with ELP levels 1–2)	Designated Sections:	Algebra
ESL II /III (ELLs at all grade levels with ELP levels 3–4)	Pre-Algebra	Social Studies
Transition ESL (ELLs at all grade levels with ELP level 5)	Health/Consumer Economics (1s/2s)	Science
Sheltered U.S. History* (or other required content course which is linguistically and academically demanding.	Computer Education (every other year)	Government (every other year)
	U.S. History (every other year)	
	ELL Reading (designated section)	
	Driver's Education or Keyboarding (or other required content course that is linguistically and academically demanding, alternated yearly)	

ELL students are placed in designated sections that often include general education students. A trained bilingual assistant can be assigned to work with teachers in designated classes to provide primary language support.

MIDDLE SCHOOL

1.5 or more ESL Teachers*

ESL courses are taught using content-based ESL methodology (looped, multi-grade).

ESL I (ELLs at all grade levels with ELP levels 1–2) or

ESL II (ELLs at all grade levels with ELP level 2)

ESL III (ELLs at all grade levels with ELP level 3)

ESL IV (ELLs in all grade levels with ELP level 4)

Transition ESL (ELLs at all grade levels with ELP level 5)

ESL Literacy (ELLs at all grade levels with ELP level 1–4)

ESL Standards-based Social Studies** all grade levels, ELP levels 1–3

ESL Standards-based Science,** all grade levels, ELP levels 1–3

Content Teachers

Courses are taught by content teachers with substantial ESL training.

Designated Sections:

ELL Reading (ELLs with ELP level 5)

Sixth grade Math

Seventh grade Math

Eighth grade Math

Exploratories (fine arts, vocational education, etc.)

Standards-based Science, levels 4–5

Social Studies (looped, multigrade) levels 4–5

Designated linguistically demanding content courses as needed

A trained bilingual assistant can be assigned to work with teachers in designated classes to provide primary language support for predominant language groups. An ESL assistant can be assigned to help other ELLs.

HIGH SCHOOL

1.5 or more ESL Teacher*

ESL courses are taught using content-based ESL methodology (looped, multi-grade)

ESL I (ELLs in all grade levels with ELP levels 1–2)

ESL II (ELLs in all grade levels with ELP levels 2–3)

ESL III (ELLs in all grade levels with ELP level 4)

Transition ESL (ELLs at all grade levels with ELP level 5)

ESL Literacy (all grade levels)

Sheltered U.S. History** (and other required content courses which are linguistically and academically demanding).

Content Teachers

Courses are taught by content teachers with substantial ESL training.

Designated Sections:

Pre-Algebra   Algebra

Health/Consumer Economics (1s/2s)   Social Studies

Computer Education***   Science

U.S. History***   Government***

Driver's Education or Keyboarding alternated yearly with other required content course that is linguistically and academically demanding

A trained bilingual assistant can be assigned to work with teachers in designated classes to provide primary language support.

---

* The number of ESL teachers needed will depend on the number of ELLs served.

** ESL teacher must have certification in this area.

*** This course can be rotated every other year in schools with less than 30 ELLs.

Table 13.11 Secondary Bilingual Education Program

Promising Program for More Than 50 English Language Learners from One Language Group (and Several English Language Learners from Other Language Groups)

MIDDLE SCHOOL

ESL Teachers*	Bilingual Teachers*	Content Teachers
ESL courses are taught using content-based ESL.	Courses are mostly taught in the primary language with planned use of English (L2).	Courses are taught by content teachers with substantial ESL training.
ESL I (ELLs at all grade levels with ELP levels 1–2)	Standards-based math for ELLs with limited formal schooling	Designated Sections of:
ESL II (ELLs at all grade levels with ELP level 3)	Sixth grade Math	Math at various levels
ESL III (ELLs at all grade levels with ELP level 4)	Seventh grade Math	General Science (looped, multigrade for ELLs in low-incidence language groups)
Transition ESL (ELLs at all grade levels with ELP level 5)	Eighth grade Math	Exploratories (fine arts, vocational education, etc.)
ESL Literacy	Social Studies	Reading (for ELLs with ELP levels 4–5)
ESL Social Studies	Science	Computer Education/Keyboarding
or other locally appropriate content-based ESL courses	Spanish for Native Speakers (2 levels)	

HIGH SCHOOL

ESL Teachers*	Bilingual Teachers*	General Education Content Teachers
ESL courses are taught using content-based ESL.	Required courses are mostly taught in the primary language with planned use of English (L2).	Designated sections: Courses are taught by general education teachers with substantial ESL training.
ESL I (ELLs in all grade levels with ELP levels 1–2)	Pre-Algebra	Advanced math courses
ESL II (ELLs at all grade levels with ELP level 3)	Algebra	U.S. History
ESL III (ELLs at all grade levels with ELP level 4)	Geometry	Health (alternated with another one-semester course)
Transition ESL (ELLs at all grade levels with ELP level 5)	Health/Consumer Economics (1st & 2nd sem.)	Biology; alternated with Earth Science
ESL Literacy	Two or more science courses	Government/Economics
Other locally appropriate content-based ESL courses	U.S. History	Keyboarding/Typing, alternated with Computer Education
	Government/Economics	Reading for ELLs (designated section)
	Spanish for Primary Speakers or Heritage Language classes (2 titles)	Spanish for Primary Speakers, Heritage Language, 2 levels
	Driver's education (when possible)	Popular electives such as Drivers Education, Drafting
	Other locally appropriate required courses	

(text continued from page 218)

programs have optimal opportunities to progress successfully toward graduation. Comprehensive secondary bilingual education programs can allocate certified ESL, bilingual, and content teachers to provide instruction that actively engages ELL students from one specific language group as well as several ELLs from other language groups.

Secondary English as a Second Language Programs. Secondary ESL programs are often implemented in middle and high schools with small numbers of ELLs in states where policy makers have set restrictions on the use of primary language instruction or where bilingual certified teachers are not available. When administrators and teachers in these programs recognize that the use of the primary language is a valuable resource, they realize that ESL programs do not have to be English-*only* programs. Schools that have ELP level 1, 2 and 3 ELLs can consider hiring bilingual assistants and/or bilingual adult tutors that can be assigned to provide primary language support in designated content sections, especially in required courses. The noncertified bilingual assistants should not follow individual students' schedules but should be assigned to work in specific content courses under the supervision of specific teachers with ESL training. The ESL and content teachers should work together to plan and implement the training of the assistants, including how the primary language can be used (without direct translation) to support learning.

Detailed descriptions of two promising secondary ESL programs are described previously in Table 13.10. This table demonstrates how ESL and sheltered content courses can be implemented in secondary schools with fewer than 20 ELL students and in schools with more than 20 ELL students. The number of ESL teachers needed will depend on the number of ELLs at the school. Even where there are few ELLs, they must be appropriately served; therefore, at least one ESL teacher will be needed. In some districts, there will be situations in which the ESL teacher does not have certification in specific content areas and therefore is not qualified to teach certain courses. In these situations, it may be possible for the ESL teacher and a content teacher to team teach the course. In schools where there are very few ELLs, the designated sections for ELL students will also serve general education students. Some of the nonsequential courses may not be offered every year so courses must be alternated yearly or rotated in a three-year cycle. It is important to mention that this program can only be effective if content teachers receive substantial ESL training. While many of the twelve key practices can be implemented in designated content classrooms, the key practices of teaching meaning-based literacy and embracing additive bilingualism will be a huge challenge, especially for the teachers of secondary ELLs with levels 1 and 2 English language proficiency (Table 13.12).

As the language education committee works with secondary program planners, they realize that using the twelve key practices to guide their

Table 13.12 Strengths and Challenges of Secondary English as a Second Language Programs

STRENGTHS	CHALLENGES
• When there are only a few ELLs from many different language backgrounds at one school, this model appears the most feasible and efficient.	• New ELLs with ELP level 1 and level 2 will have trouble understanding many concepts and may not be active, engaged learners.
• Literacy improvement can be addressed in ESL classrooms.	• ELLs who arrive with low literacy levels and are far behind in academic knowledge will have difficulty learning at the secondary level when primary language instruction is unavailable.
• In many of their content classes, ELLs receive comprehensible sheltered instruction.	• Limited English parents cannot communicate regularly with their children's teachers.
• ELL students, who come with social English fluency but are behind academically, will benefit from the sheltered instruction in designated sections.	• Scheduling ELLs into ESL and single sections of many different courses in different class periods is problematic.
• Content-based ESL materials and resources are readily available at all ELP levels.	• Mainstream content teachers may need help finding appropriately adapted materials, trade books, and other resources.
• The ESL teacher can find ways to value the ELLs' primary language and culture.	• Many content teachers in several different departments must have training in sheltered instruction methods.
	• Language-rich environments are not always available in secondary content classrooms, especially when teachers do not have their own assigned classrooms.
	• On-going professional development on key practices topics will help sustain quality instruction in all areas.

decision-making is more challenging than at the elementary level (see Table 13.10). The ELLs are enrolled in so many different courses in so many departments that it becomes difficult for mainstream and language education teachers to collaborate on a regular basis. Short-term professional development can be arranged to introduce and provide training in the Key Practices according to the roles of the certified staff members. Principals, assistant principals, department heads, and counselors can receive training on implementing key practices 1, 2, and 4 (school and classroom environment, collaboration, and additive bilingualism). Content teachers can receive training in key practices 3, 10, and 11 (student assessment, literacy, and content area instruction). In addition, all teachers can receive training about implementing the four common classroom practices. Long-term professional development can focus on providing on-going training in sheltered instruction.

Preparing Program Recommendations through a Comprehensive, Collaborative Process

After the language education committee has studied the program options and has developed program configurations that they believe are appropriate for their district, school, and community, they need to prepare program recommendations through a process that defines the purpose of the language education program, includes short- and long-term professional development plans, and shares information with parents and other stakeholders. First, they need to clarify the philosophy about educating ELLs that has guided their decision-making. They can engage the representatives from the ELL-focused PLC (principals, school leadership teams, various teacher teams) in this process. As a large group, the teams can compose a philosophy statement that encompasses the district's values and responsibilities about educating ELLs.

Defining the Purpose and Philosophy for the Language Education Program

The philosophy statement and the purpose statement that the teams develop must align with the restructured configurations. For example, if the district's purpose statement is, "the purpose of the language education program is to ensure that all ELLs develop literacy, academic knowledge, and English language proficiency in classroom environments which value diversity," the committee must make sure that enough time is allotted to teach effective literacy development, academic content instruction, and academic English language instruction. The committee must also provide professional development about cultural diversity and equitable school environments. The *Developing Philosophy and Purpose Statements for Educating English Language Learners Template* is designed to help establish a philosophy and define the purpose for the language education programs that the committee is recommending. Although we offer specific suggestions, the committee should make their philosophy and purpose statements locally appropriate by using language that matches the district's mission statement for all students.

Grounding the Language Education Program in Standards

District decision-makers often struggle with the allocation of limited resources, particularly when changes to their program require more time, more teachers, better materials, and increased costs. Grounding program decisions in standards provides the anchor that will secure the increased ELL academic performance that district personnel have been searching for. Standards-based instruction for ELLs refers not only to core state standards but to English language development (ELD) standards and language arts standards in English and, in some states, primary language standards. The language education committee can provide opportunities for professional development about standards-based instruction that provides a common language for district educators to discuss language proficiency levels of ELL students.

The vision of standards-based instruction is not limited to classroom instruction. Texts and supplementary materials that are purchased for ELLs should be linked to core state standards and ELD standards. The WIDA Consortium has designed the Protocol for Review of Instructional Materials for ELLs (PRIME). This protocol assists publishers in correlating materials to the ELD standards. (Completed PRIME inventories can be viewed online.) Copies of the state's ELD (or, in some states, ELP) standards and resource guides should be available to all teachers who work with ELLs. Professional development and time for mainstream and language education teachers to collaborate can be provided to ensure that instruction for ELLs is coordinated and aligned with standards.

Developing Short- and Long-Term Professional Development Plans

Throughout the restructuring process in year 1 (phase 1), the committee can begin addressing professional development needs for various stakeholder groups. The first priority is to initiate professional development that is essential to successfully implement the twelve key practices in the newly restructured programs. Providing training in sheltered instruction for mainstream teachers who have ELLs in their classrooms is paramount. As stated previously, we define substantial sheltered instruction methodology training as training that is similar to a graduate course, consisting of more than five all-day sessions at least one week apart so that participants can practice and reflect about what they have learned. At the elementary level, it is helpful to have at least one teacher at each grade level trained in sheltered instruction methodology. At the secondary level, targeting two or more teachers within every secondary department or division will help train the teachers who will teach designated course sections for ELLs. We provide a detailed chart that matches educators' roles to multiple professional development topics. The language education committee can immediately begin to arrange professional development opportunities for the topics that have high priority for different groups of stakeholders.

If the district plans to initiate primary language instruction/support for the first time, district personnel need to understand the concept of additive bilingualism and learn how primary language instruction facilitates English language development, helps children learn to read and write, and helps them learn academic concepts. If the restructuring plan calls for additional bilingual support staff, training should be arranged on the topic of effective use of bilingual assistants and tutors.

Informing Parents and Community

As the committee develops or restructures programs for ELLs, they must inform the language-minority parents and the community. The community member and parent who have served on the committee will be able to provide insights into the best time, place, and format for a parent meeting. Meetings with parents of ELLs should always begin by building relationships. Committee members can introduce themselves and ask questions about the families' countries, geographic areas, and schools. Then, after getting acquainted, the committee can inform the parents about how and why the ESL or bilingual program is being developed or restructured to improve instruction for their children.

If the committee is implementing bilingual classrooms for the first time, it is very important to share the rationale for the bilingual programs. The language education committee presenters should be prepared to answer the following questions: "Why are our children learning in Spanish (or other primary language) if English is what they need to succeed in school?" "How do they learn English and how long does it take?" "If you teach them to read in Spanish, how do our children learn to read in English?" "How can we (the parents) help?" When answering these questions, presenters can explain that children only have to learn to read once and their children will be learning to read and write in the language that they know best. The language education coordinator or the committee presenters can point out that in bilingual classrooms, the children with beginning levels of ELP will be able to understand and learn all of the academic concepts required at their grade level. The presenters can explain that literacy skills learned in the home language will transfer into English as the children improve their English fluency. They can explain to the parents that they can be more involved in their children's learning since they will be able to communicate with the bilingual teachers. The presenters can point out the economic benefits of being bilingual and biliterate in the work force. The meeting will show the parents that their language and culture are respected and valued; they will be pleased that the committee took the time to share this important information.

Presenting Recommendations to the School Board

At the end of the planning phase (year 1), the district language education committee will undoubtedly present their findings, recommendations, and action plans to the school board. A well-planned presentation to the school board provides a wonderful opportunity to educate the board members and other parents in the community about what the committee has learned. The committee members should share some research about educating ELLs and describe the process that led to their decisions and recommendations. The recommendations will most likely involve budget increases due to requests to hire additional teachers, assistants, and/or other staff. The presentation, along with the philosophy and purpose statements, will clarify the need to make changes. The committee may want to suggest implementing the changes over a period of two or three years in order to gradually absorb budget increases. For example, they can suggest adding bilingual staff members each year as other district personnel retire. The board will respect the time, commitment, and processes undertaken by the committee. If a board member serves on the committee, he/she can offer his/her perspective about how to make the case for change and how to provide the needed information for the board members. Once the restructuring decisions have been made and approved by the school board, all district personnel should be informed about the newly restructured language education programs. They will also need to understand the committee processes that led to the changes that were made.

Implementing, Monitoring, and Evaluating the Program

In year 2 (phase 2), as the implementation of the newly constructed or restructured programs is underway, the district language committee still has a significant role. Now their focus shifts to implementing and monitoring the new or restructured program by assessing professional development needs and reviewing student data to evaluate the ELLs' progress. The committee can meet with principals and school leadership teams to share information and coordinate responsibilities as they monitor and implement the new programs. The language education coordinator and the language education committee members will want to talk with the language education and mainstream teachers to find out what is working and not working in the new or restructured programs. What issues are popping up? What research-based information, materials, and professional development do the teachers need to work out the bugs? Planning and restructuring language education programs is an on-going task. Every school year brings new students, new situations, and new challenges. In any building, at any grade level, the program approach may need to be adjusted to match the needs of the current ELLs.

Refining Long-Term Professional Development Needs

For effective change to follow effective decision-making, all district teachers need to fully understand the rationale and significance of the restructuring decisions and receive ongoing professional development about their roles and responsibilities in implementing the key practices within the context of the restructured programs. Feedback from the various PLC teams will probably indicate that continued professional development is needed. General education teachers may find that they need training about incorporating ELD standards and big ideas into daily lesson plans. Noncertified staff members may need to be reminded that the primary languages of ELLs are valuable resources. For example, children should never be admonished for speaking in their home language while talking with friends in the lunchrooms, playgrounds, or buses.

It is extremely important that two stakeholder groups be specifically targeted for substantial training during the implementation phase: the building administrators and the language education program teachers. Without the full support of building-level administrators, the language education program will not be implemented consistently across the district. Time and again, we have seen problems with restructuring efforts at the building level because of the administrator's lack of knowledge about the goals of the district's program. We have talked with bilingual teachers who have abandoned their carefully planned language allocation plans when their building administrator tells them not to teach the ELLs in their primary language. These types of misguided directives can be avoided if the committee intentionally targets this group of administrators with professional development.

It is equally important that the language education teachers be fully aware of the twelve key practices and the processes that the committee undertook. Even though they are certified language education teachers, they should receive ongoing training. Otherwise, the restructured program may be relabeled—but implemented with no significant instructional changes. For example, an ESL teacher may have previously only focused on traditional ESL instruction and the restructured program calls for content-based ESL instruction. If the teacher is on summer vacation when content-based ESL training takes place, the teacher may continue to do what he/she has always done.

During year 2 (phase 2), the language education committee can revisit and revise their long-term professional development plan and make recommendations for the next few years. Using the *Matching Professional Development to Educators' Roles Template* at the end of Key Practice 1, they can plan cycles of professional development about specific topics for specific stakeholders through various formats at meetings, after-school workshops, summer training, and presentations infused into regular teacher institutes and in-service days.

Developing a District Language Education Handbook

Toward the end of year 2 (phase 2), a designated committee can gather to prepare a district handbook that will guide language education program procedures. The handbook can provide articulated, philosophy-driven, research-based procedures which will continue long after administrators and teachers who serve ELL students change roles or move out of the district. Once created, this handbook should be reviewed and updated annually. A summer committee consisting of bilingual/ESL teachers and mainstream teachers can handle this task. The committee may decide to print and distribute a hard copy of the handbook each year for building administrators and language education teachers. Also, the committee may choose to have portions of the handbook available for parents in their primary language. The *Checklist for District Language Education Handbook Template* provides a checklist of suggested information, forms, and documents for the district handbook.

Refining Assessment Procedures for Evaluating English Language Learners' Progress

The year 2 implementation phase is an ideal time for a language education assessment subcommittee to refine and improve assessment practices and procedures for English language proficiency and academic achievement. The language education coordinator and the ESL and bilingual teachers who have been administering various assessment measures for ELLs can identify issues and problems and suggest changes to the district assessment committee. For example, the entry and exit procedures that have been developed and field-tested can be adapted, if necessary. Common classroom assessment practices that have been developed in one building can be shared with other buildings and grade levels. As the various school-wide and teacher teams develop, try out, and refine assessment procedures, they should be recorded and included in the district's language education handbook.

Maintaining the Committee for Ongoing Analysis and Evaluation

The language education committee must keep in mind that high-quality language education programs evolve and maintaining effective programs is an ongoing process. We suggest that beginning in year 3, some members leave the committee, allowing for others to join. However, the majority of the committee members should carry over each year. Suggested yearly tasks for this newly restructured oversight committee are the following:

- Continue to address and make changes to the district's language education program (implementation problems, professional development initiatives, curriculum development, textbook adoptions, etc.).
- Annually review student demographic data to determine district trends and appropriate placement of ELLs by classroom and/or building.
- Monitor progress of ELLs as reported by state and local assessment data as well as authentic measures initiated by language teachers and mainstream teachers.
- Monitor exited students for at least two years to see how they are progressing in general education and content classrooms.

- Document and discuss the implications of the number of referrals of current and former ELLs to gifted programs, referrals to special education programs, high school graduation rates, and the number of parents who refuse language education services.

In the discussion of this final key practice, we have provided step-by-step guidance to help the language education committee develop and implement effective program configurations. Throughout all of the chapters, we have emphasized the role that collaborative teams have in implementing the twelve key practices and developing or restructuring language education programs. It is our hope that the key practices, discussions, templates, suggestions, and ideas provided throughout the book serve as valuable tools to help PLC teams, administrators, and teachers meet the goal of improving programs and instruction so that their ELLs have maximum opportunities to meet core state standards and English language development standards.

QUESTIONS FOR REFLECTION AND ACTION

1. Which program configurations seem to match the needs of your district's ELL student population at the primary level? At the intermediate level? At the middle school and high school levels?

2. Using the *Developing Philosophy and Purpose Statement* template, develop a philosophy statement and a purpose statement that reflects your understanding of a high quality, locally appropriate instructional program for ELLs.

Recommended Readings

Coady, M. et al. (2003). *Claiming opportunities: A handbook for improving education for English language learners through comprehensive school reform.* The Education Alliance at Brown University. Available at www.alliance.brown.edu/pubs/claiming_opportunities/.

Crawford, J. (2003). Hard sell: Why is bilingual education so unpopular with the American public? Arizona State University/EPSL/Language Policy Research Unit. Available at http://www.asu.edu/educ/epsl/LPRU/features/brief8.htm.

Genesee, F. et al. (2006). *Educating English language learners: A synthesis of research evidence.* NY: Cambridge University Press.

*Miramontes, O. et al. (2011). *Restructuring schools for linguistic diversity: Linking decision making to effective programs.* New York: Teachers College Press.

*Ovando, C. et al. (2006). *Bilingual and ESL classrooms: Teaching in multicultural contexts.* Boston: McGraw Hill.

*Thomas, Wayne P., & Collier, Virginia P. (2002). *A National study of school effectiveness for language minority students' long-term academic achievement.* Washington, D.C.: CREDE/CAL, ERIC # ED475048. Available at http://usc.edu/dept/education/CMMR/CollierThomasComplete.pdf.

---

*These resources specifically address the strengths and challenges of various typical program configurations.

CHECKLIST FOR KEY PRACTICE 12

The checklist is written using measurable statements that can be used to evaluate and monitor language education programs and instruction at the district, school, and classroom levels. The district language education committee and school leadership teams can use the checklist as a diagnostic tool to identify the areas that represent the biggest challenges during the restructuring process. Various teams can use the results of the checklist as a starting point to determine the professional development that educators need to know in order to successfully implement the practices. Teacher teams can use the checklist to evaluate their own teaching practices to recognize ways in which they can immediately make instructional improvements.

SCORING DIRECTIONS:
1 = This practice IS implemented.
2 = This practice is in progress or is in place in some classrooms.
3 = This practice is NOT currently in place.

Organizing the Key Practices into Effective Program Configurations

			Structuring the Language Education Program: Instruction is organized to effectively meet the literacy, academic, and language needs of the districts' ELL populations.
1	2	3	• A district language education committee is established to develop or restructure the language education program.
1	2	3	• The extent of the use of the ELLs' primary language is determined according to the specific academic needs of the district's ELL populations.
1	2	3	• New and restructured program configurations have been constructed by figuring out how ESL, literacy, and academic content instruction can be effectively implemented.
1	2	3	• The language education program has been developed through a collaborative process that defines the purpose of the language education program, grounds the program in standards, includes short- and long-term professional development plans, and shares information with parents and other stakeholders.
1	2	3	• The language education committee monitors the programs for ELLs by annually assessing professional development needs and reviewing student data to evaluate the ELLs' progress.

IMPLICATIONS AND COMMENTS _____

_____

_____

_____

Sample of English Language Learners Student Demographics Template

ELLs Grouped by School, Grade, ELP Level, and Language Group

School: _____

Language Group: _____ School Year: _____

ELP Level	PreK	First Grade	Second Grade	Third Grade	Fourth Grade	Fifth Grade	TOTAL
Level 1							
Level 2							
Level 3							
Level 4							
Level 5							
TOTAL							

Current Practices: Language Education Program Template

Teacher: _____   School: _____   Grade Level: _____   ELP Levels: _____   Primary language: _____

Program Description: _____   Date: _____

How are the ELLs in this classroom currently receiving	Language of Instruction	Time Allotment	Teacher/Classroom	If instruction is in English, how is it adapted for ELLs?	Implications for Change
English as a Second Language Instruction					
Literacy Instruction					
Academic Content Instruction					

COMMENTS

Factors to Consider about Implementing Primary Language Instruction and/or Primary Language Support Template

School _____ Language Group _____	Several answers in this column suggest primary language instruction	Several answers in this column suggest primary language support	Rationale for question
Are there 20 or more ELLs at the primary level to facilitate primary language literacy instruction?	yes	no	A school must have enough ELLs from the same language group to justify hiring a certified bilingual teacher.
Do families within this language group have a history of a high rate of mobility to and from other school districts?	no	yes	If ELLs are from a language group that is always changing, long-range planning is difficult.
Do children (age 8 and older) from this language group often arrive in your district with gaps in their schooling?	yes	no	If yes, this group needs primary language instruction to build a strong foundation and efficiently reduce the gaps in school knowledge.
Do children (age 8 and older) from this language group usually arrive with grade-level literacy skills and knowledge?	no	yes	If yes, the strong foundation in these students' primary language will help them learn literacy and concepts in English.
Do the parents in this language group generally have enough schooling to support their children's learning when instruction is only in English?	Often no	Usually yes	If no, teachers must actively work to help immigrant parents learn ways to support their childrens' learning.
Are certified bilingual teachers available in this language?	yes	no	Primary language instruction is not feasible without a pool of highly qualified certified bilingual teachers.
Are there substantial literacy texts, content texts, and supplemental materials available in this language?	yes	no	Children can't learn to read in a language if there is not an abundance of appropriate reading materials.
Which philosophy about bilingualism generally matches the thinking of the community, the school board, the teaching staff?	Additive bilingualism	Subtractive bilingualism	The answer to this question should *not* be the reason to reject primary language instruction and/or support. However, negative views of bilingualism do indicate that substantial professional development for these groups will be necessary.

Long-Term Language Education for Elementary Schools Program Planning Template

School: _____ Grade Levels: _____

ELP Levels: _____ Primary Language Group: _____

Description (or label) of Program Option _____

Language Education Program Plan

		Language of Instruction	Time Needed	Teacher (General Ed., ESL, Bilingual)	Type of Classroom (e.g.,self-contained, resource classroom, pull-out)	Professional Development Needed for Sustained Implementation
Comprehensible Instruction for ELLs	**English as a Second Language Instruction**	English				Short Term: Long Term:
	Literacy Instruction					Short Term: Long Term:
	Academic Content Instruction					Short Term: Long Term:

COMMENTS

Planning for Elementary ESL or Bilingual Programs

School: _____   Grade Levels _____   Number of ELLs _____

Language Groups _____

#____ Bilingual or ESL Teacher(s) Bilingual teacher may serve as an ESL teacher when working with students from other language groups.	Integrated Time ELLs are grouped with their fluent English speaking peers.	General Education Classroom Teachers Subjects are taught by general education teachers with substantial ESL training.
		Bilingual assistant can be scheduled to provide primary language support in content areas.

Program Configuration Template

Planning for Secondary Bilingual Programs

School _____ Number of ELLs _____

Language Groups _____

MIDDLE or HIGH SCHOOL

# _____ ESL Teacher(s)* ESL courses are taught using content-based ESL methodology.	_____ Bilingual Teacher(s)* Bilingual courses are mostly taught in the primary language with planned use of sheltered English.	Content Teachers Courses are taught by content teachers with substantial ESL training.
		Bilingual assistant can be scheduled to assist content teachers.

* Bilingual and ESL teachers must have appropriate teacher certification.

Planning for Secondary ESL Programs

School _____

Language Groups _____   Number of ELLs _____

MIDDLE or HIGH SCHOOL

# _____ ESL Teacher(s) ESL courses are taught using content-based ESL methodology (looped, multigrade).*	Content Teachers Courses are taught by content teachers with substantial ESL training.*
	Designated Sections:
	ELL students are placed in designated sections that often include general education students. A trained bilingual assistant can be assigned to work with teachers in designated classes to provide primary language support.

*ESL teachers must have appropriate teacher certification.

Short-Term Action Plan Template
Improving ESL, Literacy, and Academic Content Instruction

School _____ Grade Levels _____

Language Group _____ Date _____

Directions: Use the promising program configurations to answer the questions below.

ENGLISH AS A SECOND LANGUAGE INSTRUCTION	**What steps can be taken to maximize the STRENGTHS?** **What steps can be taken to minimize the CHALLENGES?**
LITERACY INSTRUCTION	**What steps can be taken to maximize the STRENGTHS?** **What steps can be taken to minimize the CHALLENGES?**
ACADEMIC CONTENT INSTRUCTION	**What steps can be taken to maximize the STRENGTHS?** **What steps can be taken to minimize the CHALLENGES?**

Developing Philosophy and Purpose Statements for Educating English Language Learners Template

Existing district mission statement:

_____

_____

_____

Philosophy Statement:

_____

_____

_____

Sample of Philosophy Statement:

We believe that education for all learners is the shared responsibility of the community, school, family, and students. It is our responsibility and goal to provide the English language learners the opportunity to learn in a quality program which builds upon their knowledge, culture, and experiences.

The purpose of the _____ program of School District _____ is to _____

_____

_____

_____

Suggestions:

Provide appropriate literacy instruction.

Make instruction comprehensible in all content areas.

Align content instruction with state academic standards.

Develop academic English language proficiency.

Provide instruction in a safe low-risk environment where bilingualism and diversity are valued.

Checklist for District Language Education Handbook Template

✓	
	School district mission statement
	English language learner philosophy statement
	Purpose of the language education programs
	Twelve Key Practices Checklist
	List of relevant research underpinning program philosophy and approach
	Synopsis of state rules and regulations pertaining to the language education programs
	The school district language education assessment plan, including: • Standardized testing information • District testing and common assessment procedures • Entrance criteria: home language survey, screening form, flow chart, placement considerations • Monitoring forms: including English language development, literacy development, and academic profiles • Annual responsibility charts for ESL/bilingual teacher and mainstream teacher (who is responsible for teaching and assessment in each subject each year, in what language(s) and how that subject will be taught) • Exit criteria: standardized testing criteria and authentic measures
	Completed Program Configuration templates
	Bilingual parent advisory committee (PAC) information
	Resources available for teachers
	Translated district documents which pertain to English language learners
	Parent permission forms, entry/exit forms, other parent information forms in as many languages as possible
	List of local translators, cultural informants, agencies, and local organizations that provide classes and services for immigrant groups. Include contact information (phone numbers, e-mail address, etc.)
	Language education staff directory and school calendar

GLOSSARY

Academic language proficiency: the use of language in acquiring academic content in formal schooling contexts, including specialized or technical language and discourse related to each content area (Gottlieb et al., 2007).

Additive bilingualism: the situation in which the acquisition of a second language is added to an individual or group's linguistic skills without the loss or displacement of the first language (Freeman, 2004). Educators who believe that additive bilingualism is a valuable resource develop language education programs that plan ways to use the ELL's primary language as a valuable resource for learning. In addition, they strive to maintain and improve the primary language of the ELLs while they are learning English. (See contrasting definition of subtractive bilingualism.)

Balanced assessment system: an assessment plan that uses a variety of reliable formative and summative assessment strategies. Finding out what ELLs already know and can do is the first step. Then, on-going classroom assessments monitor growth in literacy, academic achievement, and language proficiency. Finally, in addition to conducting standardized measures, authentic data is administered and gathered that document the ELLs' growth over time. The system is complete when student data help district educators inform instruction and improve language education programs.

Big ideas: broad generalizing statements, either principles (always true) or generalizations (usually true) that are developed from the concepts embedded in core state standards. These statements of essential learning, also known as enduring understandings (Wiggins & McTighe,1998), become the focus of curriculum planning, theme development, instruction, and assessment (Gordon, 2007).

Bilingual education: any program model that uses both the students' primary language and the target language for instructional purposes. There are multiple ways of implementing the use of the primary language instruction based on program philosophy and goals. The majority of bilingual programs in the U.S. are transitional bilingual education (TBE) programs that provide only one to three years of primary language instruction or support (Freeman, 2004). Late-exit bilingual programs, designed to use the primary language for five or more years, have proven to be more successful.

Clustering: the practice of locating specific groups of ELLs into particular buildings or classrooms to facilitate a particular program approach.

Comprehensible input: a term coined by Krashen (1985) that describes the scaffolding process in which teachers explicitly adjust their speech and use instructional supports so that new information is understood. ESL teachers implement comprehensible input by explaining concepts and academic tasks clearly. They use speech appropriate for students' language proficiency (slower rate, gestures, simple sentences) without using slang or idioms. They use visuals, graphic organizers, word sorts, word maps, and Venn diagrams to teach vocabulary words and support instruction throughout the lessons.

Comprehensive language education programs: instructional programs for ELLs that have been designed by a team of educators who take into consideration the literacy, academic, and English language needs of the district's ELL student populations. ESL, literacy, and content area instruction is taught by certified ESL and bilingual teachers and mainstream teachers who have substantial training in sheltered instruction methods.

Common assessments: student assessments that are used in more than one classroom. Common assessments are generally developed collaboratively by a team of teachers responsible for the same curriculum or grade level. The teachers implement these common assessments in their classrooms and mutually agree on how they will report and use the data.

Content-based ESL instruction: language instruction in which English language development is the goal. The big ideas of the content and the requisite terminology of a particular topic is the focus of the language instruction that is designed to reach English language development standards. In content-based ESL, teachers use the big ideas of content topics in various content areas (e.g., science, social studies, math, language arts) as a vehicle to learn academic language in English. In order to make second language instruction comprehensible, they implement multiple vocabulary-building strategies and use graphic, sensory, and interactive supports to differentiate instruction and assessment according to the ELLs' English proficiency levels. The origins of content-based ESL methodology, sheltered instruction, and sheltered strategies are based on Krashen's comprehensible input theory.

Cultural competence: the ability of educators to successfully teach students who come from cultures other than their own. Cultural competence entails developing certain personal and interpersonal awareness and sensitivities, developing certain bodies of cultural knowledge, and mastering a set of skills that, taken together, underlie effective cross-cultural teaching (Diller & Moule, 2005).

English language learners (ELLs): the general term used to describe linguistically and culturally diverse students who have been identified as having levels of English language proficiency that preclude them from accessing, processing, and acquiring unmodified grade-level content instruction in English (Gottlieb et al., 2007). In many states, the term English learners (ELs) is used in place of ELLs.

ESL: When we use the term *ESL,* we are describing English as a second language (ESL) as the comprehensible English instruction in which learning academic language is the goal. In some cases we use the term content-based ESL to emphasize that ESL instruction is *not* taught through a traditional approach in which conversational English is taught through grammar structures and discrete language skills. In comprehensible ESL instruction, the big ideas and requisite terminology of a particular content topic is the focus of the language instruction that is designed to reach English language development standards.

Immersion: the carefully planned learning environment for language learners in two language groups who are placed in two-way immersion (TWI) classrooms with one or two teachers who speak both English and the target language. The goal is that the non–English-speaking children will learn English and the English-speaking children will learn the other target language while both groups learn grade-level content together and become bicultural. The two student groups in a TWI (immersion) classroom have similar language proficiencies of the target language. Initially the minority language is the language of instruction for the majority of the school day. Each year, instruction is increasingly taught in English. Literacy and academic content instruction is adapted to be comprehensible for the learners in both groups and materials are specifically selected to match the students' language proficiency levels in both languages. (See contrasting definition of *submersion.*)

Language education: a broad term used to describe all types of program configurations that provide instruction and services for language learners, such as bilingual education, English as a second language education, world language education, and heritage language education programs (Freeman, 2004).

Language-minority students: students who speak a language other than the dominant societal language (Freeman, 2004). In the U.S., language-minority students speak a language other than English at home. Some language-minority students, especially those that are born in the U.S., are also English-proficient speakers. Others within this group speak the home language and have various English language proficiency levels. In other words, all ELLs are language-minority students but all language-minority students are not ELLs.

Looping: a grouping practice that allows a teacher to have the same students for two years. For example, a teacher may teach second and third graders in one room. The third graders move on to another teacher in fourth grade, but the second graders continue with this teacher in third grade.

Meaning-based literacy: literacy instruction that is meaningful and functional for the emergent readers or writers. In meaning-based literacy, the text, writing activities, skills and tasks are taught in comprehensible, concrete, and engaging contexts that the learners can relate to personally (Fife, 2006).

Primary language: describes the first language that children learn at home. In the language education field, the terms primary language, native language, and first language are synonymous.

Primary language instruction: primary language *instruction* describes language, literacy and content instruction taught in the learners' primary language by certified bilingual teachers in bilingual classroom settings.

Primary language support: describes the use of the primary language (by bilingual teachers, aides, or tutors) to support the concepts and instruction that the ELLs are taught in English in general education (elementary) and content (secondary) classrooms.

Professional learning communities (PLCs): a term that describes a group of collaborative teams that work and learn interdependently to achieve a common goal. (DuFour et al., 1998, 2006). As its name implies, successful PLCs are a community of *learners* as well as collaborators. PLCs have five attributes: supportive and shared leadership, collective creativity, shared values and visions, supportive conditions, shared practices (Hord, 1997).

Scaffolding: a term used to describe the visual, graphic, and temporary supports that help ELLs comprehend new information as they develop English language proficiency (Gibbons, 2002). These supports include modeling, questioning, feedback, student interaction, graphic organizers, and other supports (Echevarria et al., 2004).

Sensory, graphic, and interactive supports: instructional strategies that help ELLs develop academic language and understand classroom lessons. For example, sensory supports include visuals, real-life objects, songs, drawings, videos, etc. Graphic supports include multiple varieties of graphic organizers, charts, timelines, etc. Interactive supports include small group interaction, working with partners, primary language support, internet websites, instructional software, etc. (Gottlieb et al., 2007).

Sheltered instruction: a term used to describe instruction in any subject that is provided in English but taught in a manner that makes it comprehensible to ELL students while promoting their English language development. Learning the academic content is the goal (Echevarria, 2007).

Stakeholders: administrators, teachers, parents, and other adults who have specific roles in the ELLs' progress and, therefore, share the responsibilities for the students' success.

Specials: instruction in specialized subjects such as art, music, physical education, computer technology taught by teachers certified in the specific area.

Submersion: this term describes a "sink-or swim" environment in which ELLs are placed in general education classrooms with English-speaking students and a monolingual English-speaking teacher. With good intentions, administrators and teachers hope that the non–English-speaking children will learn English by being "immersed" in the language. The ELLs' primary language is seldom used in the classroom or used sporadically for translation purposes. Literacy and academic content instruction as well as texts and supplemental materials are usually not designed or adapted for the ELL students. In the submersion classroom, ELLs are taught as if they do not have diverse academic and linguistic needs. As a result, the ELLs, especially the beginners, often miss important concepts and are not active, engaged, learners. (See contrasting definition of *immersion.*)

Substantial sheltered instruction methodology training: training in sheltered (or content-based) ESL that is similar to a graduate course, consisting of more than five all-day sessions at least one week apart so that participants can practice and reflect about what they have learned and practiced. The training should include how to adapt literacy instruction; implement multiple vocabulary-building strategies; use graphic, sensory and interactive supports to make information comprehensible; utilize ELLs' languages, cultures and experiences in classroom activities; and learn ways to differentiate classroom tasks and assessments according to the ELLs' diverse needs and English proficiency levels.

Subtractive bilingualism: describes the philosophy that second language learners need to exchange their primary language for their new language, English. Programs with this philosophy do not use the primary language to support learning. In some cases, any use of the students' language is discouraged.

REFERENCES

Abedi, J. (2007). *English language proficiency assessment in the nation: Current status and future practice*. The Regents of the University of California. Available at http://education.ucdavis .edu/research/ELP_Report.pdf.

Across the Globe Learning Resources for Kids. (2010). *Learning resources in 47 world languages*. Available at acrosstheglobelr .com. Fort Lauderdale, FL.

Adams-Fletcher, C. (2011). Study a language, discover a world. *Atlanta Journal Constitution*, February 28, 2011. Available at http://www.ajc.com/opinion/study-a-language-discover-855946 .html.

Allen, J. (1999). *Words, words, words: Teaching vocabulary in grades 4–12*. Portland, ME: Stenhouse Publishers.

Antunez, B. (2002). English language learners and the five essential components of reading instruction. Available at http:// www.readingrockets.org/article/341.

Ariza, E. (2006). *Not for ESOL teachers: What every classroom teacher needs to know about the linguistically, culturally, and ethnically diverse student*. Boston: Pearson.

Asher, J. (1982). *Learning another language through actions: The complete teachers' guidebook*. Los Gatos, CA: Sky Oaks.

August, D. A., & Hakuta, K. (1997). *Improving schooling for minority-language children: A research agenda*. Washington, D.C.: National Academy Press.

August, D., & Shanahan, T. (2006). *Developing literacy in second language learners: A report of the National Literacy Panel on Minority-Language Children and Youth*. Mahwah, NJ: Lawrence Erlbaum Associates.

August, D. et al. (2005). The critical role of vocabulary development for English language learners. *Learning Disabilities Research & Practice, 20* (1), 50–57.

Baker, C. (1993). *Foundations of bilingual education and bilingualism*. Clevedon, UK: Multilingual Matters.

Beeman, K., & Urow, C. (2010). Dual language program design and implementation. Workshop presented April 21, 2010, at the Illinois Resource Center, Arlington Heights, Illinois.

Beeman, K., & Urow, C. (In press). *Teaching for biliteracy: Strengthening bridges between languages*. Philadelphia: Caslon Publishing.

Benjamin, A. (2003). *Differentiated instruction: a guide for elementary school teachers*. Larchmont, NY: Eye On Education.

Brandi-Miller, J. (2005*). Retelling stories*. Available at http://www .colorincolorado.org/article/13282.

Brisk, M. (1991). Toward multilingual and multicultural mainstream education. *Journal of Education, 173*(2), 114–129.

Brisk, M., & Harrington, M. (2007). *Literacy and bilingualism: A handbook for ALL teachers*. Mahwah, NJ: Lawrence Erlbaum Associates.

Cappellini, M. (2005). *Balancing reading and language learning: A resource for teaching English language learners, K–5*. Portland, ME: Stenhouse Publishers.

Castañeda v. Pickard (1981). U.S. Department of Education (2009). Programs for English language learners, Office for Civil Rights. Available at http://www.ed.gov/about/offices/list/ocr/ell/edlite -glossary.html.

Center for Applied Linguistics. (2008). *English language learners: Immigrant education*. Available at http://www.cal.org/topics/ ell/immigrantEd.html.

Center for Equity and Excellence in Education. (2005). *Promoting excellence series: Guiding principles*. Arlington, VA: George Washington University. Available at http://ceee.gwu.edu/CEEE %20Guide-Princ-010909.pdf.

Center for Great Public Schools. (2008). *Promoting educators' cultural competence to better serve culturally diverse students*. NEA Policy Brief #13, Washington, D.C.

Chamberlain, P. (2008). *Going on an exemplary classroom hunt*. Keynote Presentation, Annual Statewide Conference for Teachers Serving Linguistically and Culturally Diverse Students, January 8, 2008, Oak Brook, Illinois.

Clay, M. (1991). *Becoming literate: The construction of inner control*. Portsmouth, NH: Heinemann.

Cloud, N. et al. (2000). *Dual language instruction: A handbook for enriched education*. Boston: Heinle.

Cloud, N. et al. (2009). *Literacy instruction for English language learners: A teacher's guide to research-based practices*. Portsmouth, NH: Heinemann.

Coady, M. et al. (2003). *Claiming opportunities: A handbook for improving education for English language learners through comprehensive school reform*. The Education Alliance at Brown University. Available at www.alliance.brown.edu/pubs/claiming _opportunities/.

Coggins, D. et al. (2007). *English language learners in the mathematics classroom*. Thousand Oaks, CA: Sage Publications.

Collier, V., & Thomas, W. (1992). A synthesis of studies examining long-term language minority student data on academic achievement. *Bilingual Research Journal, 16* (1–2), 187–212.

Colorín Colorado. (2007). *Selecting vocabulary words to teach English language learners*. Available at http://www.colorin colorado.org/educators/content/vocabulary.

Commins, N. (2010). *Orchestrating a school-wide response to linguistic diversity: The critical role of administrators*. Presentation, Annual Statewide Conference for Teachers Serving Linguistically and Culturally Diverse Students, December 8, 2010, Oak Brook, Illinois.

Commins, N., & Miramontes, O. (2005). *Linguistic diversity and teaching*. Mahwah, N.J.: Lawrence Erlbaum Associates.

Cook, H.G. (2007). WIDA research brief 2007:2: Guidance on annual measurable achievement objectives. Available at http:// www.wida.us/Research/Policy/Policy.aspx.

Cook, H.G. (2009). WIDA focus on growth. Madison, WI: WIDA Consortium.

Crawford, J. (2003). Hard sell: Why is bilingual education so unpopular with the American public? *Arizona State University/ EPSL/Language Policy Research Unit*. Available at http://www .asu.edu/educ/epsl/LPRU/features/brief8.htm.

Crawford, J., & Krashen, S. (2007). *English learners in American classrooms: 100 questions, 100 answers*. New York: Scholastic.

Cruz, B., & Thornton, S. (2008). *Teaching social studies to English language learners*. New York: Routledge.

Cummins, J. (1980). The construct of language proficiency in bilingual education. In J. E. Alatis (Ed.), *Georgetown University Round Table on Languages and Linguistics* (pp. 81–103). Washington, D.C.: Georgetown University Press.

Cummins, J. (1984). Wanted: A theoretical framework for relating language proficiency to academic achievement among bilingual students. In C. Rivera (Ed.), *Language Proficiency and Academic Achievement* (pp. 2–19). Clevedon, UK: Multilingual Matters.

Cummins, J. (1989). *Empowering minority students*. Los Angeles: California Association for Bilingual Education.

Cummins, J. (1994). The acquisition of English as a second language. In K. Spangenberg-Urbschat, & R. Pritchard (Eds.), *Reading Instruction for ESL Students* (pp. 36–64). Delaware: International Reading Association.

Cummins, J. (2000). *Language, power, and pedagogy: Bilingual children in the crossfire.* Clevedon, UK: Multilingual Matters.

Cummins, J. (2012). How long does it take for an English language learner to become proficient in a second language? In E. Hamayan & R. Freeman (Eds.) *English language learners at school: A guide for administrators* (pp. 37–39). Philadelphia: Caslon Publishing.

DeJong, E. (2011). *Foundations for multilingualism in education: From principles to practice.* Philadelphia: Caslon Publishing.

Diller, J.V., & Moule, J. (2005). *Cultural competence: A primer for educators.* Belmont, CA: Thomas Wadsworth.

DuFour, R. (2004). What is a Professional Learning Community? *Educational Leadership, 61*(8), 6–11.

DuFour, R., & Eaker, R. (1998). *Professional learning communities at work: Best practices for enhancing student achievement.* Alexandria, VA: Association for Supervision and Curriculum Development.

DuFour, R. et al. (2006). *Learning by doing: A handbook for professional learning communities at work.* Bloomington, IN: Solution Tree.

Echevarria, J. (2012). How do we ensure that the general education teachers and English as a second language teachers collaborate to address the content and language needs of English language learners? In E. Hamayan & R. Freeman (Eds.); *English language learners in school: A guide for administrators* (pp. 147–149). Philadelphia: Caslon Publishing.

Echevarria, J., & Graves, A. (2006). *Sheltered content instruction: Teaching English language learners with diverse abilities.* Boston: Allyn & Bacon.

Echevarria, J. et al. (2004). *Making content comprehensible for English language learners: the SIOP model.* Boston: Pearson.

Ellis, E. et al. (2005). Big ideas about teaching big ideas. *Teaching Exceptional Children, 38*(1), 34–40. Available at http://www.graphicorganizers.com/images/stories/pdf/Big%20Ideas%20About%20Teaching%20Big%20Ideas.pdf.

Ellis, R. (1984). *Classroom second language development.* Oxford: Pergamon.

Enright, D.S., & McClosky, M.L. (1988). *Integrating English: Developing English language and literacy in the multilingual classroom.* Reading, MA: Addison-Wesley.

Escamilla, K. (1987). The relationship of native language reading achievement and oral English proficiency to future achievement in reading English as a second language. Unpublished doctoral dissertation, University of California, Los Angeles.

Escamilla, K. (1999). Teaching literacy in Spanish. In R. D. V. J. T. (Eds.) *The power of two languages 2000* (pp. 12–141). New York: Macmillan/McGraw-Hill.

Escamilla, K. (2000). *Bilingual means two: Assessment issues, early literacy and Spanish-speaking children.* Presentation, A Research Symposium on High Standards in Reading for Students from Diverse Language Groups, April 19–20, 2000, Washington, D.C. Available at http://nepc.colorado.edu/files/Report.pdf.

Escamilla, K. (2006). Monolingual assessment and emerging bilinguals: A case study in the US. In O. Garcia, T. Skutnabb-Kangas, and M. Torres-Guzman (Eds.), *Imagining Multilingual Schools* (pp. 184–199). Clevedon, UK: Multilingual Matters.

Escamilla, K., & Coady, M. (2001). Assessing the writing of Spanish speaking students: Issues and suggestions. In J. Tinajero and S. Hurley (Eds.), *Handbook for Literacy Assessment for Bilingual Learners* (pp. 43–63). Boston: Allyn & Bacon.

Escamilla, K. et al. (2010). *Transitions to biliteracy: Literacy squared.* Final Technical Report (2004–2009). Boulder: Bueno Center, University of Colorado. Available at http://literacysquared.org/home.htm.

Fairbairn, S., & Jones-Vo, S. (2010). *Differentiating instruction and assessment for English language learners: A guide for K-12 teachers.* Philadelphia: Caslon Publishing.

Faltis, C., & Hudelson, S. (1997). *Bilingual education in elementary and secondary school communities: Toward understanding and caring.* Boston: Allyn & Bacon.

Fang, Z,. & Schleppegrell, M.J. (2008). *Reading in secondary content areas: A language-based pedagogy.* Ann Arbor, MI: Michigan Teacher Training.

Fife, M. (2006). *A meaning-based instruction to enhance literacy learning in a dual language kindergarten classroom.* Thesis, Brigham Young University. Available at http://contentdm.lib.byu.edu/ETD/image/etd1192.pdf.

Fountas. I., & Pinnell, G. (2001). *Guiding readers and writers/ grades 3–6.* Portsmouth, NH: Heinemann.

Freeman, D., & Freeman, Y. (2000). *Teaching reading in multilingual classrooms.* Portsmouth, NH: Heinemann.

Freeman, D., & Freeman, Y. (2004). *Essential linguistics: what you need to know to teach reading, ESL, spelling, phonics, grammar.* Portsmouth, NH: Heinemann.

Freeman, R. (2004). *Building on community bilingualism.* Philadelphia: Caslon Publishing.

Freeman, Y., & Freeman, D. (1996). *Teaching reading and writing in Spanish in the bilingual classroom.* Portsmouth, NH: Heinemann.

Freeman, Y., & Freeman, D. (2007). *Teaching reading and writing in Spanish and English in bilingual and dual language classrooms.* Portsmouth, NH: Heinemann.

Freeman, Y., & Freeman, D. (2008). *Academic language for English language learners and struggling readers: How to help students succeed across content areas.* Portsmouth, NH: Heinemann.

Freeman, Y. et al. (2002). *Closing the achievement gap: How to reach limited-formal-schooling and long-term English learners.* Portsmouth, NH: Heinemann.

Garcia, O., & Baker, C. (Eds.). (1995). *Policy and practice in bilingual education: Extending the foundations.* Clevedon, UK: Multilingual Matters.

Genessee, F. (1987). *Learning through two languages: Studies of immersion and bilingual education.* Cambridge, MA: Newbury House.

Genesee, F. et al. (2006). *Educating English language learners: A synthesis of research evidence.* NY: Cambridge University Press.

Genesee, F., et al. (2011). *Dual language development in disorders: A handbook on bilingualism and second language.* Baltimore: Paul H. Brookes Publishing.

Giacobbe, M. (1990). The writing workshop: support for word learning. In G. Fountas & I. Pinnell (1998) *Word matters: Teaching phonics and spelling in the reading/writing classroom* (pp. 000). Portsmouth, NH: Heinemann.

Gibbons, P. (2002). *Scaffolding language, scaffolding learning: Teaching second language learners in the mainstream classroom.* Portsmouth, NH: Heinemann.

Goldenberg, C. (2008). *Teaching English language learners: What the research does—and does not—say.* Available at http://www.edweek.org/media/ell_final.pdf.

Gomez, E. (2000). *Assessment portfolios: Including English language learners in large-scale assessments.* Washington, D.C.: ERIC Digest, EDO-FL-00-10.

Gonzalez, J., & Darling-Hammond, L. (1997). *New concepts for new challenges; Professional development for teachers of immigrant youth.* Chicago: Delta Systems.

González, N., & Moll, L. (2002). Cruzando el puente: Building bridges to funds of knowledge. *Educational Policy, 16*(4), 623–641.

Goodman, K. (1996). *A commonsense look at the nature of language and the science of reading.* Portsmouth, NH: Heinemann.

Gordon, J. (2007). *Identifying, teaching and assessing big ideas.* Presentation, Annual Statewide Conference for Teachers of Linguistically and Culturally Diverse Students, Oak Brook, Illinois.

Gordon, J. (2011). *General suggestions for selecting ESL materials 2011 IRC's resources for ESL materials.* Arlington Heights, IL: Illinois Resource Center. Available at http://esl-methods.wiki spaces.com/MATERIALS.

Gottlieb, M. (2006). *Assessing English language learners: Bridges from language proficiency to academic achievement.* Thousand Oaks, CA: Corwin Press.

Gottlieb, M. (2011). *Common language assessment for English learners.* Bloomington, IN: Solution Tree.

Gottlieb, M., & Nguyen, D. (2007). *Assessment and accountability in language education programs: A guide for teachers and administrators.* Philadelphia: Caslon Publishing.

Gottlieb, M. et al. (2006). *PreK-12 English language proficiency standards.* Alexandria, VA: Teachers of English to Speakers of Other Languages.

Gottlieb, M. et al. (2007a). Understanding the WIDA English language proficiency standards: A resource guide. Madison: University of Wisconsin. Available at http://www.wida.us/standards/Resource_Guide_web.pdf.

Gottlieb, M. et al. (2007b). English language proficiency standards and resource guide. Madison, WI: WIDA Consortium.

Griego-Jones, T. (1993). Biliteracy from the students' points of view. In *The Power of Two Languages* (pp. 234–240). MacMillan/McGraw Hill.

Hakuta, K. (1986). *Mirror of language: The debate on bilingualism.* New York: Basic Books.

Hakuta, K. et al. (2000). How long does it take English learners to attain proficiency. University of California Linguistic Minority Research Institute.

Hamayan, E. (2009). *Readers' writing and writers' readings.* Presentation, Annual Statewide Conference for Teachers Serving Linguistically and Culturally Diverse Students, January 9, 2009, Oak Brook, Illinois.

Hamayan, E., & Freeman, R. (Eds.). (2012). *English language learners at school: A guide for administrators.* Philadelphia: Caslon Publishing.

Hamayan, E. et al. (2007). *Special education considerations for English language learners: Delivering a continuum of services.* Philadelphia: Caslon Publishing.

Helman, L. (Ed). (2009). *Literacy development with English learners: Research-based instruction in grades K–6.* New York: Guilford Press.

Herrell, A., & Jordan, M. (2007). *Fifty strategies for teaching English language learners.* Boston: Prentice Hall/Pearson.

Hill, J., & Flynn, K. (2006). *Classroom instruction that works with English language learners.* Alexandria, VA: Association for Supervision and Curriculum Development.

Hord, S. M. (1997). Professional learning communities: What are they and why are they important? Available at http://www.sedl.org/change/issues/issues61.html.

Hord, S., & Sommers, W. (2007). *Leading professional learning communities: Voices from research and practice.* Thousand Oaks, CA: Corwin Press.

Horwitz, A. et al. (2009). *Succeeding with English Language Learners: Lessons learned from the Great City Schools.* Washington, D.C.: The Council of the Great City Schools.

Hurley, S., & Tinajero, J. (2001). *Literacy assessment of English language learners.* Boston: Allyn & Bacon.

Illinois State Board of Education. Home Language Survey. Available at http://www.isbe.net/bilingual/htmls/tbe_tpi.htm.

Illinois State Learning Standards (1985). Available at http://www isbe.state.il.us/ils/science/standards.htm.

International Reading Association. (2001, January). *Second-language literacy instruction: A position statement of the International Reading Association.* Available at http://reading.org/Libraries/Position_Statements_and_Resolutions/ps1046_second_language.sflb.ashx.

Jameson, J. (2003). *Enriching content classes for secondary ESOL students.* Washington, D.C.: Delta Systems.

Jameson, J. (1998). Teaching the text backwards: A practical framework that helps English language learners understand textbooks. Washington, D.C.: Center for Applied Linguistics.

Kagan, S. (1994). *Kagan cooperative learning.* San Clemente, CA: Kagan Cooperative Learning Publishing Company.

Kagan, S., & Kagan, M. (2010). *Kagan cooperative learning.* San Clemente, CA: Kagan Cooperative Learning Publishing Company. Available at http://www.kaganonline.com/catalog/cooperative_learning.php.

Kendall, J., & Khuon, O. (2005). *Making sense: Small-group comprehension lessons for English language learners.* Portland, ME: Stenhouse Publishers.

Kendall, J., & Khuon, O. (2006). *Writing sense: Integrated reading and writing lessons for English language learners.* Portland, ME: Stenhouse Publishers.

Kersaint, G. et al. (2008). *Teaching mathematics to English language learners.* New York: Routledge.

Krashen, S. (1981). *Second language acquisition and second language learning.* Oxford: Pergamon.

Krashen, S. (1982). *Principles and practice in second language acquisition.* Oxford: Pergamon.

Krashen, S. (1985). *The input hypothesis: Issues and implications.* New York: Longman.

Krashen, S. (1994). *Bilingual education and second language acquisition theory.* In Bilingual Education Office (Ed.), *Schooling and language-minority students: A theoretical framework* (47–75). Los Angeles: Evaluation Dissemination and Assessment Center, California State University.

Krashen, S. (1996). *Under attack: The case against bilingual education.* Culver City, CA: Language Education Associates.

Krashen, S. (2004). *The power of reading.* Westport, CT: Libraries Unlimited and Portsmouth, NH: Heinemann.

Krashen, S., & Terrell, T. (1983). *The natural approach.* Hayward, CA: Alemany Press.

Krashen, S., & Terrell, T. (1992). *The natural approach: Language acquisition in the classroom.* West Trenton, NJ: Janus/Alemany Press.

Lambert, W. E. (1975). Culture and language as factors in learning and education. In A. Wolfgang (Ed.), *Education of immigrant students* (pp. 55–83). Toronto: Ontario Institute for Studies in Education.

Laturnau J. (2010). *Standards-based instruction for English language learners.* Honolulu: Pacific Resources for Education and Learning. Available at http://www.prel.org/products/pc_/standards-based.htm.

Lau v. Nichols (1974). Brown v. the Board of Education, Supreme Court ruling. Available at http://www.ed.gov/about/offices/list/ocr/ell/edlite-glossary.html#lau).

Lenters, K. (2004). No half measures: Reading instruction for young second-language learners. *The Reading Teacher, 58*, 328–336.

Lindfors, J. (1989). The classroom: A good environment for language learning. In P. Rigg & V.G. Allen (Eds.), *When they don't all speak English: Integrating the ESL student into the general classroom* (pp. 55–64). Urbana, IL: National Council of Teachers of English Press.

Lindholm-Leary, K. (2000). *Biliteracy for a global society: An idea book on dual education*. Washington, D.C.: National Clearinghouse for Bilingual Education.

Lindholm-Leary, K. (2001). *Dual language education*. Clevedon, UK: Multilingual Matters.

Lindholm-Leary, K. (2012). What are the most effective kinds of programs for English language learners? In E. Hamayan & R. Field (Eds.), *English language learners at school: A guide for administrators* (pp. 105–106). Philadelphia: Caslon Publishing.

Lucas, T., & Katz, A. (1993). Reframing the debate: The roles of native languages in English-only programs for language minority students. *TESOL Quarterly, 28*, 537–561.

Lucas, T. et al. (1990). Promoting the success of Latino language minority students: An exploratory study of six high schools. *Harvard Educational Review, 60*, 315–340.

Marzano, R. (2004). *Building background knowledge for academic achievement: Research on what works in schools*. Alexandria, VA: Association for Supervision and Curriculum Development (ASCD) Publications.

Marzano, R., & Pickering, D. (2005). *Building academic vocabulary: Teacher's manual*. Alexandria, VA: Association for Supervision and Curriculum Development (ASCD) Publications.

Marzano, R. et al. (2004). *Classroom instruction that works: Research-based strategies for increasing student achievement*. Upper Saddle River, NJ: Prentice Hall/Pearson.

Mather, M. (2010). *Children of immigrants: Charting a new path*. Presentation, Population Reference Bureau (prb.org). Available at http://www.voicesforchildren.com/pdf/Kids%20Count/Children_of_Immigrants_MarkMather.pdf.

McGroarty, M., & Calderón, M. (2005). Cooperative learning for second language learners: Models, applications and challenges. In P. A. Richard-Amato and M. A. Snow (Eds.), *Academic success for English language learners: Strategies for K-12 mainstream teachers* (pp. 174–194). White Plains, NY: Pearson.

McLaughlin, B. (1992). *Myths and misconceptions about second language learning: What every teacher needs to unlearn*. Available at http://www.ncela.gwu.edu/miscpubs/ncrcdsll/epr5.htm.

Menken, K. et al. (2007). *Pilot study: Meeting the needs of long-term English language learners in high school*. Available at http://web.gc.cuny.edu/dept/lingu/rislus/projects/LTELL/materials.html.

Miramontes, O. et al. (1997). *Restructuring schools for linguistic diversity: Linking decision making to effective programs*. New York: Teachers College Press.

Miramontes, O. et al. (2011). *Restructuring schools for linguistic diversity: Linking decision making to effective programs*. Second edition. New York: Teachers College Press.

Mitchell, D. E., & Mitchell, R. E. (1999). *The impact of California's Class Size Reduction initiative on student achievement: Detailed findings from eight school districts*. Riverside, CA: University of California, California Educational Research Cooperative.

Modiano, N. (1968). National or mother tongue in beginning reading: A comparative study. *Research in the Teaching of English, II*(1), 32–43.

Montgomery, Judy K. (2007). Vocabulary intervention for RTI: Tiers 1, 2, 3. Available at www.superduperinc.com/handouts/pdf/182VocabularyTiers.pdf.

Mooney, M. (1990). *Reading to, with, and by children*. Katonah, NY: Richard C. Owen Publishers, Inc.

Mooney, M. (1995). Guided reading: The reader in control. *Teaching K-8, 25*, 57–58.

Mora. J, (2007). Differentiating instruction for English learners: The four by four model. In T. Young, and N. Hadaway (Eds.), *Supporting the literacy development of English learners: Increasing success in all classrooms* (pp. 24–40). Newark, DE: International Reading Association.

Mora. J. (2010). *Dr. Mora's cross-cultural language & academic development (CLAD) instructional models*. San Diego, CA: San Diego State University. Available at http://www.moramodules.com/.

Moss, M., & Puma, M. (1995). *Prospects: The Congressionally mandated study of educational growth and opportunity. First-year report on language minority and limited English proficient students*. Washington, D.C.: U.S. Department of Education.

National Center for Educational Statistics. (2002). The Condition of education. Washington, D.C.: U.S. Department of Education. Available at http://nces.ed.gov/pubsearch/pubsinfo.asp?pubid=2002025.

National Council of Teachers of English. (2008). English language learners: A policy research brief. Urbana, IL: National Council of Teachers of English.

National Institute of Child Health and Human Development. (2000). *Report of the National Reading Panel. Teaching children to read: An evidence-based assessment of the scientific research literature on reading and its implications for reading instruction*. Washington, D.C.: U.S. Government Printing Office, NIH Publication No. 00-4769.

Nieto, S. (1999). *The light in their eyes: Creating multicultural learning communities*. New York: Teachers College Press.

Nieto, S. (2000). *Affirming diversity: The sociopolitical context of multicultural education*. New York: Addison Wesley Longman.

Norwood, J. (2007). Professional learning communities to increase student achievement. *Essays in Education, 20*, 33–42.

Ogle, D. (1986). K-W-L: A teaching model that develops active reading of expository text. *The Reading Teacher, 39*, 564–570.

Ohio Department of Education. Teaching to the standards: Teaching, learning, lessons and units. Available at http://ims.ode.state.oh.us/ODE/IMS/Lessons/.

O'Malley, M., & Valdez-Pierce, L. (1996). *Authentic assessment for English language learners: Practical approaches for teachers*. Reading, MA: Addison-Wesley.

Opitz, M,. & Rasinski, T., (2003). *The fluent reader: Oral reading strategies for building word recognition, fluency, and comprehension*. New York: Scholastic.

Opitz, M., & Rasinski, T. (2008). *Good-bye round robin: 25 effective oral reading strategies*. Portsmouth, NH.: Heinemann.

Ovando, C. et al. (2006). *Bilingual and ESL classrooms: Teaching in multicultural contexts*. Boston: McGraw-Hill.

Peregoy, S., & Boyle, O. (2008). *Reading, writing and learning in ESL: A resource book for teaching K-12 English learners*. Columbus: Allyn & Bacon.

Perez, B., & Torres, M. E. (Eds.). (1996). *Learning in two worlds: An integrated Spanish/English biliteracy approach*. White Plains, NY: Longman.

Pinnell, G., & Fountas, I. (2007). *The continuum of literacy learning: A guide to teaching*. Portsmouth, NH: Heinemann.

Ramirez, J. et al. (1991). *Final report: Longitudinal study of structured English immersion strategy, early-exit, and late-exit bilingual education programs for language-minority students*. Vols. I and II. San Mateo, CA: Aguirre International (ERIC #EJ460172).

Richard-Amato, P. (2003). *Making it happen: From interactive to participatory language teaching*. New York: Longman.

Richard-Amato, P., & Snow, M. A. (2005). *Academic success for English language learners: Strategies for K-12 mainstream teachers*. White Plains, NY: Longman.

Robertson (2006). Increase student interaction with "think-pair-shares" and "circle chats." Available at http://www.colorin colorado.org/article/13346/.

Rodríguez, A. (1988). Research in reading and writing in bilingual education and English as a second language. In A. Ambert (Ed.), *Bilingual Education and English as a Second Language: A research handbook* (pp. 61–117). New York: Garland Publishing.

Rodriguez-Brown, F. (2008). *The home-school connection.* New York: Routledge.

Roit, M. (2006). Essential comprehension strategies for English learners. In T. Young & N. Hadaway (Eds.), *Supporting the literacy development of English learners* (pp. 80–95). Newark: International Reading Association.

Rosebery, A., & Warren, B. (Eds.). (2008). *Teaching science to English language learners: Building on students' strengths.* Arlington, VA: National Science Teachers Association.

Rothenberg, C., & Fisher, D. (2007). *Teaching English language learners: A differentiated approach.* Upper Saddle River, NJ: Pearson.

Routman, R. (1991). *Invitations.* Portsmouth, NH: Heinemann.

Routman, R. (2000). *Conversations: Strategies for teaching, learning, evaluating.* Portsmouth, NH: Heinemann.

Ruebling, C. (2006). *Redesigning schools for success: Implementing small learning communities and teacher collaboration.* Longville, MN: AuthorHouse.

Samway, K.D., & McKeon, D. (2007). *Myths and realities: Best practices for English language learners.* Portsmouth, NH: Heinemann.

Sanchez-Lopez, C., & Young, T. (2011). *Monolingual educators in multilingual classrooms.* Presentation, Annual Statewide Conference for Teachers Serving Linguistically and Culturally Diverse Students, December 8, 2011, Oakbrook, Illinois.

Scarcella, R. (2003). Academic English: A conceptual framework. *University of California Linguistic Minority Research Institute.* Available at http://www.lmri.ucsb.edu/publications/03_scarcella .pdf.

Scarcella, R. (2009). English language learners and academic language. Available at www.colorincolorado.org/webcasts/ academiclanguage.

Scarcella, R, & Rumerberger, R. (2000). Academic English key to long-term success in school. *University of California Linguistic Minority Research Institute Newsletter, 9*(4). Santa Barbara, CA: University of California.

Schooltube.com. (2011). Safe, fun & free video sharing for K-12 schools. Available at www.schooltube.com.

Shanahan, T. (2007). The Chicago reading framework, Shanahan on literacy, Nov. 12, 2007, available online at: http://www .shanahanonliteracy.com/2007/11/for-several-years-i-have-used -basic.html.

Shore, R. (1997). *Rethinking the brain: New insights into early development.* New York: Families and Work Institute.

Short, D. (2002). Keynote address, Annual Statewide Conference for Teachers of Linguistically and Culturally Diverse Students, Hyatt Regency, January 23, 2002, Oak Brook, Illinois.

Short, D., & Fitzsimmons, S. (2007). *Double the work: Challenges and solutions to acquiring language and academic literacy for adolescent English language learners.* A report to the Carnegie Corporation of New York. Washington, D.C.: Alliance for Excellent Education.

Snow, C. E. (1992). Perspectives on second-language development: Implications for bilingual education. *Educational Researcher, 21*(March), 16–18.

Snow, C. et al. (Eds.). (1998). *Preventing reading difficulties in young children.* Washington, D.C.: National Academy Press. Available at http://www.nap.edu/readingroom/books/reading/.

Sobul, D. (1995). *Specially designed academic instruction in English.* Education Resources Information (ERIC), Instructional Center, Paper # ED391357.

Stauffer, R. (1971). Slave, puppet, or teacher? *The Reading Teacher, 25,* 24–29.

Swanson, C. (2009). *Perspectives on a population: English-language learners in American schools.* Bethesda, MD: Editorial Projects in Education, Inc.

Tabors, P. (2008). *One child, two languages: A guide for early childhood educators of children learning English as a second language.* Baltimore: Paul H. Brooks Publishing Co.

Temple, C. et al. (2010). *All children read.* Boston: Allyn & Bacon.

Thomas, W., & Collier, V. (2002). *A national study of school effectiveness for language minority students' long-term academic achievement.* Washington, D.C: CREDE/CAL, ERIC # ED475048.

Tomlinson, C., & McTighe, J. (2006). *Integrating differentiated instruction and understanding by design.* Alexandria, VA: Association for Supervision and Curriculum Development.

Trelease, J. (2006). *The read-aloud handbook.* New York: Penguin USA.

University of California Linguistic Minority Research Institute. Available at http://repositories.cdlib.org/lmri/pr/hakuta.

Urow, C., & Beeman, K. (2008). *Integrating English and Spanish instruction in the bilingual classroom.* Presentation, Annual Statewide Conference for Teachers of Linguistically and Culturally Diverse Students, January 10, 2008. Oak Brook, Illinois.

Urow, C., & Beeman, K. (2009). *The effective bridging of skills and concepts between L1 and L2 in the bilingual classroom.* Presentation, Annual Statewide Conference for Teachers of Linguistically and Culturally Diverse Students, December 8, 2009. Oak Brook, Illinois.

Valdez-Pierce, L. Assessment of English language learners. Webcast available at http://www.readingrockets.org/webcasts/on demand/1003.

Van Lier, L. (2004). The ecology of language learning. Monterey Institute of International Studies. Presented paper, UC Language Consortium Conference on Theoretical and Pedagogical Perspectives, March 26-28, 2004. Available at http://uccllt .ucdavis.edu/leo.cfm.

Vaughn, S., & Linan-Thompson, S. (2004). *Research-based methods of reading instruction: Grades K-3.* Alexandria, VA: Association for Supervision and Curriculum Development.

Vialpando, J. et al. (2005). *Educating English language learners: Implementing instructional practices.* The National Council of La Raza, Brown University. Available at www.nclr.org/content/ publications/detail/36199.

Vygotsky, L. (1978). *Mind in society: The development of higher psychological processes.* Cambridge: Harvard University Press.

Wagner, S. (2001). *Crossing classroom borders: Pathways to the mainstream through teacher collaboration.* Ph.D. dissertation. Chicago: University of Illinois at Chicago.

Walqui, A. (2000). *Contextual factors in second language acquisition.* Washington, D.C.: Center for Applied Linguistics Digest, #EDO-FL-00-05.

Walmsley, S. (2010.) *Teaching big ideas.* University of Albany. Available at http://www.albany.edu/reading/documents/IRABig Idea2a.pdf.

Waterman, R., & Harry, B. (2008). Building collaboration between schools and parents of English language learners: Transcending barriers, creating opportunities. National Center for Culturally Responsive Educational Systems. Available at http://www .nccrest.org/Briefs/PractitionerBrief_BuildingCollaboration.pdf.

WIDA Consortium. (2007). *World-class instructional design and assessment's guiding principles of language development.* Available at http://www.wida.us/AcademicLanguage/index.aspx.

WIDA Consortium (2009). CLIMBS professional development training program. Madison, WI: Wisconsin Center for Educational Research.

Wiggins, G., & McTighe, J. (2005). *Understanding by design.* Upper Saddle River, NJ: Prentice Hall.

Wong Filmore, L. (1991). A question for early-childhood programs: English first or families first? *10* (39). Available at http://virtual.yosemite.cc.ca.us/Childdevelopment/Cheryl/125/EnglishFirst FamiliesFirst.pdf.

Wood, K. (1987). Fostering cooperative learning in middle and secondary level classrooms. *Journal of Reading,* 10–18.

Wright, W. (2010). *Foundations for teaching English language learners: Research, theory, policy, and practice.* Philadelphia: Caslon Publishing.

Young, T., & Hadaway, N. (Eds.). (2006). *Supporting the literacy development of English learners: Increasing success in all classrooms.* Newark: International Reading Association.

Zehler, A. et al. (2003). *Policy report: Summary of findings related to LEP and Sped-LEP students.* Washington, D.C.: Center for Equity and Excellence in Education, George Washington University.

Zehr, M. (2009). *Buzz words, trends and policy shifts in the world of ELLs.* Presentation, Annual Statewide Conference for Teachers Serving Linguistically and Culturally Diverse Students, January 6, 2009, Oak Brook, Illinois.

Zemelman, S. et al. (2005). *Best practice: Today's standards for teaching and learning in America's schools.* Portsmouth, NH: Heinemann.

Zwier, J. (2008). *Building academic language: Essential practices for content classrooms, grades 5–12.* San Francisco, CA: John Wiley and Sons, Inc.

Twelve Key Practices Framework

Shared Practices at The District, School, and Classroom Levels

Key Practice 1. Structuring Equitable School and Classroom Environments
Literacy, content, and ESL instruction is implemented in language rich, low-anxiety environments that affirm diversity and value bilingualism.

Key Practice 2. Educating English Language Learners through Collaboration
The challenges of educating ELL student populations are addressed through collaborative teams who share common goals, common language, and common practices.

Key Practice 3. Implementing a Balanced Student Assessment System
Standardized measures, common assessments, and classroom assessments in literacy, academic achievement, and language proficiency are used to inform instructional and programmatic decisions.

Key Practice 4. Embracing an Additive Bilingualism Perspective
Instructional and linguistic decisions for ELLs are based on understanding that ELLs are emerging bilingual students who use two languages for social and academic purposes.

Common Classroom Practices for All ELL Educators

Key Practice 5. Using Big Ideas to Plan Instruction
Curriculum and instruction are planned that specifically target the "big ideas" (statements of essential learning) that lead to core state standards.

Key Practice 6. Implementing Meaningful Vocabulary-Building Instruction
Teachers pre-teach vocabulary words necessary to understand lessons and passages. New words in context are taught during the lessons/passages, and practice is provided for students to use the words in various contexts after the lessons/passages.

Key Practice 7. Activating Students' Prior Knowledge
Teachers structure activities that connect ELLs' previous knowledge and cultural experiences to current lessons and build a comprehensible context for learning.

Key Practice 8. Structuring Student Interaction
Opportunities for academic development and language practice are provided by implementing activities that require students to talk with each other about what they are learning.

The Core Instructional Practices of Every Program for ELLs

Key Practice 9. Implementing English as a Second Language Instruction
Daily ESL instruction in the four language domains (listening, speaking, reading, and writing) is planned and implemented. Instruction is focused on the academic language that ELLs need to understand and express essential grade-level concepts.

Key Practice 10. Implementing Meaning-Based Literacy Instruction
Whenever possible, initial literacy instruction is taught in the primary language; when literacy is taught in English, teachers plan and implement meaning-based literacy instruction that builds on students' oral language and uses comprehensible text at appropriate English language proficiency levels.

Key Practice 11. Implementing Comprehensible Academic Content Instruction
Teachers model and teach academic content using language a little above the ELLs' current English proficiency levels, making new information comprehensible by using appropriate instructional supports.

Organizing the Key Practices into Effective Program Configurations

Key Practice 12. Structuring the Language Education Program
Instruction is organized to effectively meet the literacy, academic, and language needs of the districts' ELL populations.